The East Yorkshire Village Book

THE VILLAGES OF BRITAIN SERIES

Other counties in this series include

Avon
Bedfordshire
Berkshire
Buckinghamshire
Cambridgeshire
Cheshire
Cleveland
Cornwall
Cumbria
Derbyshire
Devon
Dorset
Essex
Gloucestershire
Hampshire
Herefordshire
Hertfordshire
Kent
Lancashire
Leicestershire & Rutland
Lincolnshire
Middlesex
Norfolk
Northamptonshire
Nottinghamshire
Oxfordshire
Powys Montgomeryshire
Shropshire
Somerset
Staffordshire
Suffolk
Surrey
East Sussex
West Sussex
Warwickshire
West Midlands
Wiltshire
Worcestershire
North Yorkshire
South & West Yorkshire

Most are published in conjunction with County Federations of Women's Institutes

The East Yorkshire Village Book

Compiled by the East Yorkshire
Federation of Women's Institutes from notes
and illustrations sent by Institutes in the County

Published jointly by
Countryside Books, Newbury
and the E.Y.F.W.I., Beverley

First Published 1991

Countryside Books
3 Catherine Road
Newbury, Berkshire

ISBN 1 85306 138 7

Cover Photograph of Rudston
taken by Michael Race

Produced through MRM Associates Ltd., Reading
Typeset by Acorn Bookwork, Salisbury
Printed in England by J. W. Arrowsmith Ltd., Bristol

Foreword

The sub-title of Winifred Holtby's novel *South Riding*, 'An English Landscape', is an appropriate description of East Yorkshire, South Riding being in fact the south-east part of Yorkshire, a district Winifred Holtby knew well. The East Yorkshire village of Rudston was her birthplace, and she is buried in the churchyard.

The landscape shows great contrasts, from the cliffs of Flamborough to the seaside of Hornsea, through the beautiful Wolds villages down to the river Humber and the plain of Holderness.

There is much to entertain and interest the visitor to the area. There is the RSPB reserve at Bempton with its gannetry, while at Burnby Hall in Pocklington there is one of the finest water lily collections in Europe. There is an abundance of beautiful churches ranging in size from St Andrew's church, Bainton, known locally as the 'Cathedral of the Wolds', to the historic Minsters of Beverley and Howden, not forgetting St Patrick's, Patrington, the church Sir John Betjeman described as 'one of the great buildings of England'. The villages of Sledmere, Burton Agnes and Burton Constable boast three most attractive houses which are open to the public.

The WI members who have contributed to this book may not have the literary talents of *South Riding*'s Winifred Holtby, but they have penned village portraits of the places they know and love, to interest and intrigue both the reader and the visitor. This is but a taste of the pleasures the visitor may experience by visiting the villages in the area covered by the East Yorkshire Federation of Women's Institutes.

Ann Barber
County Chairman

Acknowledgements

The East Yorkshire Federation of Women's Institutes wish to thank all the members who have submitted contributions for this book; to Mrs Enid Tracy and Mrs Ruth Pattison for their help, and a special thank you to Mrs Audrey Race, the co-ordinator for the project.

We gratefully acknowledge the co-operation of the following non-members who have made this book possible:

The Pocklington Times
Mr Mason, Mason Publications
Miss R. M. Nicholls
Mr J. Dunning
Mrs G. H. White
Mr L. P. Unsworth
Mrs D. Ward
Miss R. H. R. Wells
Mrs M. Wastling
Mr G. Blewett
Mr & Mrs M. Walker
Mr S. G. Gordon
Mr P. S. Atkinson
Mrs J. Roberts
Mr J. B. Rabbets
Mr H. Jackson
Miss J. Skinn
Miss K. Spurr
Miss J. Whitley
Mrs B. Robinson
Mrs L. Brown
Mr G. Hirst
Mr R. V. Fenton
Mr C. Axford
Mr D. M. Clark
Mrs J. Hoyes
Mr R. A. Bethell
Mr P. Wykes
Mrs A. Marozzi
Mr F. G. Courtney
Mrs A. M. Johnson
Mr G. W. Nellist
Mrs M. Holmes
Mrs M. Grayson
Mrs J. Pick
Mrs C. J. Woodcock
Mrs A. Stothard
Mrs R. Hague
Mr D. Cookson
Dr. R. M. Scrowston
Mr P. Garvey

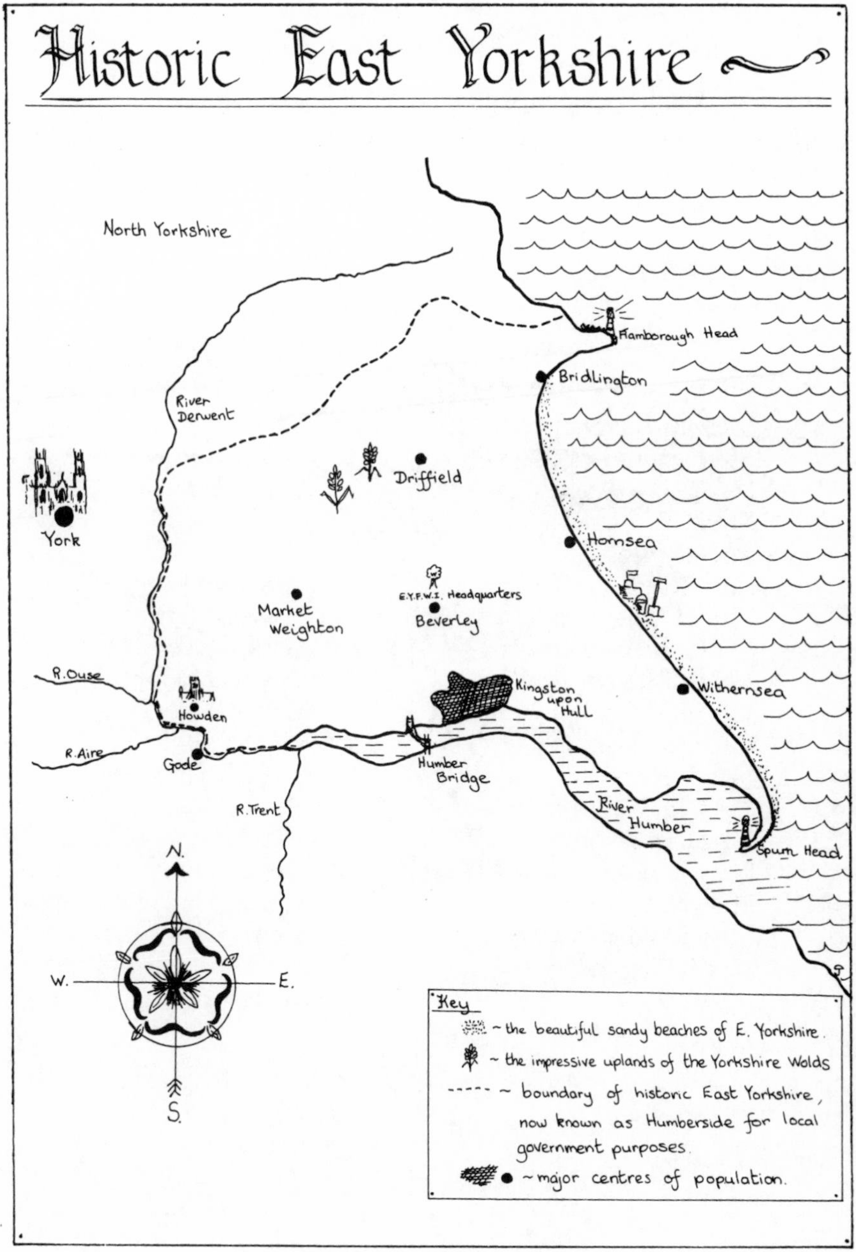

Historic East Yorkshire

North Yorkshire
River Derwent
York
Driffield
Flamborough Head
Bridlington
Hornsea
Market Weighton
E.Y.F.W.I. Headquarters
Beverley
R. Ouse
Howden
R. Aire
Goole
Kingston upon Hull
Withernsea
Humber Bridge
R. Trent
River Humber
Spurn Head
N.
W.
E.
S.

Key
~ the beautiful sandy beaches of E. Yorkshire.
~ the impressive uplands of the Yorkshire Wolds
----- ~ boundary of historic East Yorkshire, now known as Humberside for local government purposes.
~ major centres of population.

Airmyn

Airmyn today is still making its life by the river Aire as it did centuries ago. Its waters join the Ouse flowing out to the Humber, then the sea claims it all.

There is still the flat farmland, a church, school, public house, and shop-cum-post office. The long High Street has many of the old cottages and the Hall, which has long since been separate dwellings but still maintains some of its bygone wide gardens at the back. Old cottages have had face lifts, but many retain the old style of the Airmyn doors with their ridges and curves at the top. New estates of houses are now at the back of the High Street, with immaculate gardens.

No longer is there a ferry boat to meet you to cross the river but instead a swing bridge, Boothferry Bridge, allows ships to pass on with the tide, and there is also a fine motor bridge on the M62.

There is more water, and rising tides, so the river bank level is being rebuilt. The river has always been the important factor, people were dependent upon it for water, fish, wild fowl, reeds and warp for building materials; also for transport which the boats provided. Airmyn was in fact a small port. From the Middle Ages to the 18th century Airmyn's dead were taken by boat to Snaith to be buried. It was a much shorter journey than by road with horses.

River pollution was a problem in 1875; salmon as well as other fine fish were killed, to say nothing of the drinking water which was polluted. Today, river pollution is still with us.

Airmyn is well known for its fine clock tower by the side of the school. Money from the villagers paid for the building in 1866 to honour the memory of the second Earl of Beverley, who paid for the school to be built.

A small church has been on the site since 1318. On an outer wall of the present church a coat of arms bears the date 1676. Today it is kept in good order along with its lychgate and graveyard.

The school at Airmyn

Each year the village has a gala in which everyone plays a part, with many sporting events, and a yearly trip is organised for the pensioners. Airmyn, now modern, has outgrown the old village, but somehow it still manages to maintain a foothold in the past.

Aldbrough

Aldbrough is an unpretentious village situated in the Vale of Holderness. It is some ten miles from Hull, eight miles south of Hornsea and approximately one mile from the sea. This distance gets shorter by the year due to the problem of coastal erosion which is threatening the whole of this area. It seems likely that Aldbrough is not the first village of this name, others may already have disappeared into the sea.

The name Aldbrough has had many variations of spelling over the years. The suffix 'brough' or 'burg' is of Saxon-Norman origins and means castle or entrenchment. Aldbrough does not have any castle remains but it could be that these have also disappeared into the sea. In the Domesday Book the name is 'Ullenburg' and then 'Aldenburg'. The first name could refer to a nobleman called Ulph who held lands in this area before the Conquest. The latter seems to recall a nobleman called Aldene who held lands after the Norman conquest.

The church is built mainly in the Norman style with evidence of Saxon architecture around the windows and doors, probably from an earlier church. The building does not date from one particular time and like many other village churches is a mixture of styles. Inside it can boast the tomb of Sir John de Melsa, a six ft six inch warrior of great note, who was governor of York from 1292–1296. His helmet is still in existence and is one of only two known of the age. At one point it was used as a coal scuttle when school was held inside the church. Now it is housed in the Tower of London for safety.

Also housed inside the church is an ancient stone, maybe a sundial, inscribed with the words 'Ulf commanded this church to be built for the souls of Hanum and Gundhart'. This stone may well have come from an earlier building, perhaps a Saxon church which is now under the sea. The name Ulf crops up often in this area. An 'Ulf' willed his lands to the church and sealed the pact with a magnificent drinking horn which is still kept in York Minster. Another 'Ulf' was related to Danish King Cnut. They may even be the same man. Nothing is certain. Also set into the wall of the church is a small Roman figure. This is the only evidence from the Roman period but old documents do speak of Roman road remains. The coastline has shrunk since Roman times so it could be that the road, like many other early remains, is now under the sea.

The present day village is expanding and thriving. It has a population of about 1,200 and with the continuing building of new houses this figure is likely to rise. It could now be said that Aldbrough is not so much a farming community as a dormitory village.

The population is well catered for in many ways. For those without cars most requirements can be found within the village. The five local shops are a post office/general store, greengrocer/delicatessen, hairdresser's, fish and chip shop and hardware store. Other commodities can be purchased from visiting vans – butcher, fishmonger, tea man and coalman. For those wishing to make an excursion out of the village, there is still a daily bus service in addition to a private coach operator who runs many and varied excursions as well as transporting local schoolchildren. The daily pinta arrives even in the most adverse weather conditions as there is a village dairy. For those unfortunate enough to fall ill there is a regular doctor's surgery and dispensary as well as a fortnightly child health clinic.

Reversing the trend of village school closures, Aldbrough primary school in recent years has witnessed a considerable rise in pupil numbers. It now has about 150 children on roll. The present school building dates from 1862 with its most recent renovations and additions in 1979. The present school was built from the proceeds of Towrys Trust, which is still in operation. Record books from the charity show that there has been a school in the village since 1663 when the charity was founded. At this time 16 or 17 boys and the same number of girls were sent to school.

The village has three public houses; two in the village itself and one at the Cliff Top, which also serves the caravan camp. The George and Dragon still has its original beams and is one of the oldest coaching inns in Holderness.

A description of village life cannot be complete without a mention of Aldbrough's summer population. From spring to autumn caravanners visit regularly and have their own social activities at the camp as well as joining in those already occurring in the village itself.

Anlaby

The village name is associated with that of Anlaf, a Viking nobleman, but after the Norman Conquest in 1066 it is recorded that Thomas Anlabie was given land here, on which to build dykes and plant trees and hedges for the improvement of the land.

French pottery, medieval tiles and a Constantine coin were found in a flat bottomed, eight ft deep moat here: Constantine, King of Scotland in AD 920, did establish his kingdom and mint his coins in Northumbria.

In 1587, Christoper Legarde of Anlaby Old Hall received a letter from Queen Elizabeth, who required money for 'the Defense of England, against the Spanish Armada'. The letter is kept in a Hull museum. Anlaby Old Hall was demolished in 1790; due to there being many springs in this area, several large houses had to be demolished, some only 120 years old.

Anlaby House was built with a flight of twelve steps up to its first floor: it is now an annexe of the Beverley Borough Council. It was built by the Voase family, of a shipping line company, who entertained in grand style, their London relatives visiting them by steamer.

In 1844 William Voase died childless, and the heiress was the aunt of Mary Smith, the future wife of Arthur Wilson of the Wilson shipping line, who in 1874 started to build Tranby Croft on 34 acres of rising land in Anlaby.

The features already there, a two-storey cottage, a boating lake and cricket pitch, and a double flight of balustraded steps, remained as part of the grand plan. Indeed, work first started on the gardens. Plants and trees were easily brought in from overseas; a lily pond, and a double bank of rhododendrons of every hue, which were to last for over a century, were established. There were three vineries, peach and nectarine houses, and a kitchen garden 280 ft square was surrounded by a twelve ft high wall. There was stabling for 19 horses.

The villagers, population 494, were allowed to watch the development of Tranby Croft, and how their tongues wagged! Tranby Croft was to have 80 rooms, lighting and some heating were to be by electricity; there were crystal chandeliers, huge gilded mirrors, extensive ornate plaster work and carvings, five heraldic beasts for the corner posts on the wide staircase and ornate tiling. The blue room was decorated in Wedgwood design, with silver stars set in the ceiling.

Tranby Croft was ready in two years, for lavish entertaining and social climbing. The Wilsons had seven children, sound family principles and were philanthropic.

St Peter's church, Anlaby, built in 1880, had to be destroyed in 1883, the roof being too heavy for the main structure. The cost of rebuilding was £1,500. The Wilsons worshipped there.

Mary Wilson's first bazaar not only raised £800, but recruited many ladies' sewing groups. Bazaars, charity work and children's balls became a way of life in Anlaby. A three day bazaar would include a tableau vivant, which required a group pose, wearing appropriate dress, to remain for two minutes absolutely still whilst representing perhaps a painting, or an historical event, such as Cleopatra, or the Martyrdom of the Saints. Such a bazaar might raise £1,500. Children's fancy dress balls were popular: children would entertain as they progressed to the refreshments – the 'clown' would try to juggle all the way, the 'gnome' propel himself along on a big ball, trying not to fall off, and some would dance the hornpipe or Scottish dances. In 1888 one bazaar, opened by the Duke of Edinburgh and his wife the Grande Duchess Marie of Russia, raised £5,000 and funded the building of an orphanage in Hull; many ships 'went down' in those days.

In 1890, Field House, not a Wilson venture, was built near Lowfield Road for the mentally ill and had 28 male and 15 female patients.

Anlaby has a frog watch! Thousands of frogs come here to mate in September, and Anlaby people are concerned about 'Frog Road Safety'.

Today Anlaby's greatest attraction is its situation: a mile from the Humber Bridge, three miles from the airport and three from North Sea ferries for Holland and Belgium. The population is 12,000.

Atwick

The first sight of the village of Atwick, the most northerly in Holderness, comes when travelling up the East Coast road from Hornsea to Bridlington, as this road runs through the centre of the village.

A picturesque village green, with floral tubs in season, is bounded by the Black Horse public house and the village stores and post office. The outbuildings behind the Black Horse are the original stables which were used as the overnight stop in the days of horse and cart deliveries in the early 1900s. The blacksmith's shop which stood on the corner is now long gone.

Immediately behind the post office is the village hall, which was originally the school, built in 1877. This school was closed in 1961 and the children are now taken by bus to neighbouring Bewholme. After many years of lying empty, the school was renovated and altered into a village hall by the hard work of residents and friends, raising money in many ways for the conversion.

On the green, in front of the village hall, stands an ancient stone cross raised on three steps, which is of unknown origin. It is said to have been three miles from the sea in 1786. The sea over the last 200 years has worn away the glacial clay of which the cliffs in this area are formed, to now less than half a mile away, the complete village of Attenwick now being under the sea.

At the western end of the village, the church of St Lawrence is the third church to be built on that site, and the earliest church registers date back to 1061. It had links with Meaux Monastery. The well, a short distance from the church, is reputed to have been used by the monks for ceremonial purposes, hence its present name of Holy Well. The first church went into disuse at the time of the Great Plague. The second was a cobbled building, but little is known of this, and the present one, rebuilt in 1876 at a cost of £1,725, is of brick with a saddleback tower. The open nave is arched at the chancel, the pews of which are of oak and pitchpine. The oldest part of the church is the cylindrical font which is of stone and reputed to have been hand chiselled.

The vicarage behind is now private living accommodation, and the parish is now served by the same vicar as Hornsea.

In 1821 a small Methodist chapel was built but this has now closed, and is due for conversion into living accommodation.

The major industry of the village is farming, comprising both arable and dairy farms, but just to the north of the village, in the hamlet of Skirlington, are large caravan sites catering for many visitors in the summer months. A recent addition to the site is a Sunday market which boasts nearly 200 stalls.

Also on the northern edge of Atwick is a very large establishment belonging to British Gas. After a geological survey it was found that this was the only area in England that had a deep layer of salt which was suitable for the storage and containment of gas from the North Sea Fields. In the early 1970s British Gas developed a site one mile north of Atwick, and started by conventional oil well techniques to drill underground, to create caverns. To date there are now seven such caverns at a depth of 6,000 ft. The original salt is dissolved in a controlled manner to create teardrop-shaped caverns each 150 metres high and 150 metres in diameter. This process, using sea water, takes approximately two years to form each cavity. The dissolved brine is discharged by a system of diffusers back into the sea one mile off shore. The gas is drawn through the national transmission system and forced into the cavity, displacing the brine, and is stored at pressure, each cavity holding the equivalent of 1,200 conventional gas holders. At times of high demand, gas is released from storage through varying systems to lower the pressure and any entrained moisture into the national gas system. This vital role balances demands of consumers all over the country.

The development of such a large site has in no way impaired the beauty of this rural area, and indeed, at night provides a spectacular sight with hundreds of lights illuminating the evening sky.

Bainton

Bagenton, Baynton, Bayngton, Bainton; such have been the changes in spelling through the centuries of this attractive East Yorkshire village. First mentioned in the Domesday Book and with Scandinavian connections, Bainton is situated at the foot of the Wolds, surrounded by rich agricultural land and sliced down the middle by the busy B1248 Beverley to Malton road. Hull, York and Bridlington are almost equal distances away, and easily reached. The present population is around 300 and is unlikely to be increased as Bainton is a non-development village.

There are several listed buildings, one of which – Manor House – stands on the edge of the village, close to a traffic roundabout. This old house is notable as the former court house for Bainton Beacon petty sessions, and where offenders could be locked up whilst awaiting trial. The beacon used to stand a few hundred yards from Manor House on the Driffield road. Recently an extremely high street light was erected on the roundabout, and is visible for miles around – Bainton Beacon Mark II! In the spring daffodils bloom in their hundreds on the grass at 'Manor corner' and more were planted in the village around a seat, given by the local WI members to commemorate the movement's Golden Jubilee in 1965. Manor Farm, as it is usually called, was once a coaching house – the New inn, a resting place for travellers and horses alike, en route from York to Scarborough.

Majestic St Andrew's church stands on a raised site, and is thought to be the fourth in this position. Known locally as the Cathedral of the Wolds, it contains a Norman tub font. The east window is modern, replacing the one inserted in 1844 which was severely damaged during the Second World War by a blast from a land mine. The old market cross stump is now situated in the churchyard.

Another notable building is the Methodist chapel. Modern in design, it was built to replace the old Wesleyan chapel in 1957. Funds to meet the building costs came from the many and varied efforts of enthusiastic members, both local and from neighbouring villages. Financial support came also from the Joseph Rank Benevolent Trust, the Department of Chapel Affairs and the Driffield Methodist Grants. The foundation stones were laid on 5th October 1957 and a joyous celebration, just over two years after the project began, took place to mark the opening of the chapel on 14th June 1958. It has been in regular use since that time.

A Bainton family has ancestors who were pond builders and well known for their skills over a large area. A few years ago, a secret hoard of silver coins was unearthed on their land. Dated 1180 and numbering 133, the coins were thought to have been deliberately hidden and this made them treasure trove. As a result of the most unusual inquest – the first to be heard in these parts for over 30 years – the coins were immediately forfeited to the Queen's Treasury.

The residents take a pride in their village and with conservation in mind approached the local council about several unsightly aspects. The outcome was that numerous 'eyesores' were either removed or improved, a broken seat on the side of the main road was repaired and new trees planted to replace elms, destroyed by Dutch elm disease. A dangerous stretch of road was given a wider footpath and a piece of neglected land in front of the village hall was given a facelift. A local couple undertook the job of clearing away rubbish which was spoiling the look of the village hall and then planted a variety of shrubs and trees.

Neighbouring Neswick is also recorded in the Domesday Book. In the mid 18th century the estates of Bainton and Neswick became united. Today the population is only a fraction of what it used to be. Neswick Hall, long since demolished, was the home of the lord of the manor, for centuries the principal landowner in the parish. Acres of glorious pastureland with a farm and one or two tastefully restored private dwellings are all that remain. Neswick can be reached a mile or so along a peaceful tree-lined lane which runs by the side of Bainton church.

Barmby Moor

Looking down on Barmby Moor from a vantage point high on the Yorkshire Wolds, the village seems enshrouded in trees, only the graceful spire of the village church soaring above them. Ancient elms, a black poplar (very rare in this area) and a majestic avenue of horse chestnuts are just some of the trees which form this leafy frame.

The horse chestnuts, which stand south of the York to Hull road and opposite the Barmby Moor Country Hotel, are a much admired feature of the village. Throughout the seasons, from the 'sticky bud' time of early spring, through the massed white candles of May and June, to the nut-brown conkers of autumn, the trees present a magnificent sight. The avenue is alive with snowdrops and daffodils in the early months – and with small boys when the much prized conkers begin to fall.

The hotel opposite the avenue is a place of much interest historically. Originally called the Bunch of Grapes, and later the Wilmer Arms, this elegant Georgian house was a famous coaching inn during the 18th and 19th centuries. It was a regular stopping place for the eleven coaches which passed daily through the village along with the miscellany of chaises, waggons and packhorses which also came this way.

It is reputed that Queen Victoria herself once stayed a night at the hostelry – one particular bedroom is still referred to as the 'Queen's room'. What is certain is that the Court Leet usually adjourned there for dinner. And it is possible, likely even, that earlier Henry VIII and his queen, Catherine Howard, journeying from York to Holme, would have changed horses at this inn.

The manor house is also a place of both beauty and interest. It stands on the site of a much older building; parts of an ancient moat can still be traced, the remainder now lying beneath a modern housing estate. It is said that the Tenth Legion camped here on their way from York. Many Roman coins and artefacts found in fields close to the village south of the York–Hull road, lend credence to such a theory.

Incidentally, 'Hemp Pits' field (on the same farm) is a reminder of the area's thriving 19th century rope and twine industry.

The village church, rebuilt in 1851–52, is stone built in the Perpendicular style. It has an embattled and pinnacled tower, surmounted by a graceful spire. Features of special interest are the font, thought to be 13th century and recently restored, and the inlaid Minton floor tiles. These latter were the gift of Herbert Minton (Stoke-on-Trent), brother-in-law to the first resident vicar, Robert Taylor, whose vicariate ran from 1840 to 1885.

There is a curious stone, about six ft high, on the south side of the church. It is some 22 inches in width at its wide end, tapering to about 15 inches at the narrow one. Rain water sometimes lodges in a weathered basin on its surface, and in times long past it was believed that this water was a certain cure for warts. It is thought to be a prehistoric monolith, and judging by the fact that the church was built so close to it, it may have been invested with some sort of religious character. That there has been a settlement at Barmby since very ancient times seems certain. Evidence of Stone Age inhabitants has been shown in the stone axes etc which have been found here in the ground.

The village is mentioned in the Domesday Book. Apparently it was once a market town of some importance and had a weekly market. When this discontinued, an annual market was held to supply meat for the village feast. The feast was traditionally held on the first Thursday after 11th July and was originally a religious observance, the night being largely spent in prayer. It later developed a secular side, and is held to this day, beginning now on the Friday, with the main events and celebrations on the Saturday.

At one time the village was referred to as 'Black Barmby' because of the 'evil deeds' which were done on the moor – a then wild stretch of country on each side of the road to York. Happily to relate, the said 'evil deeds' were not committed, as a rule, by the residents of Barmby, but by the robbers, foot-pads and highwaymen who preyed on hapless travellers. The Public Records Office in London houses accounts of these dastardly deeds. The perpetrators of these crimes were hanged at York, but sometimes their bodies were brought back and hung on the moor in chains. It must have been a grisly sight.

Formerly an agricultural village in essence, Barmby Moor, because of development over the last few decades, could now almost be described as a 'commuter' village. But happily it has not lost its village ambience, enjoys a strong sense of community, and is an extremely pleasant place in which to live.

Barmby-on-the-Marsh

Barmby-on-the-Marsh is a small village set in the confluence of the rivers Ouse and Derwent. It was named in the Domesday Book as Barnebic and later as Barmby-on-Derwent. Its 1,500 acres of warp and sand are some of the richest in the county.

Its ancient church, St Helen's, was originally a tithe barn. Eventually the brick eastern tower with two bells was added. The chancel was restored in 1870. The register dates from 1790; previous records from 1500 are included in the Howden data. There were two chapels, only one built in 1833 remains and is in regular use.

The National school near the church was erected in 1834. It is used as a parish meeting place for social occasions. The present school replaced the old one in 1878 and is well attended by children from Barmby and adjoining villages from the ages of five until eleven, after which they travel to Howden four miles away.

An 18th century census gives a population of 500, later counts average 300, about the same as today. Occupations other than farming were sail and rope making and weaving – flax was grown here. The extraction of linseed was undertaken at the flax mill before the straw was retted for fibre preparation and, rather surprisingly, there was salmon fishing. There has always been lively river traffic of grain and other crops which were transported to market and mill, with coal and other stores coming in on the return journey. The Hull and Barnsley railway line came to the village in 1896 – this is now closed.

The common lands were enclosed in 1853 and old maps of the village show the old strip systems of field boundaries.

In the churchyard is a spring, St Helen's Well, rich in iron. Also nearby is St Peter's Well, which is rich in sulphur and is said to have ensured health and longevity. They did protect the population from an outbreak of cholera in 1854.

The village benefits from a number of charities. Early benefactors left land to the village trustees in order that rents from the land enriched life, helping to educate young people and to give to them a start in their chosen careers. Generous gifts each Christmas are given towards the cost of fuel for heating the homes of the senior citizens.

For relaxation it is recorded that horse racing took place for three days, starting on the last Thursday in June. However, the need for horse power declined. Barmby Feast was a day when every house was cleaned and spruced up, tables laden with food and doors wide open to relatives and friends. Travelling funfairs set up swings and roundabouts, everyone dressed in their Sunday best and all thoroughly enjoyed themselves to the music of steam organs.

Prior to work on the river banks and the installation of pumps and drainage systems, the marshlands flooded in winter. Skating on the frozen meadows was a winter pastime. Progress, as it is called, has now put an end to this. The marshes are now drained and cultivated, although the modern tractor and plough can come to a sudden stop when encountering a long dead blackened tree trunk working its way upwards, a reminder of the forests that once clothed the land.

The need for farm working folk has declined and there may not be the need to put every acre under corn. Present-day growers produce today's needs for salad crops, no cows graze the marshlands but goats supply milk for health foods. A wealth of talent exists in the production of high quality leather goods, artistic painting and china decorating.

Barmston

Barmston is a village you can easily pass by without noticing because the only road through it leads nowhere except into the North Sea, but should you be travelling along the A165 between Hull and Bridlington and spot the signpost, why not explore a little.

Six miles south of Bridlington, where the road sweeps round the bend, Barmston Lane End is flanked on the north by a display of holiday homes and on the south by a branch of the 'Little Chef' catering chain. In complete contrast to these images of modernity, only a few hundred yards away stands ancient All Saints' church and the remains of the manor house (now a farmhouse known as the Old Hall) with traces of its surrounding moat. The de Monceux family were lords of Barmston from the beginning of the 12th century until the male line died out in 1446, and the manor passed to the de la See family. Sir Martyn de la See was one of the first supporters of the future Henry IV when he landed further down the coast at Ravenspurn with about 7,000 men. Like so many other villages along the coast, Ravenspurn has been washed away.

From the de la Sees, Barmston passed into the hands of the Boynton family but they only lived in the manor house until the end of the 17th century when they moved a few miles away to Burton Agnes, having acquired that estate through marriage with a Griffith heiress.

The church contains a pre-Conquest 'hog back', a 12th century tub font on its original base, with moulded edge and diapered body, and an alabaster tomb with a recumbent effigy of a knight in armour believed to represent William, the last of the de Monceux line. More recent treasures include a screen carved by the village joiner whose family were in business in the village over many years, and a blue and gold altar frontal and pulpit and lectern falls made from the fabric used in Westminster Abbey at the Coronation of Queen Elizabeth II. There is also an unusual 'leper's squint' giving a view of the altar from the Lady chapel.

Amongst the rectors of Barmston commemorated on a wall tablet are several members of the Boynton family, but possibly the most distinguished incumbent was Cuthbert Tunstal, presented with his first living by Lady Margaret Boynton in 1506. He became Bishop of London and later of Durham and lived through the reigns of Henry VIII, Edward VI and Mary, and into the reign of Elizabeth I. The parish includes the hamlet of Fraisthorpe to the north and outlying farms and cottages, but the present day rector is also responsible for the churches of Ulrome and Skipsea to the south.

The Barmston estate was owned by the Boynton family until the late 1940s when it was sold to a business consortium known as Glendon Estates. One of the new landlords who lived in the village for some years was responsible for the erection of a 'memorial to death' on top of a mound known as Trusey Hill, believed to be the site of an ancient monastery. Known locally as 'Woodhenge', the monument consists of stark trunks of dead elms reaching skywards, and underneath are buried a skeleton found on the site and part of a First World War gun carriage which was washed up on the beach.

Main Street or Sands Lane straggles for about a mile until it reaches the cliff edge. Beyond the cricket field and village hall the rectory, a comparatively modern house, stands next to the former one, a sprawling Georgian building now in private ownership. For half a mile or so 'the village', a mixture of varying styles of architecture, lines both sides of the road. Whitewashed cottages, former almshouses proclaiming 'This hospital erected 1726' and Manor Farm date 1768 mingle with several styles of council houses and newer bungalows. Half way along, the pub, the Black Bull, built in the 1930s, stands opposite the village pond. The Methodist chapel is close by. Further along a road leads to Hamilton Hill, site of a beacon in former times.

The one time blacksmith's is now the village shop and post office and when nearby Hollycroft, a bungalow estate, was built in the early 1970s the village doubled in size. There are now about 260 people on the electoral roll. Like holiday-makers for many decades, quite a number of the new residents came from the industrial parts of Yorkshire but Barmston is such a friendly place that those who wish soon become part of the village community. A free monthly newsletter 'Village Voice' keeps everyone informed of the activities of the parish council, village hall committee, church, chapel, cricket club, Wednesday Fellowship and of course the Women's Institute.

The Holderness coast between Bridlington and Spurn at the mouth of the Humber has the fastest rate of erosion in the country and numerous villages built on the soft mixture of boulder clay, sand and gravel left behind by the glaciers of the Ice Age, are now under the waves. Within a few years, bungalows built many yards from the cliff edge only just before the Second World War had been demolished after being left unsafe following particularly high tides. After this the WI sent a delegation to London and succeeded in stopping large scale removal of sand and gravel from the mouth of Barmston Drain by contractors.

Beyond the main part of the village, a stretch of open fields leads to the cliff top and a holiday caravan site with club, shops and amenities for families to enjoy a break by the sea, and all that the locals appreciate all the year round – the peace of the countryside, the open air and a walk along the beach. Only a mile, but a mile full of interest.

Beeford

The village of Beeford is situated around the crossroads where the B1249 Driffield to Hornsea road crosses the A165 Hull to Bridlington road. Beeford was mentioned in the Domesday Book and was originally known as Byford, the name being derived from the fact that whichever way you approached the village, a ford had to be crossed. The Main Street stretches for about a mile, with small estates and lanes branching off it. One could not describe it as being picturesque, the landscape being very flat all round. It has a population of about 800.

It is a thriving farming area, surrounded by many large farms. One large concern in particular employs quite a number of people from the village and surrounding area, and hybrid pigs are exported to many parts of the world from here.

There is a large playing field where tennis, bowls, football and cricket can be enjoyed, and a play park for the children. Funds have been raised and a new community centre has been built on a site acquired near the school. The old meeting place was a small building over 200 years old, which was originally built as an infants school. In later years it was used as reading room, and housed a billiard table and a dart board where the young men met in their leisure time. During the Second World War it was the headquarters for the air raid wardens, and a first aid post. Later its use was a builder's store, and subsequently the ladies of the WRVS restored it and formed a Darby and Joan Club.

To the north of the village stands the lovely old stone church of St Leonard. It has a 15th century embattled western tower with crocketed pinnacles, containing three bells. In the chancel lies a very well-known effigy of Rev Thomas Tonge, a former rector, dated 1472, which is searched out by brass rubbers as being of particular interest.

On the Main Street there is a Methodist chapel which was built in 1868, and a primary school. Clustered around the crossroads there is a post office, a general store and a bakery, two public houses, and a fish shop which is of some renown. It has quite a history to it, having served many different purposes; originally a blacksmith's shop, then a cycle repair shop, and during the First World War a soldiers' washroom. Later it was occupied by a monumental mason, fish shop, and a poultry dealer as a plucking house. During the Second World War it was the Home Guard's headquarters. After that it was a plumber's and electrician's showroom, before finally being converted into a fish shop again. It was partly constructed of wood and in 1970 it was destroyed by fire, but it was built again into the fish shop as it stands today.

There is a butcher's, a wrought iron shop, two garages, a doctor's surgery, and a veterinary practice; also a village policeman, builders, joiners, blacksmith and a saddler's. The only thing the village seems to lack is a good bus service. Beeford is a friendly village, and although it cannot claim to have any scenic beauty, it is a village many people hold dear to their hearts.

Bempton & Buckton

Bempton, an area of approximately 2,000 acres, stands 200 ft above sea level on the Yorkshire coast, on the northern side of Flamborough Head, four miles from Bridlington. It was probably an Anglian settlement, and the eastern boundary with Flamborough is formed by the prehistoric Danes Dyke.

One mile north of the village are the awe-inspiring Bempton Cliffs, which are in places 400 ft high (twice the height of York Minster!). This is the Heritage coast, where the Yorkshire Wolds end in an almost perpendicular drop to the sea, and where 80,000 pairs of seabirds breed, the largest colony in England.

The RSPB established a nature reserve here in 1970, with a summer warden and information centre. A new car park was laid out and landscaped in 1988, to cater for the hundreds of visitors who come to observe and photograph the eight species of birds nesting precariously on the narrow ledges in the sheer cliffs. The kittiwakes, who build their nest of seaweed on the tiniest nooks and ledges, are the most numerous. There are three species of auk: guillemots, razorbills and the engaging puffins with brightly coloured beaks who, though as small as a dove, ride out the winter storms at sea. There are also fulmars, herring gulls, about 20 pairs of shags, and over 600 pairs of gannets.

Bempton is the only mainland gannetry where these spectacular birds breed every year. The size of a goose, they have a wingspan of six ft, and a streamlined body for plunging head first into the water from up to 100 ft in the air. Many other birds frequent the cliff tops and 200 species of wild flowers have also been recorded on the reserve.

The Norman church, founded on the site of an earlier Saxon building, dates from 1120 and stands in a picturesque setting near the duckpond and village green. It has often been altered through the centuries. The old rectory and the new vicarage are now private houses for there is no longer a resident clergyman.

The first chapel was built in 1825 by the Wesleyans, and replaced with a new one of red brick and terracotta in 1903. As Protestant dissent increased in the 19th century, it was said that ‘nearly all’ the inhabitants of Bempton were Wesleyan or Primitive Methodist. In 1843 the latter built a small chapel in Bolam Lane; it is now used as a furniture store.

Until the late 1960s the population was about 300, living in cottages and farms mostly built in the 19th century. The main occupation was farming; there was also a blacksmith’s and a joiner’s shop. Since then most of the small farms have gone; nearly all the paddocks and spare land have been used for building houses and bungalows, and the population now numbers about 1,000. People commute to work in Bridlington, Scarborough, Beverley and Hull. Many of the newcomers are from the West Riding, though Bempton is now a sought after location for people retiring from the south as well. There used to be three shops and a post office, but only the combined shop and post office remains. There is also a garage, an antiques shop, a hairdresser’s, a caravan park and club situated on the old RAF camp site, and a family business specialising in breeding tropical fish and aquatic plants.

Many holidaymakers visit the three caravan sites on the outskirts of Bempton; and a well known landmark in the village is the unusual bright blue roof of the White Horse public house. Landmarks of an earlier trade are the stumps of two windmills on the skyline. The East Coast Railway, Hull to Scarborough line, runs through Bempton; the station is on the site of the lost hamlet of Newsham, of which there is little trace except for the solitary ‘mystery grave’ of Henry Jarrat, lord of the manor of Bempton-cum-Newsholme, who died on 14th January, 1721.

In 1618–19 an unlicensed schoolmaster taught at Bempton; by 1819 there were two schools containing altogether 32 pupils each paying a penny ha’penny a week, and in 1854 a National school was built by subscription. A red brick building with stone mullioned windows, it stands at the corner of the churchyard and is now in use as a hairdresser’s and men’s clubroom. The present building in School Lane dates from 1912. At one time it was threatened with closure, but a new intake of young people has secured it for the foreseeable future. There are bus services to take children over eleven to the Headlands School and the villagers to shop in Bridlington.

In times past there were many small freeholders in the village, with no record of anyone really important, but Bempton was famous for its 'climmers'. These were the daring men who, from the 18th century, worked the cliffs round the coast of Bempton, Speeton and Flamborough mainly for guillemots' eggs. The best known climmer between the wars was Sam Leng. Using a winch and ropes, one man would climb down to the nests and fill canvas bags attached to his harness, while the others waited on top of the cliffs to heave him up and transfer the eggs to the baskets. In Victorian times the popular holiday 'sport' was the shooting of massive numbers of seabirds from boats which, until it was banned in 1869, affected the climmers' livelihood. Sir Christopher Sykes of Sledmere was known as 'The Gulls' Friend' because he introduced the Bill into Parliament to stop the wholesale slaughter.

Egg collectors and dealers came from all over the country and the world to buy the eggs at the cliff top, for no two guillemot eggs have the same markings. Any left were sold for food in markets at Bridlington or Leeds. Climming was made illegal in 1954. Although the practice was condemned as 'robbing the nests', the climmers rented their stretch of the cliffs and 'farmed' it, clearing loose rocks before they started going down for the eggs, and always leaving enough eggs to ensure the continuation of the species. A different section of their area was left unclimbed each year, to recover. They also took eggs from the common gulls, predators of the smaller, rarer birds, to keep the numbers under control, and the climmers, with their great experience of the cliff face, were also able to foretell, and warn about imminent rock falls.

Bewholme with Nunkeeling

It is difficult to know which came first, Bewholme or Nunkeeling, or even where the boundary lay. Both are mentioned in the Domesday survey, Begum, the old name for Bewholme, meaning 'at the bends of the stream' and Nunkeeling or Chilinge, from 'Cylla and his people', dating back to AD 700.

The only claim to fame is that a Benedictine nunnery was established in 1150 at Nunkeeling with an average complement of twelve nuns. This was surrendered to the king in 1540 and the church and buildings demolished. Another church was built on the site; this fell into decay, and another church was built in 1810. The only remains now are the walls and churchyard, which the Bewholme parish council is maintaining as a site of historical interest.

Most of the population then lived in Bewholme and a chapel of ease was established there, and in 1900 a new church with churchyard was built in the centre of the village. In 1831 a Wesleyan Methodist chapel was built, but on its closure in the 1920s it was converted to a house, now known as Wesley House. In 1839 a Primitive Methodist chapel was built and services are still held there as well as at the church.

Even with the addition of the hamlets of High and Low Bonwick and Dunnington in 1935, which increased the acreage from 2,200 to 3,700, and the building of 14 council houses in the 1940s, the population remained the same as the 1851 census of 240 persons.

With only a limited amount of infilling allowed for houses and the advent of modern transport, the village shop has given way to the town supermarket, although the post office is still open. As people seek recreation facilities further afield it has led to a decrease in village activities and a loss of community spirit. Very few of the old families are now represented in the village.

A village school was built in 1848 and extended in 1910, the average attendance being between 60 and 70. Now, even with the attendance of the children from Atwick, the number is only between 30 and 40, with older children going on to secondary school at Hornsea.

The land, mainly of heavy clay soil, is low lying and not until after the Second World War when most of it was redrained and the advent of heavy machinery made working conditions easier, did it realise its full potential. It was farmed on a two field system until it was enclosed by an Act of Parliament in 1740, and the present landscape of scattered farms and hedged fields created.

The village was more or less self supporting, with all the men employed on the land or in the workshops in the village. In the 1851 census blacksmiths, wheelwrights, joiners, shoemakers and masons were some of the enterprises making up the village community. Now with the farms fully mechanised only one or two men are needed on a farm and so all the rest of the workforce has to leave the village for other work in industry.

There are one or two interesting farmhouses and an imposing vicarage built in 1865 by William Burgess of London. The shaft of an ancient stone cross about six ft high stands against the wall of a cottage in Nunkeeling.

Bilton

Bilton is a small village in the parish of Bilton, Wyton and Ganstead in South Holderness, four miles north-east of Hull. At the time of the Domesday survey it was called Bilestone and was owned by a Baron Droge de Beuvere.

In the reign of Henry VIII, John Flower sold the manor to Sir William Knowles, from whom it passed to the Stanhopes. In 1820 Lord Viscount Downe was lord of the manor and the sole proprietor with the exception of about 30 acres.

Lord Downe's sister, the Hon Lydia Dawnay, very generously paid for the village church (St Peter's) to be rebuilt in 1852. The previous one dating back to Saxon times had been demolished in 1851. The entrance to the churchyard is through a lychgate. The church has a porch on the south side, a small vestry on the north side and beautiful stained glass windows, one of which is dedicated by the parishioners to Rev Henry Quilter, a much loved vicar of the parish and canon of York.

The chancel is divided from the nave by a screen of Caen stone and a beautiful carved reredos of the same material was erected at the expense of the vicar in 1886. The belfry has two bells. Up to the beginning of the Second World War the bell tolled at two minute intervals for a quarter of an hour whenever anyone died.

A school was built by Captain Dawnay in 1870 with an adjoining school house and like many schools during this period was organised and run by the church. A new school was built in 1937. With the growth of the population it was used as a primary school only, with the older children going to the nearby county school, now a comprehensive school at Preston.

In 1908 the village of Bilton was sold, the farmers got their own land, and the sale of the labourers' cottages was planned so that they could remain in them. For many years there were just farm houses and cottages. In the 1920s a bus service commenced but was not reliable and many had to walk to Hull. Water pipes were laid and gas and electricity gradually arrived in the village during this period.

Up to 1926 there were a total of 65 houses in the true parish of Bilton. By the late 1930s about 300 houses had been built. In the post-war years 300 houses were built on land sold by the owners of High Farm. It was named Lime Tree estate, the roads and avenues being named after old Bilton families, eg Dawnay Road, Ingram Avenue, England Road.

The first shop was built in 1933, a typical village shop which sold just about everything, but when the Asda store opened (half a mile away) in May 1982, trade dwindled and the shop was sold and converted to a house. The post office, two newsagent's shops and a fish and chip shop remain on the main road, and a hairdressing salon and greengrocer's shop on the Lime Tree estate.

The old village hall was built on land given by Mr England in 1932. A new attractive village hall was opened in May 1985 after many years of fund raising by a dedicated team of workers and is in constant use.

The British Legion hall was built in 1948; a hospital-type Nissen hut was erected near the old village hall on land given by Mr Ingram. This has since been rebuilt and serves as a club for the village. A church hall was erected and on 18th July 1975 was dedicated by the Archbishop of York, the Very Rev Stuart Blanch.

Bishop Burton

Bishop Burton lies in a dip of the Wolds, on the main road between York and Beverley. The road not only dips but takes a curve here, out of respect to the pond which is the chief glory of the village.

Burton is a common name, particularly in the east where the Anglian invaders settled in the 5th century AD; the name is a derivative of the Old English Burgh-tun meaning a fortified place. It was originally called South Burton to distinguish it from its neighbour North or Cherry Burton, but became known as Bishop Burton due no doubt to its early association with the Archbishops of York who had a palace within the parish, Archbishop Romanus dying there in 1296.

There is evidence of much earlier occupation of the area in the form of many tumuli, just to the west of the village, dating from the early Bronze Age. There are also Neolithic enclosures, trackways and at least two sites of very early habitation and the possibility of a Roman road running in a south-westerly direction from the village towards Newbald. Although it is recorded in Gent's *Ancient History of Ripon* that a ploughman while ploughing in Bishop Burton field discovered a fine tessellated pavement, its whereabouts remain unknown and its existence now seems doubtful.

At the Dissolution of the Monasteries the manor was surrendered to Henry VIII and remained in Royal hands until 1591 when it was purchased by Thomas Crompton, auditor to Queen Elizabeth. After his death it was sold by his heir to William Gee of Beverley. The estate was owned by their family for 180 years. William was a wealthy merchant, who was knighted for his services to the Crown and was buried in York Minster where there is a fine monument to his memory. The family were well known for their charitable work. Elizabeth Gee left in her will £100 for the education of poor children in the parish. Her trustees purchased a ten acre field, the rent of which at the time was £2 per acre, which still provides the income for this charity.

The estate was sold again in 1783 to Liverpool merchant Richard Watt, who had acquired a vast fortune as a sugar planter and trader in Jamaica. On his death it passed to his nephew and in turn to his son Richard the 3rd, the racehorse breeder and trainer who renamed the public house after one of his St Leger winners, *Altisadora*. It was his sons William and Francis who carried out extensive restoration of the parish church and High Hall. On the death of William the estate came into the possession, through the female line, of Richard Bradley Hall. He received the legacy on condition that he took the name of Watt, which he did on his coming of age and so became known as Hall-Watt. It was his son Alvery who sold the Hall and estate to O. S. Hellyer who in turn sold the Hall and one farm to the county council in 1951. The Hall was then demolished and a new building erected on the site that was opened as an agricultural college for 28 male students and twelve female in 1954.

The church, although much restored, is built on ancient foundations for tradition says that it was founded by Earl Puch before the Conquest and was given to the Dean and Chapter of York in 1194. The earliest surviving fabric is the gabled west door and the lower courses of the tower. Other features of interest include the brasses in the chancel, particularly the chalice brass to a previous vicar, Peter Johnson, who died in 1460; a small Saxon figurine on the wall by the south door; a monumental slab to Tobias Hodson; and a fine alabaster monument to Rachel and Elizabeth Gee. In 1679 John Wesley is reputed to have preached beneath an elm tree on the village green. This tree was struck by lightning in 1836 and the squire Richard Watt had a bust carved from its remains. This much admired carving of John Wesley can be seen in the church on the south wall of the south aisle, being placed there by Rev Brass in 1964.

The village had a licensed schoolmaster in 1743, and in 1834 there were 94 children attending schools within the village. In 1860 a new school was built by the Watt family, when there were 60 pupils. In 1984 the school was closed when only 24 pupils were attending.

Within the parish is one of the three remaining Beverley Minster sanctuary stones, situated just south of the A1079 near the Beverley bypass roundabout. The right of sanctuary was granted by King Athelstan on his return from subduing the Scots in AD 938.

Bishop Burton, being on the main Hull–York road that was turnpiked in 1764, had a toll bar that was situated just east of the village. The farmers of Bishop Burton were allowed through free of toll; they had 'T F' painted on their carts. It was demolished in 1885.

Bishop Wilton

Bishop Wilton is beautifully situated under the high escarpment of the Wolds. The eastern end is well sheltered by the chalky hills and is slightly higher than the rest of the village which slopes gently downwards, with a variety of picturesque houses and cottages – many with pantiled roofs – set on either side of a pretty stream, known locally as 't'beck'.

Narrow roads criss-cross the green, as well as making roads for vehicles or pathways for pedestrians. A flight of stone steps with white hand rails crosses the green opposite the church gates. In far-off days there was a carriage road down the centre of the green, running alongside the stream, and horse-drawn vehicles halted beside the steps.

The church, with the unusual dedication to St Edith, is a very beautiful building of which to be proud. It was restored by Sir Tatton Sykes in the mid 19th century having previously fallen into a ruinous condition. There are two Norman arches, the one in the porch being noted for the fine stone carvings. The floor is a copy in mosaic of one in the Vatican and elderly residents of the village recall tales of the visits of Italian craftsmen who lodged here while engaged on this intricate work.

Near the church there stood, until the end of the 19th century, an old Hall with fishponds nearby and an impressive dovecote. An old photograph shows the Hall in its last days before demolition and the ponds are now almost dry.

In the centre of the village, known as 'The Bridge', two roads meet. One goes to the local town of Pocklington, five miles away, and the other skirts the slopes of Garrowby Hill to join the York–Bridlington road, with a great volume of traffic on fine Sundays and Bank Holidays.

Garrowby Hill is one of the largest and steepest hills in this part of Yorkshire, rising from 200 ft to 800 ft, the highest point of the Wolds where the old Wilton Beacon once sent warnings across the countryside. There are magnificent views across the plain of York to the distant Pennines which appear as a bluish blur on the horizon, with the white horse of Kilburn visible on very clear days as a bright dot on the side of Roulston Scar. On the roadside near the summit of Garrowby Hill is a crucifix erected by the first Earl of Halifax in memory of King George VI. In winter weather the hill becomes dangerous to traffic and is often snowbound.

Garrowby estate, owned by the Halifax family since 1804, stretches over several thousand acres. At one time the village was mainly agricultural with many estate workers housed in 'Garrowby'-owned property. Now, with changing times, there are cottage conversions and many people commute to work in the towns, though a conservation order preserves the character of the village.

The village is lucky still to have its Church of England school, with some 40 pupils. The late Victorian building has in recent years been upgraded and is a happy and successful school. Older pupils go by bus to Woldgate comprehensive in Pocklington. In a field opposite the school one can see the remains, in humps and bumps, of the old Archbishop's Palace, with part of the medieval moat still visible.

The village shop and post office still flourishes and near the Bridge the old firm of Fishers Agricultural Engineers gives valuable service to farmers. Their office is a quaint little building, the first known school in the village. On the opposite corner stands the Fleece inn – a popular hostelry.

Interesting old postcards show such activities as sheep washing in the beck and a fair on the green. The village at one time had two chapels and three pubs. Times have changed but this is still the centre of a rural community with a friendly 'good neighbour' atmosphere in this very beautiful corner of Yorkshire's East Riding.

Boynton

Boynton is a small village with a population of just over 100. It is situated on the edge of the Yorkshire Wolds, approximately three miles to the west of the coastal resort of Bridlington, and to the north of the stream called the Gypsey Race. It is listed in the Domesday Book as Bouingtone.

The church of St Andrew is at the southern end of the village. The tower of the present church dates from the 14th century, though there was certainly an earlier place of worship in the village, possibly a chapel attached to the priory in Bridlington. In the middle of the 18th century the nave of the existing church was destroyed by fire, and was rebuilt by Sir George Strickland whose family had succeeded the Boynton family as lords of the manor. At the east end of the new nave was added a mortuary chapel for the Strickland family, where memorials to the family can still be seen. The Strickland coat of arms and the church lectern both feature the turkey, which William Strickland, who sailed with Sebastian Cabot to the New World in the 16th century, is credited with introducing into Britain.

It was the same William Strickland who pulled down the existing manor house and replaced it with Boynton Hall, which stands to the south of the Gypsey Race. During the Civil War, Sir William Strickland and his brother were prominent Parliamentarians, but this did not prevent the family giving shelter to Queen Henrietta Maria, wife of Charles I, who was returning to this country from Holland. Her ship was blown off course into Bridlington Bay, and she stayed at Boynton on her way overland to Newcastle. She is reputed to have taken with her the family silver, leaving a portrait of herself as payment.

The Hall, still basically the original Elizabethan mansion,

though Georgianised by later members of the family, remained in the Strickland family until the early 1950s, when both the Hall and estate were sold. The Hall itself was bought by the present owners, themselves descendants of the Strickland family, in 1980.

Brandesburton

The village of Brandesburton is pleasantly situated about eight miles north-east of Beverley and six miles west of Hornsea on the Bridlington road. It first prospered under the church of St John of Beverley, who was given the land by King Athelstan, but this was soon superseded by the St Quintins who came over from France at the time of William the Conqueror. By the start of the 14th century the St Quintins' hold on the village had slackened and the title descended by marriage eventually to Gregory, Lord Dacre, and his wife Anna. Their marriage was childless and when she died in 1595 she left the manor to the Lord Mayor of London, in trust for the benefit of Emmanuel Hospital, Westminster, which she had founded. This bequest was to influence the shape of the village for many years to come. The Dacres maintained strong links with the village. The school, a neat red brick building, was erected in 1843 by the Lord Mayor and Corporation of London.

The market cross still stands on the small green. It is on a base ascended by three steps, but the carving at the top was so damaged years ago by village vandals as to be unrecognizable.

The church dates from Norman times and is dedicated to St Mary. It is of considerable size, built of sea cobbles and a large portion of brick with windows, doors, mouldings and ornaments of stone. It has a square embattled tower at the west end. The east window is a fine pointed one with five lights and delicate tracery.

On a large blue stone slab in the chancel are two brasses of life size figures of a knight and his lady, beautifully decorated in fine costume. A piece bearing the knight's head has broken off. He is Sir John St Quintin who died in 1397 and the lady is his wife, Lora, who died in 1369. Another brass bears the half length figure of William Darrell, rector of Halsham and Brandesburton, who died in 1364.

Dr Hymers was once rector here and when he died in 1887 he left all his wealth, upwards of £150,000, for the foundation and endowment of a college in Hull for 'training intelligence in whatsoever rank of life it may be found'. The bequest was invalid under the statute of mortmain and reverted to his brother, Robert Hymers, who voluntarily gave £50,000 to the Corporation to carry out his brother's wishes.

In the churchyard are a number of war graves of airmen lost in the area in the Second World War. There are 13 German, nine Canadian, 14 British, six Australian, two New Zealand and one Polish airmen. The war memorial is in the school grounds.

The rectory is mainly Georgian, but it is now privately owned and a new rectory has been built. There are two public houses in the village, the Dacre Arms and the Black Swan. There is also a post office, a craft shop and a general store. Once there were two chapels, a Primitive Methodist and a Wesleyan, but in 1937 they amalgamated and a new Methodist chapel was built in the Main Street.

There are very good sports facilities in the village, which has always boasted a good football team and cricket team. There are also bowls, tennis and squash courts, as well as billiards, table tennis and badminton in the parish hall. This was an RAF cinema and dining hall and after the war was given by the Mewburn family to the village and converted by voluntary labour.

Brandesburton Hall was built in 1772. Colonel Harrison lived there but he spent much of his time abroad, big game hunting. He brought home some pygmies from one trip and they lived for some time in the grounds of the Hall. They used to go to the blacksmith's shop, which is no longer there, to get nail clinchings to tip their arrows in order to shoot rabbits. The Hall is now used as a mental hospital, although its future is uncertain.

The Franklin Dead Brief is a charity peculiar to the area. Over 150 years ago a man died at Brandesburton Moor and there was no money to bury him, so people gave one shilling each for the purpose. This started the charity, which still exists with a membership of over 300. They each contribute 20p when a member dies. A dinner is held every Candlemas at the Dacre Arms for members.

A Mutual Improvement Society was formed in 1852. There was a reading room in connection with it and a library but these no longer exist, as a mobile library now comes to the village. There was also a village institute but this has reverted back to a house.

Catfoss aerodrome was on the outskirts of the village before the Second World War. After Lawrence of Arabia left the Middle East he joined the Air Force under the name of Shaw. He served some of his time at Catfoss and was a familiar figure in the village riding his Brough Superior motor cycle, although not many people then knew who he was. During the war Catfoss was a Coastal Command training school and later Central Gunnery School.

There have been large deposits of gravel in the village, a two mile stretch known as Brandesburton Barfe. It has long served the inhabitants for the repair of roads but gravel pits have been worked for over 70 years, although deposits now seem to be coming to an end. Many fossilized remains have been found there. Some of the gravel pits have now been filled in and returned to agricultural use, others are used by fishermen, and for water skiing and other water sports. Many birds are attracted to them.

Originally the village was mainly agricultural but the coming of the gravel pits provided another source of employment. There are now two industrial sites just outside the village providing a variety of work.

Brantingham

Brantingham lies near Brough, twelve miles to the west of Kingston upon Hull. Relics found at the foot of Spout Hill, in the present village, show positive signs of habitation in the area during the Bronze Age, the Iron Age and by the Romans. The Scandinavian word 'bret', meaning 'steep', gives a clue to the first known name of the village, Bretinha, and no doubt refers to the topography of the Brantingham dale. The location of a water supply provided by the springs in the dale suggests the existence of a Saxon settlement near the present church in the 5th or 6th century.

The Domesday survey of 1086 recorded the Bishop of Durham as having land under cultivation in the parish at that time. The earliest parts of the present church are clearly Norman (12th century), eg the main south door, the small doorway in the south side of the chancel, the font, a window in the north side of the nave and the arches of the transepts. The medieval period is represented in the tower, the tower arch and two main windows in the nave. The church was appropriated to the Prior and Convent of Durham in 1458 but the sum of 20 marks was retained in the parish for the yearly maintenance of the perpetual vicar.

The land enclosures of 1765 saw 449 acres allocated to the church. The enclosures also brought the erection of a number of the existing buildings on the present site of the village in the mouth of the dale, where level land was available, more suitable for farming than in the narrowness of the dale near the church.

The largest residence in the village is that of Brantinghamthorpe, to the south of the village proper. Parts of the house date from the 16th century but considerable additions were made during the mid 19th century. This latter period saw the house occupied by Christopher Sykes, younger son of the first Sir Tatton Sykes of Sledmere and a close friend of the Prince of Wales, later King Edward VII. It was whilst the Prince was a guest of Brantinghamthorpe that he became an innocent party to the baccarat scandal at nearby Tranby Croft.

It is many years since the Thorpe was central to the Brantingham estate and the proprietor of the estate now lives at Brantingham Hall, in the centre of the village. The greater part of the village was owned by the estate until comparatively recently and the compact, relatively unspoilt nature of the village owes much to the sympathetic manner in which that ownership has been discharged. Many of the older houses and cottages in the village are still owned by the estate and these, together with the village green, pond, church, dale and adjacent agricultural land, present a tranquil, rural scene.

Broomfleet

The tiny village of Broomfleet, with its population of 246 in 1981, is an isolated community situated on the north bank of the river Humber between Brough and the Market Weighton canal.

Today the village has no resident doctor, policeman or vicar and no garage or cafe. But for villagers and visitors alike it has the friendly Red Lion pub, the well kept village church and the modern village hall, which is the venue for educational and social events. As there is no bus service, and neighbouring villages are three miles distant, the inhabitants, especially those without motorised transport, are grateful that the post office and village store still occupy a prominent position in the centre of the village.

Broomfleet is boxed in by the Humber to the south, the canal to the west and the railway to the north and east. As the railway station is approximately one mile from the village and the trains few, this form of transport is almost negligible.

Today the Humber is a total barrier but it was not always thus, as the village owes its very existence to the river. The tributaries rush down from the Pennines carrying large amounts of sediment which is deposited when the water reaches the slower, low-lying Humber. In modern days it can be seen as mud and sandbanks in the broad river, but before the days of man-made drains and Humber banks, the flood water flowed over the fens (Wallingfen) and the marrs (Marr Farm) and left its rich deposits when the water receded. The compacted sediment laid down long before Christ, became the clays from which the Romans made their pots and tiles at the present Market Weighton Lock. In the 1839 tithe survey there were four brickyards at Broomfleet landing and today in the same area Santoft Ltd's large modern brickworks is being extended to produce roof tiles which are made from the old clay dug from nearby fields.

The later, well drained alluvial deposits make fertile agricultural land for cereal growing. At the beginning of the 20th century a large deposit of about 300 acres was enclosed and drained and became the Island Farm.

Before the days of pollution the river was rich in eels, perch, roach and salmon, and fisheries abounded on the river bank. Near the Lock there was a haven and the catches were salted and transported by boat to up-river towns. In the 13th century the then owners of the village, St Leonard's Hospital, York, noted that on the menu was Brungareflet salmon. The very name of the village could have connotations with the river. 'Flete' was a creek or tidal stream and Brungar a Scandinavian surname.

From the pig of lead (approximately AD 150) and fragments of pottery excavated at the Lock, it is certain Romans were acquainted with the area. Fishermen would have been afraid of Viking longboats landing at their haven and may have stared in bewilderment when the fleet carrying Harold Hardrada of Norway and his warriors sailed by on their way to their doom at the battle of Stamford Bridge in 1066.

Later, but before the coming of the railway in 1840, packets and market boats plied their way along the river calling at Blacktoft and the Lock to allow goods and passengers to alight or be taken on board.

Broomfleet has much history and has had many notable days. On 17th March 1302 King Edward I stopped here on his return to Westminster during a lull in his attempted conquest of the Scots. King Edward VII, when Prince of Wales, went wildfowling and was given a pick-a-back over marshy ground by one of the strong men of the village. After the Second World War, Sir Peter Scott, the naturalist, visited Island Farm to study the huge skeins of wild geese which made the river their autumnal evening roost.

With the increasing number of motor vehicles, which are essential to the modern community, all the children and many adults travel away to their education or employment. The decreasing number who work locally are engaged in agriculture or are employed at the brickworks.

The village has attractions for the discerning visitors who seek the quiet countryside. In the summer, amateur fishermen enjoy their weekend sport with rod and line on the banks of the Market Weighton canal, but it is to the many thousands of river birds that Broomfleet is an all year haven where there is peace and an abundance of food. In 1954 the Humber Refuge was created which stretches from Brough to Faxfleet Ness and recently the shore was designated an area of special scientific interest. No shooting is allowed in the refuge and the great flocks of teal and widgeon, as well as many less known species, dwell and feed in undisturbed peace and plenty.

The success in taming the Humber, draining and resisting its floods and putting its resources to productive use is due chiefly to the determination, tenacity and hard labour of the inhabitants of Broomfleet over the last 2,000 years. The new homes which are presently being built and the number of 'outsiders' who choose to join this isolated community augers well for the future.

Bubwith

Bubwith is a small village, dating back to Viking times, situated on the east bank of the river Derwent in the vale of York, and on the A163 road eight miles from Selby. The counties of North Yorkshire and Humberside are divided by the river, thus leaving Bubwith in the county of Humberside, or as Yorkshire folk prefer it to be called, the historic East Riding of Yorkshire.

In times gone by Bubwith must have been a very busy village. Being on the river Derwent a lot of trade was brought to the village on barges which negotiated the river between Malton and the ports of Goole and Hull, joining the river Ouse at Barmby-on-the-Marsh some eight miles south of Bubwith. Until a few years ago the river was tidal, then a barrage was built across the mouth of the river at Barmby preventing the tidal flow. During the winter months the ings around the village often flood forming a temporary wildlife sanctuary for migrating birds, and a lot of interest is created when some rare species is spotted, causing a stir among ornithologists. The meadowlands, which are flooded in winter, are also home to a number of rare species of grasses and wild flowers during the summer, and are protected by English Nature.

In the past Bubwith supported quite a number of different trades which have now died out. One of these was the growing of teasels which were used for the combing of wool in the spinning and weaving industry in the West Riding mills.

The village church is of special interest, dating back to the 12th century. The stone of which it is built was brought up the river in barges, and like the nearby village churches of Aughton and Ellerton it is built on the river bank. The church is well worth a visit, and the churchyard contains a memorial recently dedicated to the airmen of the 78th Squadron, who were based at nearby Breighton airfield during the Second World War. A special service is held every two years in the church when men who served in the squadron are reunited. A plaque has also been placed in the church in memory of the airmen who died.

Nowadays the village is a thriving community and boasts a variety of village interests, with all age groups being catered for. All sports are provided for in the recently built sports centre, and on the playing field. Every year a village queen is chosen and on Gala Day she is crowned; the celebrations last for a week when money is raised for the upkeep of the playing field.

In the past Bubwith was mainly a farming community, but thanks to the combustion engine and the new era of movement in communities, Bubwith, like so many other villages, is growing. The formation of the Selby coalfield has brought an influx of miners from the West Riding, and the building of the M62 has brought commuters from the surrounding cities. With the incoming of new people has come new interests. A former farm on the outskirts of the village has been turned into an art centre specialising in the production of television. This centre is known as the Advanced Residential Theatre and Television School International, and draws students from around the world to study and perform plays. It boasts a theatre and workshops and is open to the public to go and watch their productions.

Bugthorpe

Bugthorpe is much prettier than its name. Nestling among the 'little hills' of the Yorkshire Wolds, it is completely at home in its peaceful rural setting. Red-roofed cottages and farmhouses stand around the green, their pantile roofs and hand-made bricks lending a picture-book charm of times long past to the scene.

Standing in a commanding position on a wayside bank close to the green is the village church. A long building, it seems large in relation to the rest of the hamlet. Begun by the Normans, the church is chiefly 14th century with a 15th century embattled tower at the west end of the nave. A door in the chancel leads to a winding stairway in the turret, which projects at one corner. The window lighting the stair affords a fine view of the surrounding countryside.

Dedicated to St Andrew, the interior walls are white. This gives a delightful air of spaciousness and a certain quaintness to the building, but it is thought by some that successive applications of the wash may have led to the curious carvings on the Saxon arch in the chancel being less distinct than they otherwise might have been. Among these carvings is one which shows a bird on an animal's back, and another showing a man on a two-headed dragon.

In stark contrast with the large church is the old Wesleyan chapel in Beck Row. A tiny building, attached to the side of a house, it seats about 30 people. It has banked pews and a small pulpit. Originally there were two chapels in Bugthorpe, both in Beck Row. The Primitive Methodist chapel was demolished in 1947 after a huge tree was blown down across it.

Before 1875 both chapels were used as schools – one for boys and the other for girls. The Wesleyan chapel, though still in use as a place of worship, has now no connection with the Methodist church.

Within the vicinity, Bugthorpe is famous for its Butter Cake. Local tradition has it that in days gone by, a travelling fair of some kind came to the village every year round about the middle of

October. On this occasion the villagers would make their Butter Cake. Much visiting among neighbours would take place for the sampling of each other's cake, and according to rumour, the partaking of a 'little tipple' along with it. The fair no longer visits the village, but the Butter Cake tradition has been kept alive by the school. The annual school sale is held around 10th October and is called 'The Butter Cake Fair'. A traditional cake is made for the occasion and is either raffled or used in a guess-the-weight competition.

Burstwick

Burstwick, mentioned in the Domesday Book, is situated midway between Withernsea and Hull, approximately eight miles from each. Its position is just south of the B1362 and north of the A1033.

The castle or manor was bequeathed by William the Conqueror to the Earls of Albemarle and in 1306 the Countess of Carrick, queen of Robert the Bruce, was imprisoned in the castle for a year by Edward I.

There was a tunnel leading from this building to the parish church which was built in 1228. An unusual feature is the squint, enabling the chantry priest to gain a view of the high altar and so synchronise the service of the masses to the congregation in the chapel. At the present time there is a very enthusiastic team of bell ringers who not only ring the church bells each Sunday but also visit other parts of the country in competitions.

In this once very religious village there were four chapels, starting in 1825 (no longer in existence). In 1848 and 1854 came the second and third (these are now in existence as residences). The fourth was built in 1898 at a total cost of £1,000 and is still used for worship today. The present buildings, the church at the north and the chapel at the south, stand proudly as guardians of the faith, lending distinction to this historic village.

The original school, built in 1875, which stood proudly prominent and will long be remembered with affection by its former pupils, has now been converted into dwellings. The new school was built in 1970 and is of modern design. It caters for 120 pupils at the present time.

There was a very successful railway and the station was built in 1845. At one time this line from Hull to Withernsea had a considerable impact upon village life, until Dr Beeching axed the service in the 1960s. However, the station property now houses a children's nursery and a tool hire firm, and the track lends itself as a pleasant nature walk.

At one time, apart from the farms, there were only two companies who employed local people. One of them (Hedon Growers) is the largest producer of cucumbers in the United Kingdom, growing 10% of its requirements. There is now a small industrial estate and work can be undertaken in electronics, joinery, animal feeds, printing, double glazing and much more. One third of the industries export to other countries produce as varied as sows of Hybrid Piggeries and computer software.

There are two local hostelries, one of which serves food, two shops, one incorporating the post office, and a butcher, to serve the community.

Burstwick is now the proud owner of a playing field which has been provided by the community and the residents are able to enjoy the outdoor pursuits of football and cricket, whilst the youngsters enjoy themselves on the play area which contains swings etc. Other leisure activities include riding, with windsurfing, water skiing and fishing on the disused gravel quarries.

The population figures are gradually rising and there are plans for further expansion. It is anticipated that soon the population of Burstwick will have risen to 2,000 and many of the properties being built are the work of the local builders and the village people employed by them.

Burton Agnes

Burton Agnes lies on the southern edge of the Wolds nearly six miles from Bridlington. The population of Burton Agnes civil parish, which includes Thornholme and Gransmoor, was 510 in the mid 1980s.

It was one of many Burtons mentioned in the Domesday Book, but from the mid 12th century it has been known as either Agnes Burton or Burton Agnes. There were three ladies of about this time named Agnes who could have given the village its distinctive suffix, but it was probably Agnes, daughter of Geoffrey Baynard, for whom the village was named. She married Robert de Brus who then became overlord of the manor. It is likely that this Geoffrey Baynard was the man renting the manor from the King in 1086. The Domesday Book states that prior to 1066 the manor was held by Morcar.

The demesne lord of Burton Agnes in the later 12th century was Roger de Stuteville, who built the original manor house which stands today, although much altered, beside the great 17th century mansion. After the building of the present Hall, the old building became service quarters, at one time being a laundry. A date stone of 1712 set into the east wall suggests a date for the drastic alterations giving the building the appearance we see today. A 12th century well is nearby, with a donkey wheel probably of the 17th century. This manor house is now in the care of English Heritage.

Burton Agnes was a comparatively large village in the Middle Ages, owing its local importance to a Tuesday market and an annual fair, the charter for which was granted in 1257. This probably carried on until the mid 1300s when the Black Death decimated the population causing many village markets and fairs to cease. A water mill and windmill are mentioned in documents of 1265. They belonged to the manor, and tenants were obliged to have their corn ground there, paying a fee to the lord of the manor for doing so. The mills were still working in 1840, but had

Burton Agnes Village

apparently ceased by 1850 when 'Old Mill' stood by the pond and 'Mill House' marked the site of the windmill north of the park. The site of the gallows and pillory has been lost, but the gallows was probably at the top of Rudston road near the parish boundary and the pillory near the church.

The present church, dedicated to St Martin, was built about 1100 to replace an earlier one on the same site. Much altered and added to over the centuries, the church contains some curious features. Behind the pew of the lords of the manor, in the north aisle is a fine alabaster tomb chest on which rest the effigies of Sir Walter Griffith (died 1481) and his wife. A rather macabre memorial to Sir Henry Griffith (died 1645) and his two wives is on the north wall of the church. Below three black coffins is a tomb chest decorated with a panel carved with a jumble of bones and skulls. Among other monuments is one to Robert Wilberforce, son of William Wilberforce the reformer, who was sometime rector here. The parish registers date from 1700.

The jewel of Burton Agnes, and, many would argue, the whole of the East Riding, is the present Hall. In 1599 Sir Henry Griffith was appointed to the Council of the North which had its headquarters in York. Living in Staffordshire, Sir Henry had only occasionally visited Burton Agnes, but now, needing a base nearer York, he decided to live here. The old manor house was by now very decayed, so he started to build his new house in 1601. A plan of the building was found, after his death, among the papers of Robert Smythson, master mason to Queen Elizabeth I, architect of Longleat and Hardwick Hall. Apart from internal alterations about 1730, Burton Agnes Hall has changed little over the years. The symmetry of the south front was obtained by putting the entrance at the side of one of the projecting bays. In its beautiful setting it remains today a tribute to a golden age of domestic building.

Burton Agnes Hall has the rare distinction of never having changed hands through sale. The family now resident can trace their ancestry back to Roger de Stuteville. The Hall has been open to the public since 1949.

A famous visitor to Burton Agnes in 1697 was Celia Fiennes, cousin to Sir Griffith Boynton, who travelled the country on horseback keeping a diary of the places she visited. Giving a good description of the house and gardens, she remarks that from the gallery windows, 'you view the whole country around, and discover ships at sail, though at a good distance'.

Another visitor to Burton Agnes was Charlotte Bronte whose friend Ellen Nussey's brother, Henry, was a curate here. It was on his recommendation that Charlotte and Ellen took a holiday in Bridlington in 1839 after Charlotte had refused Henry's offer of marriage.

A school existed in 1540 when a vicar of that time left money to provide an income for a schoolmaster. Children from Burton Agnes had free tuition, but others had to pay for it. The school was then in a chapel to the north of the church, which was replaced in 1835 by a building which was demolished in 1956. A new school was built by Sir Henry Somerville Boynton in 1871 on Rudston Road. This forms part of the present school.

The pond, from which Mill beck flows, has unfortunately suffered in recent years from a combination of dry summers and the abstraction of water higher up on the Wolds and is now little more than a puddle. Hopefully this will be remedied in the near future and the area will once again be a picturesque haven for wildfowl. At one time the beck fed several fish ponds and in the 17th century a washing stone was set in it, above which, a byelaw ruled nobody might wash 'puddings, fish, clothes or any other filthy things'.

The character of the village in the 20th century has been affected by the volume of traffic on the Bridlington road. Improvements were facilitated in 1939 by the demolition of some old almshouses and cutting back the hillside near the crossroads. Recent road widening accommodates the even greater flow of modern traffic through the village, effectively cutting it in half.

Burton Constable

Burton Constable is a small hamlet about eight miles north-east of Hull. Mentioned in the Domesday Book as Santriburtone, the name came from its owner Erneburg de Burton who married Ulbert le Constable.

The first documentary evidence of a large house on the estate dates back to 1294 when Simon Constable left a mansion house, dovecote, windmill and 13 cottages to his heir. The Constables continued for many years accumulating honours and land by their prowess in numerous battles, or by marriage to wealthy peeresses until 1559, when Sir John Constable built the present Hall onto the old manor house. The building as it is now bears no resemblance to the original. Two wings were added to the old manor, and these are now used as private living accommodation for the family.

From 1750–1780, £40,000 was spent on the Hall and parkland; the experts of the day were employed, namely Chippendale, Wyatt, Lightoller of York, and Capability Brown. There are many beautiful paintings in the long gallery, and a priceless stained glass window. It is said that there are 365 windows in the Hall and 52 doors. The suite of furniture made by Chippendale cost £1,000, a great deal of money in 1840. The hand-painted wallpaper in the Chinese Room cost 18 shillings per piece. The Hepplewhite-style dining table and chairs were made by the estate joiner, who must have been a very clever man, considering it was made 20 years before George Hepplewhite's designs were published.

The Golden Bedroom is supposedly haunted by William Constable, who was evidently seen last by the present owner's grandmother. Another ghost goes back to the 17th century. A nun is said to float down the long gallery, by-passing the priest's hiding hole. The ghost most frequently seen, however, is that of Nurse Dowdall, who was nanny to the children of Clifford Constable. The present owner is Mr John R. Chichester-Constable, 46th Lord Paramount of the Seignory of Holderness.

This old Elizabethan building is set in parkland and woods with a 22 acre lake. The surrounding villages of West Newton, Marton, Ellerby and Sproatley were at one time a small part of the estate, but much of the land in these villages has now been sold for private building.

The Elizabethan Constables were obstinate in their refusal to acknowledge the supremacy of the Crown concerning religion, and continued to adhere to the tenets of the Roman Catholic Church. Consequently, the beautiful chapel had to be hidden away. This can be seen today, as also can the church and presbytery built in the woods surrounding the estate at Marton. The drive through the woods is very attractive in the springtime, but on a dark, dreary night the sense of history can be felt in this corner of Holderness. Perhaps the ghosts are not just confined to the Hall itself!

Burton Fleming

The village of Burton Fleming lies in the valley of the Gipsey Race in the north of the Wolds. Mentioned in the Domesday Book as Burtone, the Fleming was probably added from the Flemyng family in the 12th century. Two hundred years later the village was referred to as North Burton, which may have been to distinguish it from nearby Burton Agnes. it has now reverted to Burton Fleming, but there are still those who refer to it as 'Noth Botton'.

The course of the Gipsey Race runs through the village and can remain dry for several years and then begin to flow in the spring, and on occasions in the past, when it was in full spate, has flooded the streets. An old legend says that such a strong flow heralded a national disaster and the years of 1665 (the Great Plague) and 1939 (the Second World War) are often quoted as examples.

In former years there was a custom that villagers went out to meet the arrival of the waters, but in recent years a new custom of guessing the date of its arrival at the crossroads has taken over.

The old village pump, Black Jack, with its two handles, still stands at the crossroads although no longer used to give water.

The church of St Cuthbert dates back to Norman times, as a chapel of ease belonging to the mother church of Hunmanby, and the first known vicar was recorded in 1302. The registers begin in 1538. Inside the church is a board relating to the Sawden Charity which provided bread for the poor of the parish. The loaves were put on a shelf under the board to be distributed after the morning service each Sunday. The Charity still exists, but its funds are now used at the vicar's discretion.

When weddings are held at the church, the old custom of tying the gates is still carried out. The best man is then expected to throw coins over to the waiting children who have gathered to watch.

One Methodist church survives as a place of worship but two other buildings are still in existence, one converted to a dwelling and the other used as a store.

The village has several listed buildings including the church, the Hall which was built in the early 1800s, and the Manor Farmhouse, where, during the Civil War, Queen Henrietta Maria stayed with her army on the night of 5th March 1642.

This is a farming area and in years gone by most of the village activity was connected with agriculture. There were two blacksmiths, a joiner and a wheelwright. Present businesses include an agricultural engineer, an agricultural contractor, a builder and haulage contractors as well as the remaining farms.

The village school has been closed for some years, but the post office and village store remain as well as a butcher's. A village hall has recently been built and a community bus operates to nearby towns.

Carnaby

Carnaby is a small but very pleasant village three miles from the town of Bridlington. The busy main road to Hull and York runs straight through the middle of the village.

The ancient church of St John the Baptist is situated on a hill above the village. The church was first mentioned between 1148 and 1153, and has had some restoration work done to it. There

Carnaby Temple

are two hotels, both converted from farmhouses, a post office, about 52 houses, and eight farms. The railway to the south of the village is no longer used, but the signal box is still in use.

In one garden is a statue of a horse, erected by a Mr Robinson, a farmer who lived nearby. When times were bad, he was saved because the horse won a lot of races. He had a chance to sell the horse but refused, and on its death erected the statue in its memory.

Above the village is Carnaby Temple, an octagonal red brick tower built by Sir George Strickland in the late 18th century. It was possibly built as a lookout tower, but was used in the Second World War for military purposes.

During the war FIDO (Fog Intensive Dispersal Operation) was built. It was a huge aerodrome which lit up each side to disperse the fog. Bombers returning from a raid would be diverted to FIDO when their own bases were fog-bound. It is now a thriving industrial estate. Near this estate is a very modern refuse baling plant, where the refuse is baled, buried beneath the soil, and the land returned to agriculture.

Carnaby does not have a village hall, the main meeting place being the schoolroom of the nearby Haisthorpe chapel.

Cherry Burton

The village of Cherry Burton lies some three miles north-west of Beverley, and at the eastern end of its parish. Until development started in the 1960s the village consisted of a main street stretching along a line of wells running in an east-west direction, and at the western end roads leading off it going to Etton and Bishop Burton. There were working farms along the main street, but this is no longer so, and from a village whose roots lay firmly in agriculture it has now mainly developed into a dormitory for people who work in Beverley, Hull and other nearby towns. From a population of 450 prior to development, it has now grown to nearly 2,000.

Cherry Burton has not always been called by this name. It was originally one of eight Burtons in the East Riding, but became North Burton to distinguish it from the nearby village of South Burton, now Bishop Burton. However, by the 17th century, the word 'north' had changed to 'cherry'. In spite of some argument, it is now accepted that this was because of the large numbers of cherry trees which grew in the area.

The written history of the community goes back 1,300 years, and starts about the year AD 687, when St John of Beverley is reputed to have come to consecrate the church. While in the township he cured a servant of Addi, who had been close to death. The next time that the township is recorded is some 400 years later – in the Domesday Book. Over the next 400 years there are only fleeting glimpses of the parish through such things as entries in wills and the poll tax returns of 1381.

Unfortunately little is known of the ordinary members of the community in the years which followed. Those we do know something about are such people as curate Thomas Davey who was in trouble for rushing through church services; Edmund Bonner, who as Bishop Bonner was reputed to have had at least 200 people put to death, and many more tortured during the 1530s; and then there was Thomas Micklethwaite, who was nicknamed 'Burnroast' on account of the length of his sermons.

By the end of the 18th century, life in the village was becoming more fully documented. Roads were beginning to improve, and with the sale of the manor to David Burton Fowler, the village of today started to take shape. By the 1830s the old fields which had been farmed in strips were enclosed, and the fields, hedges, and ditches, and also the wide road verges which can now be seen, were a part of Cherry Burton.

Twenty years later, in the early 1850s, the old church was pulled down, and the present one was built at a cost of about £2,000. Somewhat unusually for a village church, a clock was installed which has four faces. The church has three bells which are now run electrically. The present organ was installed in 1899. Built by Wordsworth & Co of Leeds, it has two full manuals and a separate pedal organ, and cost £305. An electric blower was installed for the organ just after the Second World War, but the hand bellows still remain in place.

When David Burton Fowler died, he left the manor to his great-nephew, David Robinson, on condition that he adopted the name Burton. Now David Burton, he and his descendants gradually built up an estate which covered about two-thirds of the parish. His son was to be the first chairman of the East Riding County Council, and another descendant, D. C. F. Burton, was to be Captain of the Yorkshire Cricket Club from 1919 until 1921. Until the sale of the estate in 1916, the Burton family played a prominent part in the life of the village, and even today, although no Burtons remain living in the village, the family still maintain an interest.

Apart from the church, a number of other buildings remain as part of the village heritage. Cherry Burton Hall, built on the site of an earlier house next to the church, dates from 1794. There is also Cherry Burton House dating from 1835, and there is the house now known as Cedar Grange, which was built as a rectory in 1878. While the Primitive Methodist chapel which stood in the Main Street opposite the village shop has now disappeared, the Wesleyan Methodist chapel was enlarged in 1928 to become the village hall. The Bay Horse public house is the only remaining licensed house of the two or three which existed at the end of the 18th century. Other buildings such as the reading room, the old village post office and the old school house are now private houses, as is the old railway station. The old school which had been built in 1872 has disappeared, to be replaced by two modern bungalows. The present village school was built in 1967.

While the railway, which was on the line from Hull and Beverley to Market Weighton and York, finally closed in 1965 having served the area along its route for almost exactly 100 years, housing development was taking place in the village. The first such development was the building of The Drive on the western edge of the village in 1963. The Meadows development started in 1965, Canada Drive in 1967, and Highcroft in 1972. The old football field and tennis courts were sold by the Borough Council to developers in 1984, and in 1989 to 1990 Elm Tree farmyard and part of a field between Canada Drive and the Etton Road was developed, as was a field on the eastern side of the Bishop Burton Road.

Apart from an active church life in the village, evening classes are held in the village school. The new sports field provides facilities for such activities as tennis, football and cricket, while there is also housing for a scout group there.

Very important to the community are the village shop and post office – these also serve a number of villages around about which lack such amenities. Visitors to the village include a mobile butcher, baker and fishmonger. The village is also regularly served by a mobile library and bus service.

Coniston

Coniston has always been a small village, but in the present time it is divided into two parts. One part consists of houses running down both sides of the A165, the Hornsea/Bridlington road. The second part is set on the old road which has been bypassed and forms the heart of the village.

There is a garage by the name of Coniston Bill which repairs cars but does not sell petrol. There is also a public house, the Blacksmith's Arms, which is a very popular meeting place for the local inhabitants and people from further afield. The post office cum local store is very well stocked and most items can be purchased there. There are two farms in Coniston village, one being a small unit and the other being the base for one of the largest farming operations in the area. Pig Tails is a computer service for pig farmers and this is also based in the village.

Mr Darley, who has now retired, carried out work as a joiner, and was also well known for renovating and restoring carriages and many items of furniture back to their former glory. Many years ago there was a blacksmith's shop but this has long since disappeared.

The Methodist chapel still holds services once a week. There is a village hall which has had extensive renovations both inside and out, which is used by the villagers and also hired out for various functions.

Cottingham

Cottingham is situated in the East Riding of Yorkshire. This part of the county was renamed Humberside in the year 1974 but most people prefer to retain the title – the Ridings of Yorkshire. The village is only seven miles from the beautiful Humber Bridge and five miles from the historic town of Beverley. Cottingham, which the local people boast as being the largest village in England, was included in the Domesday Book of 1086. The 14th century saw the building of an Augustinian monastery, the parish church of St Mary the Virgin, and the fortification and castellation of the manor house by the Wake family, which later passed to Edward Plantagenet, better known as the Black Prince. Both the church and the manor house grace the village today but the monastery has long since disappeared.

During the 19th century Kingston-upon-Hull saw a growth in economy, particularly in shipping, banking and commerce. Cottingham, being a mere four miles from the city, became a desirable place for prosperous merchants to build their large houses and so began the expansion of the shopping area in Hallgate, the main street. Between the two World Wars several Dutch growers settled in Cottingham as the land is very fertile and well suited to market gardening.

The expansion of the University of Hull has brought large numbers of students to the village and they are now accommodated in some of the large houses, now Halls of Residence. In spite of increased residential development and the influx of students, bringing the population to 20,000 the village still manages to retain a great deal of its old charm and village atmosphere. Shopping here is most pleasurable and there is little need to travel to Hull as we are served so well locally. The Thursday market, which dates back to King John, has recently been revived. During the summer months the village also hosts its own Annual Cottingham Show and Horticultural Society Show.

Among many famous people who have lived here are the Holtby family, whose daughter Winifred was the well known authoress of

St Mary's Church, Cottingham

South Riding. Holtby House still stands and is now a student house. More recent notables from the world of the arts include Brian Rix and Alan Plater.

Four primary schools and one secondary school take care of the education of the young whilst an adult education day/evening institute offers a wide variety of subjects for those wishing to extend their knowledge or take up new interests. As well as the

Anglican church of St Mary there are Catholic, Methodist and United Reformed churches and a Salvation Army hall. Six public houses are on hand to quench the thirst and satisfy the appetite of villagers and visitors alike.

The residents of Cottingham are fortunate in having a large selection of cultural, social and recreational facilities. As well as senior citizen clubs and various youth movements, there are horticultural, civic, dramatic and local history societies, choirs, the usual range of sporting activities and several women's guilds.

Cottingham, with its shopping and recreational facilities, good rail and road links, close proximity to the coast, excellent areas of housing and its sense of history, is a very pleasant place to live, full of friendly folk who take pride in their village.

Driffield

Great Driffield, Capital of the Wolds, is situated at the foot of the Yorkshire Wolds and is an agricultural town, with a thriving cattle market on Thursdays and a general market on Thursdays and Saturdays. The annual Agricultural Show and the pedigree sheep sales have made it into one of the most important small towns in what was the East Riding of Yorkshire. Little Driffield is a small village to the west. The area of Driffield and Little Driffield is approximately 2,500 acres with a population of around 8,000.

Driffield has no 'romantic history' but serious historians and archaeologists find it an intriguing area. As recently as 1989 remains of the Iron Age were found prior to building developments. In Norman times Driffield was not unimportant; the Domesday Book records eight mills and two churches – probably All Saints' and St Peter's at what are now Great Driffield and Little Driffield respectively.

All Saints' parish church has Norman origins with later Early English work incorporated. Clerestory windows, the nave and arcades are clearly Norman. The tower was added in the 15th century and restored with other portions of the church in the late 19th century. In St Mary's church, Little Driffield (originally St

Peter's), a tablet on the north wall stated that Alfred, King of Northumberland (d. AD 705) was buried in the chancel; however this has never been proved conclusively. Other places of worship include the Methodist, Roman Catholic, Congregational, Pentecostal and Primitive Methodist churches.

The oldest part of Driffield is Moot Hill at the northern end of the town, which was the meeting place of the Saxon 'Toen moot'. Opposite Moot Hill was the only windmill in the village. The medieval pinfold, for stray animals, was restored in 1973 and is to be found at the foot of the hill.

The opening of the Driffield Canal in 1772 was a major turning point in the development of the town. Grain and goods could be shipped by barge or keel directly to Hull, instead of having to be taken on the badly made roads by horse and wagon. So Driffield prospered through the 19th century.

In the past 20 years there have been many changes, not least in the development of industries. A number are allied, of course, to agriculture, but Driffield is also a well-known centre for oven-ready poultry, confectionary, shirt and clothing manufacture, printing and publishing, baby accessory and spectacle frame manufacture and a variety of other businesses including an excellent shopping centre.

A cottage hospital, the Alfred Bean (named after the donor), was opened in 1931. During the Second World War wooden huts were erected on land adjacent to the Alfred Bean and used as a hospital by the military forces. After the war, the East Riding General Hospital, as it became known, provided all the town's hospital requirements. Since the reorganisation of the Health Service the majority of the services have been transferred to other hospitals in the region. The hospital is now a community hospital and known once more as the 'Alfred Bean Hospital'.

Driffield's educational needs are served by several pre-school play groups, two infant, a junior, a special school and a large comprehensive school, the latter being the main secondary school for both rural and urban districts. On the same site as the secondary school is the Youth Centre and the College of Further Education. The town has many clubs and societies, far too numerous to mention individually, which cater for everyone – young or old.

The town is twinned with Bad Sulzeflen in Germany and a number of exchange visits have taken place, so helping to further international friendship and understanding.

Several annual events keep up the old traditions – 'scrambling' probably being one of the oldest. On the first day of January (now the second due to Bank Holidays) children gather at the southern end of the town and work their way down the main shopping street chanting for money, fruit, sweets, etc. As the shopkeepers throw out handfuls of goodies, the children scramble. A great sport!

The first Driffield Agricultural Show was held in 1854 and since then every July has brought a bigger and better show.

Driffield Trip Day originated in 1921 with children from local Sunday schools going on an outing to the coast. It has continued since then with only a short break during the war years. The trip is now the responsibility of the Trip Day Committee who raise enough money to provide each child with some pocket money and the return fare to Bridlington. Each August special trains were hired to take the thousand plus passengers to the resort. Sadly, modern trains are no longer suitable for Trip Day and now a fleet of buses empties the town of the majority of children and their parents.

As well as the commercial dealings and busy social life, Driffield has some lovely countryside very close at hand for pleasant, relaxing walks – by the trout stream (also excellent fishing), or the canal (now being restored for recreational purposes), Kings Mill (a natural beauty spot and former mill), Water Forlorns (Anglo-Saxon 'water springs'), Little Driffield with its attractive pond and historic church (now a very peaceful village since the completion of the bypass), Horsefair (where the gipsies gathered annually to meet socially and sell their horses) and 'Mucky Dick Lane' (officially Church Lane – where's the connection?).

Dunswell

Dunswell is situated on the banks of the river Hull midway between Hull and Beverley.

The river Hull was the main means of transport before and after the road was built, with ships sailing across the Dunswell fields to Beverley and others built at the yard there moored at Hull Bank Farm waiting for the tide to take them to Hull. The river traffic is now no more.

The road was built in 1303 but by 1362 the bridge at Dunswell needed repairing. The road was turnpiked in 1741 with toll bars at Newland and Woodmansey and a tarmac surface put on about 1929. The many coaches, horses and goods carts going up and down the road gave the public houses their names.

The Coach and Horses public house was originally a single storey building and was known as the Plough for a short time. The Waggon and Horses was on the opposite side of the road and, like the Coach and Horses, seems to date back to the 1600s. The building was demolished and three houses built on the site, one of which was occupied by the village joiners.

Ings Lane in Dunswell was an enclosure road from Skidby Landing on the river Hull to the main road, where the Ship inn is located, and then via Skidby Carr Lane to Skidby.

The land in the village was very wet and marshy and suffered severe floods. The Beverley Skidby Drain constructed in 1785, the steam engine at Dunswell and the Barmston Drain constructed in 1798 all helped to drain the land. The erection of the water walls also helped but caused many people's wells to dry up.

The chapel in Dunswell was built about 1816 for the Methodists and many events were organised such as the annual chapel anniversaries, Sunday school outings and the 150th anniversary celebrations in 1966. The chapel closed after the Harvest Festival service in October 1968. Church people met in the village school for many years until St Faith's was opened in April 1951.

The village school was built in 1881 for 75 pupils although the average attendance was 30. The school had a coal fire and two rooms and the 'Boys' and 'Girls' signs can still be seen even though the school has been enlarged.

The village shop opposite the school was for many years run by Douglas Errington and was fondly known as 'Dougy's', but alas the shop is no more. The keeper of the village post office, until it closed in 1989, was Mrs Wastling. The village petrol station has survived and was fully rebuilt in 1990.

The 20th century is leaving its mark on the village with the new Beverley bypass striding across the fields of Dunswell, once the parklands of Cottingham Castle.

The village is now dominated not by farmers but by horticulture with Ings Lane Garden Centre, Land Plan Landscape Gardener, a horticultural supplier and many greenhouses on the flat land. New houses spring up every year as the village expands.

Easington

Easington is known to the local community as 'East End', presumably because it is in the east of Holderness, and about half a miles from the North Sea. At the turn of the century the first landmark to be seen upon approaching the village would have been the church tower, but that is not the case today, because in 1965 British Petroleum brought their first North Sea gas ashore, and the structures of the site are visible from quite a distance away. They resemble Blackpool Illuminations, especially at night.

All Saints' church is situated in the centre of the village and stands on a great mound. In 1990 it celebrated its 800th anniversary. Lots of activities went on in the village to mark this great event and the nationally known playwright, Sheila Yeger, presented a play based on past and present-day events of the village. Many residents took part: acting, playing the music, building the stage and scenery, office work, wardrobe, and in the whole range of production tasks.

Another very old building is the tithe barn, which was built in the 14th century. It has a thatched roof, and was rethatched a few years ago. In recent years the gable-end blew down in a gale and had to be rebuilt.

Once there were four schools in the vicinity of East End: Easington, Holmpton, Spurn and Welwick. Only one school remains today, Easington C of E primary school. The Headteacher, Mr L. E. Malkin, and two of his staff have had three books published, using photographs and extracts from the old schools' log books as the main source of information. There used to be three shops in the village, but only one remains, Webster's, and this houses the post office.

The Connor and Graham bus service has served the community since the 1920s. The first buses must have been very cold and uncomfortable in those days with no heating; not like the modern coaches they use today. The Graham family still run the bus company and have improved the service immensely since those far off days.

The White Horse, the Neptune and the Granby are three local hostelries in Easington. There was a fourth called the Sun inn, but it is now the home of one of the local residents and his family.

Sad to say, the village 'stately home' Easington Hall, home of the Overton family for many years, was demolished about 100 years ago. Also vanished from this small community over the years are the coastguards and their families, who moved up the coast to Bridlington. The coastguard houses and station still stand along the main road through the village with the name to remember them by. Mr Loten's museum was another, full of interesting curios and relics collected from far and near, possibly some from shipwrecks along the coastline. Pride of place went to a supposedly mummified body of a 'little mermaid', a delight to the children who visited, but only the older residents still remember. The village had a windmill, but all that remains today is the millstone, used as a feature by the roadside at Blacksmith's Corner.

Also lost from this vicinity is the old lifeboat shed, no longer required because the Spurn lifeboat does an excellent job around the coastline. Mr Brian Bevan, the coxswain, is one of the most decorated lifeboatmen in Britain, with gold, silver and bronze

Eastrington Church

medals. Spurn is the only lifeboat station in Britain that has a full-time crew. The lifeboatmen live with their families in a small community of purpose-built homes at the end of the narrow, three mile long sand-dune peninsula known as Spurn Point, now owned by the Yorkshire Wildlife Trust and one of the best places in Britain to watch birds migrating.

Dimlington was a village about half a mile along the coast, but, also, it met with the same fate as other villages along the Holderness coast and is lost to the sea. Memories and street names are all that is left to remember them by.

Eastrington

The village of Eastrington dates from the time of the early Anglo-Saxons. The name means a farmstead (ton) belonging to a family group living to the east, probably of the major settlement of Howden. Eastrington was mentioned in the Domesday Book of 1086. It belonged to the Bishop of Durham and was surrounded by approximately 75 acres of arable land, as well as by a large common.

There was a church in the village by 1227 although Saxon and Norman work in the present building suggest the existence of a small chapel even earlier. The first permanent vicar that we know of was Robert de Heyington who was appointed in 1318. Eastrington church as it now stands is a mixture of styles. The chancel is the oldest part and was probably the original building mentioned in the 13th century. The Portington and Ousethorpe chapels date from the 14th century while the tower and clerestory are in the Perpendicular style and date from the 15th century.

The village has always been largely agricultural and a comparison of occupations in the 14th and 19th centuries shows that little changed over 500 years. Most men worked the land although a number of villagers were involved in cloth-making (wool in medieval times, flax in the 19th century). Eastrington had its own mill (standing in the yard of the present Mill Farm), butcher and carpenter. In the 14th century there was also a thatcher, replaced in the 19th century by the village brick and tile maker.

Eastrington men marched in the Pilgrimage of Grace in 1536, protesting against Henry VIII's religious policies, and mustered on the green to prepare for a Spanish invasion when Elizabeth was Queen. However, perhaps a more dramatic event for the village people was the collapse of the chancel arch in the church in 1632. This was quickly repaired using oak from nearby Spalding Moor, and a celebratory peal of bells rung in 1633.

The village has long had a school. There is a record of a schoolmaster in 1700 even before the foundation of a free school by the will of Joseph Hewley in 1726. Since then Eastrington has had a National school, a board school, and now possesses a modern 20th century building. A hundred years ago local children had a holiday on Shrove Tuesday when they scrambled for free oranges, worked hard at hay, pea and potato harvesting, missed school to attend Howden Hiring Fair, and died from 'catarrh' and 'typhoid'.

Eastrington children also traditionally had a week's holiday in June to celebrate the village feast, sports and foal show! Although now a one day event, the show is still a highlight of village life and is always held on the third Saturday in June.

The open fields around the village were enclosed early in the 19th century but the old names remain. West-field lane now leads to a council-owned nature reserve and picnic area, created from the former clay-pits of the village brickyard and from the disused bed of the Hull and Barnsley railway line. The village pinfold, where in 1771 John Lea impounded straying animals for a payment of fourpence a head, has gone – but Pinfold Street remains.

A century ago the village fields were growing crops of flax and teazles, the latter to be transported by rail to the West Riding cloth towns where they were used to raise the nap on woollen cloth. The three cottages where they were stored still remain, Teazle Cottages, as do the descendants of Thomas Holmes, the farmer who carried on the trade.

Since the 14th century, Eastrington's population has tripled. Around 650 adults now live in the village, and many new houses have been built since 1960. There is a bus and train service, a parish church, Methodist chapel and village hall. Despite the many changes, Eastrington is still a village community, surrounded on all sides by rolling arable fields.

Ellerby

The settlement is very old, and was known as Alverdebi in the Domesday Book. Today Old Ellerby and New Ellerby are two small villages almost a mile apart.

As the name implies, Old Ellerby is the original settlement, and the scattering of cottages and farmsteads which made up New Ellerby was much expanded after the arrival of the railway. Here the trains went under a hump-backed bridge in the road on their journey from Hull to the coast at Hornsea. The railway is no longer in existence, and the track makes a pleasant country walk and is a haven for wildlife. The Railway public house, which now has a popular restaurant, reminds one of those days. The main part of New Ellerby village stretches along both sides of the Hull to Hornsea road, being six miles from the coast. The village once boasted a windmill, the lower half now being incorporated into a dwelling. The Methodist chapel, 1909, is still in use, but the small shop-cum-post office has closed.

Old Ellerby, a small and scattered community, was mostly part of the Burton Constable estate, and much of it remains so today, with many of its residents still involved in agriculture.

A National school was built in 1876 to accommodate 50 children, but since closure this has been converted into two dwellings. Tradespeople such as the blacksmith, wheelwright and carpenter have long gone, the forge now converted to an attractive cottage home. In 1889 the tiny church of St James was erected; this is administered by the church of St Mary at Swine, and is still in use.

In well-wooded grounds on the outskirts of Old Ellerby is Woodhall, a once handsome mansion, now belonging to the Constable family but originally built in 1814 by Henry Maister, a prosperous Hull merchant.

In the corner of a field to the west of the village are the remains of an anti-aircraft battery, located there to protect Hull during the Second World War. Many dwellings were originally agricultural cottages, but most have now been modernised and are privately owned. Individual new properties have been slotted between the old, but no development on a large scale has spoilt the character of the village.

Ellerker

Ellerker is a small village in East Yorkshire on the old A63 road, with the Wolds on the east and Humber Bank on the south, adjoining the smaller village of Broomfleet and backing up to the much bigger village of South Cave. There is a beck flowing through the village, and a saying that you are not a true Ellerkerite unless you fall in. Many of the children do, and enjoy doing so.

Ellerker got its name from John Ellerker, who built the chapel of ease in 1100. The church was damaged by fire in 1241 and John Ellerker's great grandson repaired the church and gave lands to maintain the chantry. The Bishop of Durham gave the grantship of Ellerker to him and his heirs for his work. In 1512 Rolf Ellerker and his three sons fought for King Henry VIII in the Spanish Expedition. The King knighted them as a reward for their help. The family history can be traced back to the Norman Conquest and they played an important part in the history of the country. They have not used their title for the last hundred years and several of the later Ellerkers are buried in the graveyard in unmarked graves.

The church, St Anne's, was found to be in need of much repair in 1843 and Mr Pearson was brought in to rebuild it. He became a well-known builder of churches, one being Truro Cathedral, some saying that he practised on Ellerker church.

The church is built of local limestone, roofed with tiles and has a bellcote at the west end. There is only one bell (which is still rung) but in the past there were three bells which have disappeared. The east window is in the theme of the Ascension, with stonework tracery given in memory of Norrison Marshall Levitt in 1889, along with the brass lectern.

St Anne's still possesses a silver cup which Queen Elizabeth I decreed to be the sole article of value that could be used at Communion. The cup can be seen in the silver display at York Minster. The church has seating for 100 worshippers. It is lovingly cared for by the villagers and is well attended. An open air service with a steam organ brings in people from other villages.

Two noteworthy facts were the finding of a pig of iron (weight) in Ellerker parish on the route of the old Roman road and the finding of remains of a Roman villa at a place called Cockle Pits. Because of the shells it is thought that the Romans came up from the Humber to get to the road here.

Ellerker has a village hall which was built in 1928 and enlarged later, which is used by village organisations. The parish council meet here as well as the social club for old age pensioners, Women's Institute, drama group and many others. There are two playing fields owned by the village and looked after by the Playing Fields Association. A barn dance is held in a local barn each year supported by the villagers and friends to raise money for the upkeep of the field, Sports Day and a Christmas party for the village children.

Farming and the growing of tomatoes, cucumbers, other salad crops and rose trees, are the main occupations of Ellerker, with many working at British Aerospace in Brough or in Hull.

Ellerker has a few old, large houses which have been modernised, such as the Manor, the Hall and many farmhouses. In the past there was a mill, two public houses, a well attended Methodist chapel and a blacksmith; now all these have gone. The village school closed about 20 years ago, followed by a shop, then the post office/shop a few years ago. There are a few buses but villagers help the elderly to get their pensions and take all without cars to meetings outside the village.

Many houses have names of the past, like Mill House, Mill Cottages, Blacksmith Cottage and Penny School House (in the 1880s the children had to pay a penny to be taught). Amen Cottage once belonged to the church, where the church clerk lived free of rent in return for doing his duties. Sebastapol Cottage was so called because the stone wall around the cottage was built with the stone ballast from a Russian ship sailing from Sebastapol to Hull. The docks are about 14 miles from Ellerker.

From the crossroad at the top of Spillman Hill the yachts with their coloured sails can sometimes be seen sailing up and down the river Humber. The hill was so called because of the mill that was at the beckside at the bottom. Spillman Hill looks over the fields to the view of the Humber and the far shoreline of Lincolnshire.

Elloughton cum Brough

Elloughton cum Brough, as the name suggests, is two villages in one, situated eleven miles west of Kingston upon Hull. They have a very interesting history, dating back to Roman times when Brough (or Petuaria as the Romans called it) was the most important town on the north bank of the river Humber.

Bosses Field (now a playing field) covers an area which was a walled Roman town. There have been many interesting finds of coins, bones etc, but most unusual of all part of a large stone describing the Roman theatre. The remains of an important villa were found outside these boundaries and much more must lie beneath the soil.

Brough declined with the decline of the Roman Empire and wealthy landowners occupied most of the land until the Hull to Selby railway was built through the village. Wealthy businessmen then moved out from Kingston upon Hull and built large houses on land bought from the big estates. The motor car also hastened the exodus from Hull.

The Romans had established a ferry between Winteringham, on the south bank of the river Humber in Lincolnshire, and Brough and this continued. Steam packets ran from about 1840 to get goods down to Lincoln more quickly. Today in the village there is a Ferry inn, reputed, as are other houses, to have links with the notorious Dick Turpin.

In 1909 the Blackburn Aircraft Company began its life on the edge of the river and this grew from strength to strength and made a major contribution during the Second World War. The company was taken over by Hawker Siddeley Aviation and is now part of British Aerospace.

As the aircraft company expanded so did the village population, from 600 in 1840 to 5,500 in 1988. The increase was of course helped on its way by the new road links with Hull and the popularity of the motor car. Many of the small farms became housing estates, but the villages are fortunate to be divided by a large acreage of open land, Brough golf course, which has 18 holes. This started as a small private nine hole course in 1891.

There are two Anglican churches, one Methodist and one United Reformed church and services for Roman Catholics are now held at the Anglican church. There are several banks, shops and a library. The village has a local dramatic society and a number of other organisations. Elloughton cum Brough has now been designated as an urban area. This means that over the next 20 years the population will double again.

There are very pleasant walks along the river bank from the yacht club at Brough Haven to neighbouring villages. In the local library there is a small book written by J. Allen in 1841. It is called *Walks for the Stranger to Elloughton, Brough, Welton, Melton, Ferriby and South Cave*. J. Allen describes the Dale which lies to the north side of Elloughton:

> 'To those who are fond of retirement from the active scenes of life this will be a favourite spot, nothing can exceed the stillness that reigns all around. A considerable portion of the Dale has lofty trees on each side of the road, which meet overhead, and in the heat of summer, afford a most grateful shade. The wild flowers in this wood send forth their perfumes, which greatly add to this sequestered spot.'

Although the joint parish has changed so very much over the years, thankfully this could still describe the Dale as it is today – one lovely part of the village which has not changed.

Fangfoss with Bolton

Situated about ten miles east of York, this area has managed to escape the historical spotlight. A Roman road to Eboricum (York) passed through the west of the district. Fangfoss was an Anglian settlement when the Domesday Book was written; it mentions Frangefosse as being in the King's manor of Pocklington.

The parish is mainly agricultural, much of it formerly meadow and open-field land, with rough pasture provided by common moor in the west. Much of this flat common land was used as a bomber airfield during the Second World War. A hangar was sold to a caravan company in 1967 and a small industrial estate is developing beside it.

The centre of Fangfoss is a triangular green with the church and Fangfoss Hall to the east, and the old school to the west. The green must have been larger before the 18th and 19th century houses were built around it. Manor House Farm was built in the mid 19th century near the site of an earlier rectory. Fangfoss Hall was built in 1766 on or near the site of a house mentioned in 1563. Its carriage approach passes behind the church.

St Martin's church has been linked with Barmby Moor since about 1100. The church of the 12th century was a good size but ruinous by 1602. Repaired in the 18th century it was practically rebuilt in 1848. Norman stonework was used around the door. Known as St Mary's in 1851, and St John's in 1890, it is now rededicated to St Martin of Tours. The Methodist chapel was built in 1865, closed in 1974, and is currently a woodturner's workshop. The one remaining public house, at the entrance to the village, is the old Carpenter's Arms. The Primitive Methodist chapel (Canaan chapel) in Pocklington Road has become a carpenter's workshop and showroom.

Education has been active in the village since 1819. A school was built in 1867 and a master's house in 1869. The senior pupils were transferred to Pocklington in 1952 and the new primary school was built on the west side of the main road in 1971–72. A housing estate has grown up around the playing field, and further houses are being erected on the site of the old brickfield and claypit. The ancient road to Pocklington is the dividing line between the old and most of the new. A mile to the west the old railway station is a caravan site.

Nearer to Pocklington is Bolton village. It was held by the Archbishop of York in 1086. Later, the Bolton family lived in medieval Bolton Hall which stood on a moated site near the crossroads. There was a chapel east of the hall. The present Bolton Hall was erected in 1760 about one mile to the west. The small Wesleyan chapel dates from 1823.

Between Fangfoss and Bolton stands tiny Spittal, on land that was given to the Knights Hospitallers around 1100. There is no trace of the ancient hospital that was built in 1267. Part of the land near Spittal Bridge was leased to the Crown after the Dissolution of the church lands and was known for centuries as the King's Garth. Bramer Meadows lay between Spittal Bridge (known in 1371) and Ox Pasture to the west – both areas of former common land. Throughout the whole region straight hedges hint at areas of pre-enclosure common land, and curving hedges point to former strip cultivation.

Fimber

Blink, and you will miss this charming Wolds village nestling on the hillside twixt Fridaythorpe and Sledmere. You may think as you drive through on your way to either York to the west or Bridlington to the east that nothing ever happens in such a peaceful place; how wrong you would be.

Fimber (pronounced Fimmer by the locals) is the birthplace of John Robert Mortimer, 1825–1911, best known for his work in archaeology which led to a book being published, *Forty years Research in British and Saxon Burial Grounds of East Yorkshire.* Mortimer was in fact a corn merchant to his native village, and he built up an extensive trade both in Malton and Driffield, his interest in archaeology being purely a spare-time hobby.

The houses in Fimber in those days were thatched, with white chalk walls. Fuel was very scarce and had to be transported many miles by horse and cart, so the villagers would burn cassons, which was in fact dried cow dung.

In 1826 it was an exceptionally hot summer and water became very scarce. The village folk depended on rain water collected in village ponds, and up until this time Fimber had always allowed the people from the neighbouring village of Fridaythorpe to take water from their pond whenever theirs dried up, as they had two large ponds. However one of the ponds at Fimber too had dried up, and things began to get quite worrying. The people of Fimber withdrew their act of charity towards their neighbours, but the people of Fridaythorpe after such a long time felt that it was their right, and were determined to enforce it. This resulted in a war breaking out, with several broken heads and duckings in the pond. Women too took part in the battle between the two villages, which eventually ended with a victory for the people of Fimber.

Witchcraft was widely believed in and practised. Each village had a resident witch; at Fimber she was known as Rachel Kirby and she lived in a thatched house, the last one at the Fridaythorpe end of the village. When anything went wrong in the village it was declared to be due to Mrs Kirby's evil eye.

Mr John Coates, a neighbouring farmer from Wetwang, would visit the village with his cure for rheumatism, making passes over the parts affected. It was claimed there were many cures of people who had faith. Superstitions were rife; a howling dog near a sick person's house was a sign of death, and a crowing cock at the back door indicated a stranger approaching; the shoe of a horse or ass nailed to the door brought luck.

In the south-west corner of the village 'Auntie Jane' taught children in her father's cottage, and in 1867 a draw well was sunk to obtain spring water.

Fimber was also infamous for cock fighting, badger baiting and dog fighting but happily the village has now taken on a more peaceful and tranquil approach to life.

Fitling

Fitling is a scattered hamlet of farms and cottages, and the population has barely altered since the 19th century. In an earlier period it belonged to the brethren of the Hospital of St John and was mentioned in writings in the time of Henry VII and Queen Elizabeth I. It was known to have a population of 137 when it came under the manorship of Lord Hotham in the 1890s, when there were ten farmers, a shopkeeper, wheelwright, shoemaker and carrier. A licensed house, the Golden Ball, is now a private house and last opened for trade in 1954.

Admiral Storr, the son of a Hedon magistrate, was born here when the family held the manor in the early 18th century. The Admiral gained distinction in battles with the French fleet. On a mound near the coast some two to three miles distant from Fitling, stands Admiral Storr's Tower, built as an aid to navigation in the area, the ruins of which can still be seen today.

The current population is 91, with four farmers and no shop. Many trades have long since gone, and the children go by bus to primary and secondary school.

Flamborough

Flamborough village in the early days of this century and beyond, was a place rife with superstition. The villagers were mostly fisherfolk who scarcely ever ventured over the dyke separating them from the nearest town four miles to the south. Visitors to the village were eyed with suspicion and greetings met with a frown.

They were very clannish, resenting any intrusion or interference from outsiders, or 'foreigners' as they were called. These men were never seen in anything but navy-blue jerseys knitted by the wives in a cable, diamond and mesh, peculiar to Flamborough itself. The same is still being knitted, and worn by fishermen today, the pattern being passed down through generations of fishing families.

From 40 to 50 boats fished from the North and South Landings each day. The daily catch was spread on the beach and auctioned by the skipper of each boat. Fish-buyers signified their bids by nods and winks and other signs familiar to fishermen.

Fish was scarce and catches brought poor prices in those days. Both men and women worked long hours for very little reward. The wives were on the rocks by dawn each day, gathering bait. Afterwards long lines were baited whilst husbands were at sea, woe betide anyone who mentioned a hare or a pig whilst these lines were being prepared. That *was* asking for bad luck.

Wool was never wound in lamp-light or misfortune would befall the lines put into the sea the next day. Nothing was ever begun on a Friday and no boat ever sailed out of Flamborough on a Sunday. Donkeys were used by the fishing crews for taking their gear to the beach each day. When they were not needed two old men tended them on the village green, for a wage of sixpence per donkey per week. Imagine the noise from these beasts when all together on the green. Gradually over the years a pony and cart replaced the donkey, then a small van took over the conveying of gear to the shore.

As the children of each generation grew up the superstitions declined and the Flamborough clannishness and dialect has almost faded out, so also has the fishing fleet. Now, only five or six boats fish from the two bays and the fish auction is a thing of the past.

In the 18th century Flamborough fishermen were asked to pay tithes on their catches, though often too poor to support their families. They found, however, a champion in the lord of the manor. A John Ogle, who journeyed to London to plead their cause. Whilst there, unfortunately, he contracted 'gaol fever' and died. Such was the grief of the fishing community that a chosen crew set sail from Flamborough, bringing him home from London by sea for burial in the village. Descendants of the skipper of this boat are still fishing and manning the lifeboat at Flamborough today.

The lifeboat has always played a great part in the life of the village, the first being rowing and sailing boats stationed at both the North and South Landings. Before modern methods of navigation were discovered, wrecks were numerous around the coast. Fishermen crewed the lifeboats and saved many lives over the years. Now there is one motor lifeboat stationed at the North Landing but the life of the boatman is still a hard and dangerous one.

The most popular feature of this village is the steep, high cliffs around the Headland. Up to the middle of this century men were lowered down on ropes to gather eggs laid on the ledges by seabirds. The climbers (or climmers as they were known) were hauled to the top of the cliffs when the bags strapped around their waists were full of the large green and blue mottled eggs. The same evening these men went from door to door in the village selling them. The taste was rather fishy but greatly enjoyed by the villagers. The practice of egg-climbing is now illegal and the seabirds are left in peace, hence the cliffs are alive with a busy throng, whose comings and going never cease.

In days gone by, before a regular bus service between Flamborough and the nearest town, two carriers did the shopping for the villagers. Each man had a horse and covered wagon. They brought everything from a piece of furniture to a bottle of medicine, going daily on their many errands. These men were often left to choose personal clothing for their customers and many were the arguments over purchases chosen and found unsuitable by the recipients. However, all was quickly forgiven as both sides realised they relied on each other for their day to day living. News was gleaned from the townspeople and all the latest happenings were related on their return to the village.

When a special event was to be held in the community the 'village crier' was heard in the street. People rushed from their houses as he rang a large brass bell. Perhaps a concert was arranged, to be given in the village school, or a jumble sale was pending. Sometimes it was a meeting of the fishing-coble club, this old custom like so many has now died out.

Schoolchildren still dance the traditional Flamborough 'sword dance'. Boys in navy-blue fishermen's jerseys, white trousers and red woollen caps are a familiar sight around the village when any local event is taking place. This dance is performed with wooden swords which are all locked together at the end of the dance, or held aloft by the leader. A triumphant finale to an extremely lively and exhausting display.

The many caves around the coast are each known by name. The smuggler's cave speaks for itself. In the summertime, years ago and in more recent times, visitors were invited by the fishermen to 'sail around the caves'. Many tales were told of the exploits of the old time smugglers, some true and others largely exaggerated.

Part of the village green was once a large mere where children skated and sailed their boats. In recent years it was filled in and now boasts swings and slides and wooden seats, not so picturesque as formerly.

The first Flamborough lighthouse was built in the 17th century and the present one dates from 1806. It stands 85 ft high and 250 ft above sea level on the headland and its beams reach far across the water. The fog-siren is also on the coast and its note echoes far and wide on a foggy day. Many boats have been saved by the lights from Flamborough Head.

The church dates back to the 13th century. The rood loft front, though restored, retains much of its original work and is unique. Flamborough is mentioned in the Domesday Book of 1086, under the name of Flaneburg. More than 400 years before the Norman Conquest the country around the village was under the rule of a great Christian King named Oswald. Hence the church's name – St Oswald's.

Altogether, the village has much local heritage and a great deal to be proud of.

Foston on the Wolds

This attractive village is almost one mile in length and lies some five miles south-east of Driffield and approximately four miles inland. It stands on the bank of a small rivulet once celebrated for its trout, a tributary of the river Hull, most of its boundaries being watercourses.

Originally a Danish settlement established in the late 9th century, it was comprised of two large and two small fields, extending over some 1,108 acres, where open-style strip farming methods were used. By 1086, there was a corn-grinding watermill, and in the 16th century, three fulling mills to bleach, shrink and thicken material were operating. Following the closure of the brewery around 1910, the last flour mill closed in about 1925.

Primarily an agricultural area, by its advantageous position on the navigable Foston beck it attracted a diverse range of trades. Coal was brought from Hull up to the pool by horse-drawn barges, and collected by the coal merchant. Also resident in the village were millers, brewers, innkeepers, a butcher, blacksmith, joiner/undertaker, cartwright, tailor, draper and horsedealer, as well as carriers who took produce, and when necessary people, in their horse-drawn carts to Driffield, Beverley and Bridlington. By 1937 the majority of these had disappeared.

St Andrew's church, serving also Gembling and Brigham, dates back to 1300 and is of considerable interest historically. Originally it was in the care of rectors living elsewhere, but in 1381 the first resident vicar was appointed and this continued until 1947. Today one vicar is minister to five parishes. A Wesleyan chapel was built in 1802, but 77 years later was replaced by a new chapel on an adjacent site. The original building was converted to a memorial hall and was used for parish activities up until 1952 when it was demolished. The shell of the chapel is now used in conjunction with a piggery. A war memorial stone, sited near the chapel, was transferred to the churchyard. When the memorial hall was demolished, a new parish hall was built, funded by public subscription. Ten years ago this hall was replaced, partly by grant, and is now used by the Ladies Club, Flower Club, Church Mothers' Union, and by the school for indoor sport.

One remaining link with the past is the Gembling school, built in 1872 and situated about one mile from Foston, also serving two other villages. In 100 years the attendance has shrunk from 90 pupils to 27.

The Cross Keys public house served as a meeting place for the ancient Order of Shepherds, an old Friendly Society, and hosted annual club feasts up to 1915. Today it is a private residence. The

Plough inn, formerly a bakery, and then a two-room beer house, has been enlarged and modernised over the years to its present status.

The extractive industry of the parish has been, and still is, based on the deposits of sand and gravel. Cruckley Hill has been worked for centuries, closing and opening according to demand. Today the village has a market garden, painter/decorator, agricultural contractor, arable mixed, pig and deer farms, and the Cruckley Animal Farm attracts many visitors.

Sadly, all the old East Yorkshire characters have disappeared, the pattern of life has changed, and in common with many villages, Foston is today very much a base for commuters.

Fraisthorpe

This is a small village, three miles south of Bridlington, of 1,037 acres. The village itself contains three farms, two haulage contractors (of which one runs internationally), eight houses and scattered farms and cottages in the outlying districts of the village, 53 souls in all.

Nowadays there are no amenities in the village except a post box and telephone kiosk. In the past there was a small village shop, a blacksmith and a joinery shop, and on the outskirts a sand and gravel quarry, known as Kingsgate gravel pit. It was opened for the purpose of supplying sand and gravel for the building of Carnaby airfield, in the neighbouring village, before the Second World War. This sand and gravel was also needed for the locally called 'concrete road' which was built to bypass the village.

Fraisthorpe was part of the Boynton estate, which was purchased by William Strickland of Boynton in 1549 on his return from a voyage to the New World. This gentleman is the one who introduced turkeys to this country. Fraisthorpe was sold off to private enterprise in 1968.

The small Anglican church, built of seaside sand and cobbles, dates from 1693, replacing the original church which was washed into the sea. It is a very pretty church, seating 40 people, admirably kept by the villagers and well worth a visit.

The village continued on its quiet agricultural way until the First World War and the advent of the Dawson-Hydes at one of the larger farms in Fraisthorpe, who became renowned for never turning a supplicant from the door – many people were 'tramping' at this time. One person particularly remembered was of Turkish origin, without legs. He travelled very ably by use of his arms and stumps protected by leather patches. It was said that he was frightened by nobody, even though disabled. Any trouble and out would come his First World War revolver!

During this period the local blacksmith and joiner were kept very busy. However, as 1939 approached the coastline was heavily fortified to prevent invasion, the cliffs being very shallow. The fields and woods around Fraisthorpe were congested with tanks, ambulances and other vehicles, and staff waiting to be shipped out of Hull to the continent.

Up to this period no property had running water or electricity and, ironically, when the war began large numbers of Italian prisoners of war were housed in the village in Nissan huts and they were the first ones to gain these advantages. The highest property on the village outskirts, a three storey house, had to be demolished because it was in direct line of heavy artillery firing out to sea. There were two aircraft shot down and quite a number of land mines and incendiary devices dropped in the area.

After the war the village returned to its own quiet way for some time until more and more people came on their holidays. In the early 1950s Fraisthorpe was very popular with travelling gipsies and it became unusual not to see their caravans around the village. One local county councillor, Alderman Harry Smith, was asked to conduct a census of the gipsies encamped, so he asked the advice of a local man, Mr Tom Walker, as to how he should do this. He was told that it should not be too difficult as they were all his namesakes, Smith, Smith and Smith.

Fridaythorpe

On a journey from Driffield to York on a dark evening, the traveller will see the twinkling lights of Fridaythorpe as though perched on a hilltop in the distance. This, the highest of the Wolds villages, is 500 ft above sea level, and on a clear day the coast 20 miles away can be seen.

Danish raiding parties struck at the Wolds settlements in the 11th century, so it is possible the name Fridaythorpe came from the Danish goddess called Freya, 'thorpe' also being Danish in origin.

As in many Wolds villages, the sturdily built farmsteads and houses surround a village green and a pond. The road to York dissects what would otherwise be a quiet leisurely place.

Standing to the side of a quiet lane, and approached through a lychgate, the church of St Mary is one of the 18 East Yorkshire churches restored by the second Sir Tatton Sykes, fifth baronet, of Sledmere in the 1856–1903 period. An outstanding feature of the church is its unusual clock. Said to have been copied from one in an 18th century French chateau, it is made of wood with attractive black and white scrollwork. The inscription announces 'Time is Short, Eternity is Long'.

The village now has no school and no chapel, but there is a village shop, the Cross Keys public house, and a popular restaurant called the Manor House. A long-distance footpath from Filey Brigg on the east coast to North Ferriby on the bank of the river Humber, called the Wolds Way, runs through the village and is marked by an 'acorn' sign on the village green.

Garton on the Wolds

The village of Garton on the Wolds, being on the York to Bridlington road and having Driffield as its near neighbour, has never been as insulated as some of the more remote villages on the Yorkshire Wolds.

The village shop has been an important centre and the supplier of goods for the parish and outlying farms. As today, there were always travellers calling in the village supplying their various wares of groceries, meat, fish and fruit.

The village church of St Michael is of fine Norman origin and was restored by the first Sir Tatton Sykes in 1856/7 and then lavishly decorated in 1872/1880 by Clayton Bell on behalf of the second Sir Tatton Sykes. The church was chosen by the Pevsner Memorial Trust as a suitable commemoration to the architectural historian, the late Sir Nikolaus Pevsner, and the richly coloured 13th century biblical frescos have been restored. Garton can be proud of its church which is now a recognised tourist attraction.

There were two chapels and the anniversary at each was a red letter day when the children were all expected to recite or give a personal performance of some kind. Up to the Second World War the Wesleyan chapel, now closed, was well supported. At Christmas, carol singers were organised to visit the farms in the area to augment their running costs.

The reason that the village has maintained its attractive open aspect has been largely due to the farms and land being part of the Sledmere estate and the determination of the late owner Sir Richard Sykes to preserve its character at all costs.

In the early part of the 20th century the population was almost entirely dependent upon farming and its many subsidiary businesses, of which there were joiners, wheelwrights, undertakers, blacksmiths, tailors and cobblers. The Driffield area was renowned throughout the world for its hackney horses, and there were two very prominent breeders of hackneys in Garton.

Garton was fortunate in having a railway station, even though it was one mile south of the village. This was of great benefit to the farmers for the transport of livestock and grain to the various market towns, and then loading back to the farm with coals for the threshing machine and for heating. There were, as now, six or eight large farms in the parish and a number of smaller farms and holdings in the village which have sadly disappeared. The larger farms would employ ten or more farm workers and two maids in the farmhouse. At Manor Farm in busy times 18 men would sit down at one table for dinner, which was invariably at twelve o'clock. Manor Farm in those days comprised three sets of farm buildings, including the Church Farm which is now an art and craft gallery. At harvest time the farm staff would be supplemented by additional labour, very often Irishmen who would frequently visit the same farm year after year for the harvest months.

In those times the families were much larger; the Megginsons at Garton Field had 13 children, the Atkinsons at Highfield eleven children, the Wilsons at Cedar Farm twelve children, and the publican William Marshall had 15 children. The Megginson family had a cricket team who were more than useful performers, some of whom played for the Driffield and Garton Cricket XIs.

As recently as the 1930s cows were tented on the grass verges of the roads and in the green lanes in the parish. At that period Rev Dransfield was the vicar, a rather stout pompous character who took great pride in keeping the grass verge outside the vicarage mown and tidy. This recently mown sweet grass attracted the cows when returning home from the lanes, much to the chagrin of the vicar, who did not believe in the benefits of the organic deposits on his lawn. Consequently 'Butch' the cow tender, who had a masterly vocabulary, and the vicar would have a confrontation of words, neither of them comprehending the vehement expressions of the other!

The headmaster at the school, then attended by 100 or more Garton children aged five to 14 years, was 'Daddy' Watts. A highly respected gentleman who had a club foot, he was a great disciplinarian. 'Daddy' Watts' successor was a Mr Stainer, who is still remembered for his ability to instil knowledge into the least academic pupils. In the 1920s the late Lady Sykes visited the school to give clothing to the scholars, many of whom were only scantily clad.

Up to 1939 there was no mains water connected to Garton. For drinking water the village was entirely dependent upon various pumps situated in the parish, from which the water had to be carried home in buckets. The pond was the vital supply for livestock and horses in the summer months; frequently in the dry weather there were three or even four water carts to be seen in the pond at the same time, being filled with scoops before being led out to stock in the fields. In the hard winters, which were then more prevalent, the pond was an ideal skating rink.

Garton, like all arable areas in the UK, has experienced the complete change from horse power to tractor power with a reduction in the work force. The area in clover leys and grass has been greatly reduced and on some farms totally eliminated. Potatoes were not grown on the Yorkshire Wolds and now they are grown extensively, as are peas and oilseed rape. The numbers of cattle and sheep on the farms have been sadly reduced or, like the grass, totally eliminated. Every farm and smallholding had at least one house cow for the supply of milk, cream and butter and now there isn't a milk cow in the parish.

Garton with Grimston

The village of Garton is pleasantly situated about one and a half miles from the sea, and two and a half miles south-east of the village of Aldborough. The area of Garton with Grimston, which was made into a civil parish for local government purposes, has been much reduced by coastal erosion over the years.

Most of the area is covered by boulder clay and lies more than 15 metres above sea level, rising to 22 metres near the coast giving an unbroken line of steep cliffs down to the sea. The coast road from Hornsea to Withernsea runs through the west part of the village. The village has a linear plan, and is surrounded by open fields and countryside. The main street is formed by the Aldborough road, with a side road to Grimston.

The church of St Michael is built of boulders with ashlar dressings, and consists of chancel with south chapel, nave with south aisle, porch, and west tower. Parts survive from the 12th century, and it has been added to and parts rebuilt over the centuries. It is now in good repair and services are supported by a small congregation.

The Garton manor house recorded from 1718 was presumably the current Blue Hall, which was so called because of the colour of its roof tiles. The house is of red brick and was built in the later 17th century with an L-shaped plan. It is a Grade II listed building, and to the front there were three storeys and five bays with a central entrance. Over the years the top storey and the bays have been removed. The interior retains a 17th century staircase with heavy turned balusters, and panelled rooms with other fittings of the period. There are remains of a possible moat and walled forecourt to the front. The house was once owned by the Constable family, and Henry Constable and his sister Margaret both lived there, dying within a few days of each other in 1701.

The main street of Garton continues eastward to the sea and Moat Farm, the former site of Grimston Garth, mentioned in the 15th century when it was the seat of the Grimston family. The manor house, or a replacement on its moated site, was later known successively as Grimston Garth Farm, and Moat Farm. It is said to have burnt down during the lifetime of William Grimston, but a substantial house survived in 1772. It was not used by the family as they stayed at nearby Hilston when visiting Holderness. The old house is now derelict but the moat is still there with some fishponds, and a smaller moat near the surrounding earthwork called the Mount.

The new Grimston Garth was built by Thomas Grimston about 1781 and was used as a summer residence by the family, who also lived at Kilnwick. It is castellated and was designed by John Carr of York. It is built of brick with stone dressings, all of which were originally colourwashed. The house has been restored to its former splendour and is lived in today. The main block has a circular tower at each corner. The main reception rooms are hexagonal and are on the two first floors.

The two public houses, reading room and school have now gone, and the Methodist chapel is used as a village meeting place. Today the land is mainly owned and farmed by four farmers growing wheat, barley and oilseed rape. Smaller farms run cattle, there is one dairy farmer, and three farms have substantial pig units.

Goodmanham

In Volume Two of Sheahan & Whellan's *History and Topography of the City of York and the East Riding of Yorkshire* published in 1856, the village of Goodmanham is said to comprise 2,930 acres and 325 inhabitants. 'Its soil is a light loam, resting upon chalk, the surface is undulated, and the scenery very picturesque. This place is of very remote antiquity. Two streams which rise in this parish, unite and turn a water mill. This stream divides the parishes of Goodmanham and Market Weighton. There is a chalybeate (iron) spring in this parish.'

The ancient name Godmundingaham is derived from the Celtic 'godo', an uncovered sanctuary or temple, and 'mynyddis', meaning a hilly place.

According to some authorities, the ancient Britons had here a Druidic temple. Some antiquarians say the present village may even be the site of the Roman station Delgovitia, though this is disputed.

The Venerable Bede asserted that the Great Pagan Temple of Northumbria was situated at Goodmanham, probably on the very spot where the present church of All Hallows now stands. In AD 627, Edwin, the Saxon king of Northumbria, and Coifi, the high priest, were converted to Christianity. It was Coifi who rode up Goodmanham Lane near Market Weighton to burn down the temple and destroy its idols. Then, as the predicted calamity did not befall them, Edwin and his chiefs went to York to be baptised in a wooden church where today York Minster stands. It was Easter Day.

In 1927, a pilgrimage and a service held in the churchyard at Goodmanham gave thanks for 1,300 years of Christianity in the North. A wooden cross marking the spot where the Archbishop of

York stood then, was erected on a base of stones from Londesborough Hall. Tradition says it may have been at Londesborough that the Great Council of Northumbria met to consider the momentous question of accepting or rejecting God.

Goodmanham church, now considerably restored, stands on a prominent elevated knoll towards the north-eastern end of the village. Its oldest and principal part dates from the beginning of the 11th century. The church comprises a nave, north aisle, a south porch and a chancel. The low massive embattled tower is a mixture of styles. In its lower part are the remains of a Norman doorway on the western side, almost entirely concealed by a buttress. The 15th century belfry contains three bells and is reached by a wooden ladder with rough blocks for steps.

Today, entry to the church is through a porch and a Norman doorway on the south, enriched with zigzag carving, as is the recessed Norman chancel arch, which is quaintly awry, with a peephole to the altar on the north side. The chancel is 13th century and has two priest's doorways, one blocked. The nave, divided from the north aisle by three substantial arches, has massive roof beams. The large, handsome and elaborate 16th century font is richly carved on all eight sides of its bowl and stem. By its side is a crude hexagonal 18 inch high Saxon or Norman font said to have been used by Paulinus to baptise Coifi. Fragments of Norman carving are built into the walls.

Today, Goodmanham still has five working farms in the village itself and has a fairly stable population of just over 240 inhabitants. It has a public house, but no longer a school or village shop. The mill at its south-western end is no more, its name being perpetuated by a very fine private house. The majority of the village is, very properly, a conservation area, with just a handful of larger new properties shoehorned into spaces between houses and cottages of considerable character.

Many footpaths traverse the area in or near Goodmanham, including the Wolds Way, making the village a popular focal point for walkers and ramblers who delight in the advantages offered by the two disused railway lines which diverge and run to the north-west and south of this relatively unspoilt Wolds settlement.

Great Givendale

The village is small and consists of farms and cottages, mainly connected with agriculture. It is situated at the western foot of the Yorkshire Wolds, about 4 miles north of Pocklington. The area is very picturesque, and has many attractive walks.

The first known inhabitants were the Vikings, who dug out the bog in the dale bottom to create ponds in which to breed carp. Within the past few years Manor Farm has been given a conservation award for reclamation of the ponds. These form an attractive feature, making a habitat for wild geese, many birds and also bog-loving plants.

St Ethelburga's church dates from the 12th century, but was much restored in 1849 in the Gothic style. The Norman chancel

Givendale Church

arch was retained, and the ancient font preserved. The western turret contains two bells.

The setting is delightful, surrounded by woodland and carpeted with snowdrops and aconites in the early spring. In summer Givendale is unique for its white comfrey flowers, rarely found in the north. It is thought the white comfrey was introduced from the south of England by the monks who used it for making beer!

The village is part of the Garrowby estate belonging to Lord Halifax. Hopefully it will not suffer any major developments to spoil its quiet charm.

Great Hatfield

Man may have settled here in the era following the Ice Age when the landscape of Holderness was bog and mere; the Romans are known to have lived close by; the Danes were almost certainly in the area but it is in the Domesday Book that we first read of Haifield (Hatfield), when the fearsome Drogo de Beuvriere was the lord, under the rule of William the Conqueror. The ancient cross, the most important feature of the village, although sadly ruined, still stands. From Norman times its magnificent presence once marked the centre of a busy market place. The manor, with its moat, orchard, chantry chapel and magical well dedicated to St Helen, was the focal point of village life in the Middle Ages and hundreds of sheep grazed in the open fields.

In later times Great Hatfield acquired other buildings of significance. The Methodist chapel was built in 1862 and was added to in 1901. The village school remains (although now a private residence) and dates back to 1894. There is a fine war memorial, erected at the end of the First World War, where, thankfully, only one death is recorded among those who served. The Wrygarth inn stands at the entrance to the village, but a hundred years ago drink was served in the attractive old blacksmith's cottage. The pond opposite was used by him and the farmers to refresh the horses. It is unusual as it is half-moon shaped, brick-lined and surrounded by beech trees. Restored and landscaped by a local family it is one of the most attractive features for miles around. This has always been a farming village and still retains working farms. It also has a smallholding, and pick-your-own fruit. Sheep and horses still graze but, unexpectedly, there is a touch of the technological age with a small components factory in the old village hall.

In spring the verges are a mass of colour following the planting of bulbs by the Women's Institute, and hanging baskets and tubs of flowers adorn the front of the chapel in summer. Pride of place however must go to the village green, now fully restored from a neglected waste land. It is neatly kept, with a handsome red telephone kiosk and matching red letter box. Set around with old hedges and newly planted shrubs under which crocuses, tulips and daffodils grow, it gives an opportunity for the local residents to enjoy the rural peace. The new wooden seat placed under the horse chestnut tree is well used and the Morris dancers can be seen dancing at the summer fair.

The railway came to Great Hatfield in 1864 when the Hull to Hornsea line was opened. Sadly, it came under the Beeching axe in 1964, but now there is a beautiful nature reserve abounding with wildlife and flowers.

The people here retain a northern independent spirit and are proud to belong to East Yorkshire.

Halsham

Halsham is a scattered farming village spread over a three mile area of Holderness, four miles from the east coast. The land is very flat, which is a great advantage for a large agricultural area growing many acres of rape, barley, wheat, peas and beans. There are several pig farms, also cattle, sheep and chickens.

The church of All Saints is tucked away in a wooded corner of the village. It was built in the 12th century. In the 19th century a Victorian architect called George Edmund Street redesigned the church and it underwent general restoration, including a pitched roof to replace the flat leaden one. An organ was installed in 1906.

Nearby is the church institute, where social events and activities are held for the upkeep of the church.

From ancient times the manor was divided and known as East and West Halsham. One of the manors was held by the Constable family for over 500 years. Their manor house no longer remains but the family mausoleum is still a feature of the landscape today. The building of it commenced in 1790 and took ten years. It is a circular, domed building, and was up until recently crowned with a cross. Since that time members of the Constable family have been interred here, and it is said that it can fulfill its purpose till the crack of doom. The Constables founded a free school and alms hospital here in 1579. It became the school in the later 19th century, when it was altered to accommodate 50 children. The building has now reverted to an attractive residence, Halsham House.

Building within the village is very restricted, as the land must be kept for agriculture. There is a post office, public house, and fishing ponds. Every year a ploughing contest takes place, and Halsham once boasted a very fine cricket team, but this has recently disbanded.

Harpham

As the traffic speeds along the coastal road, few glance across the countryside to where the village of Harpham has followed its own quiet existence since pre-Roman times.

Only a mile from the main road the Early English square tower of the church rises above the trees and rooftops of the village. The church and its surrounding fields hold nearly all the clues of the history of the village. The farmers are allowed to graze the church fields but no ploughing must be done because here was the site of the ancient manor of Harpham. Only mounds and hillocks, ridges and hollows are visible, but it is here where the legend of the Drummerboy's Well originates. When archery was the all important skill, the lord of the manor, St Quintin, with his nobles was enjoying watching his soldiers at the butts. In a sudden movement he caught his drummerboy who was standing to one side and the lad, losing his balance, fell down the well. Tradition has it that the 'rat-a-tat-tat' of the drum comes from the depths of the well when a member of the St Quintin family is about to depart this life.

The village has a further claim to a place in history through the healing waters of the second well, known as St John's. It is claimed that he was born in the village in AD 640, educated at Whitby monastery, later appointed Bishop of Hexham and then became Bishop of York from AD 705–718. Towards the end of his life he founded a Christian community on a site which has now grown into the town of Beverley. He died there in AD 721 and was buried in his monastery church. His tomb is in the minster which he founded and each year it is decorated with primroses gathered in Harpham woods by the local schoolchildren. Annually on the Tuesday evening nearest to St John of Beverley's Day, the 7th of May, a choral procession (visiting choristers from the minster) walks from the church in Harpham to the decorated well at the east end of the village and back again to hold a service in church followed by a generous supper, much to the delight of the choirboys, in the village hall. The church of Harpham is dedicated to St John of Beverley and because of the healing miracles claimed in his name, he is the patron saint of the deaf and dumb throughout the world.

The St Quintin family came over with the Conqueror and the village church contains tombs and memorial tablets to them. The stained glass windows bear the family shields of 28 successive members from 1066–1490 and there are some very fine brasses from the time of Agincourt. There is a rare example of a carved tomb in alabaster and a most beautiful monument in white marble depicting the figure of Grief. The high pews are of 18th century oak and the 62 ft high tower contains three bells, two of which are dated 1615. Through the centuries great love has been shown in the care of the church and this continues even today.

The Victorian and Edwardian era was the time of the large shooting parties when the shooting lodge in the next village of Lowthorpe was filled with guests and the domestic servants from Scampston Hall were brought down to attend to all their needs.

Many of the estate workers in Harpham found themselves caught up in the excitement and hard work involved.

A brick kiln was in use in Lowthorpe at this time and the additions to several cottages in Harpham can be clearly seen. The last estate cottages to be built were in 1911.

During the 19th century the village was given the amenities of a reading room, a Methodist chapel and a village school, where the appointed mistress was responsible for educating the village children along with those from four surrounding villages. Many of these brought sandwiches for their mid-day meal and the teacher gave them mugs of hot cocoa. During the winter months the children's wet clothes were draped over a huge fireguard round a blazing coal fire. The girls produced samplers as evidence of their competence in plain sewing and the children's progress was checked by a visiting inspector.

The reading room has long since disappeared; the school continued until December 1967 and was then converted by the estate into a dwellinghouse; and the chapel closed in 1985.

Between the wars, the villagers followed their quiet routine almost unaware of the modern changes in the world about them. Wood and coal fires were their only method of heating and cooking. Oil and candles were their only source of lighting until 1935 when electricity was brought to the village by the Buckrose Light and Power Company. The whole village was entirely reliant on natural springs and boreholes until a water main was laid across the fields in 1953.

The annual event was the Home Encouragement Show when just about everyone in the village took part. Table decorations were exhibited down the full length of the centre of the schoolroom and side stalls of produce were judged and awarded prizes. Tea was served and later followed by a dance. This affair was transferred to the village hall after it was built in 1933, but during the Second World War the hall was taken over by the Army. The Royal Engineers were camped in the woods by the railway where they trained as Bomb Disposal Units.

After the war the villagers began to organise their own social lives again and the village hall became the rendezvous for many events. A piece of land was obtained to be used for cricket and another for a tennis club, and now there are many activities taking place both for the young and the older inhabitants.

The church attracts many visitors each year; the walks bring the ramblers across the fields and the St Quintin Arms is a popular meeting and eating place.

Hayton

The village of Hayton lies to the north side of the York–Hull main road, the A1079, just a few miles west of Market Weighton.

A tiny hamlet comprising some 50 to 60 houses, it has escaped any large-scale development. Truly rural in character, its name is evocative of its nature; the original meaning was probably 'hay enclosure' or 'hay homestead'. In former times there was a corn mill on Hayton beck, the last mention of a miller there being in 1933. The building, three storeys high and built of brick and slate, is used now as a dwelling. The wheel was fed from a dam.

Hayton's most noteworthy building is the parish church, tucked away among lofty trees on the eastern edge of the village. A most striking feature – immediately apparent – is the extraordinary tower, which is wider at the top than at the base, the walls leaning outwards as they rise. It is said to be largely 14th century.

The interior of the church is a little on the dark side, but has some interesting and attractive features. A fine east window depicts the Crucifixion, while windows on the south wall of the nave show, respectively, the scene in the Stable and the Flight into Egypt, the Baptism of Christ by John the Baptist, and the Last Supper. The ancient font seems to have traces of a lock, a reminder that in times past, witches were suspected of stealing holy water.

The Norman arcade leading to the aisle is noteworthy by virtue of the stiff leaf ornament decorating the square capitals of the tall, round pillars. Demon heads and roses – a curious combination – are carved on the tower arch, grotesque heads, a mixture of animal and human, decorate a Norman corbel table. A badly faded and defaced mural on one of the vestry walls is, it seems, a complete mystery to everyone. Quite large, and square in shape, it looks as though it may have been mostly terracotta in colour.

Outside the church it can be seen that, some time in the past, the aisle has been repaired in brick. The churchyard is extremely large for so small a village. The noted Pocklington benefactor, Major Stewart, is buried there.

The former village school stands on part of the site of Hayton Hall, which was demolished in 1805. Described as 'a pleasing Dutch-style villa', it was built in the 1660s by the Royalist, Sir Thomas Rudston, baronet.

A suggestion has been made by one or two local people that there may have been some sort of battle close to the village during the Civil War, but there is no documentary evidence of this at all. However, it is on record that 'John Hotham, with about 1,000 men, marched from York to Beverley about August 1643', and that there were 'skirmishes along the route'. Perhaps one of these took place near Hayton . . . who can tell?

Hedon

Hedon is situated six miles east of the city of Kingston-upon-Hull. It lies in the fertile and pleasant countryside known as Holderness; the peninsula between the North Sea coast and the estuary of the river Humber.

Having its own natural haven, Hedon gained its early prosperity in the 12th century by becoming the major port on the north bank of the Humber. Gradually as the trading ships became larger and the haven more difficult to keep clear of silt, more and more trade moved to the growing port of Hull.

The church of St Augustine, from its position at the junction of Market Hill and Church Lane, dominates the town and is perhaps the only remaining monument of those earlier prosperous times. With its cathedral-like proportions, it is known as the 'King of Holderness'. Work began on it between 1180 and 1190 and took nearly 400 years to complete, there being many interruptions to the building due to the lack of money, strikes and the Black Death.

Today, St Augustine's is the focus of a major Restoration Appeal.

The first proven charter was granted by Henry II in 1158, but it was Edward III in 1348 who granted a Charter of Incorporation to Hedon which gave the burgesses of the borough the right to elect a mayor and other officers and so become self-governing. This state of affairs lasted well over 600 years until the Local Government Reorganisation Act in 1976 removed the borough status and Hedon became a town.

Following a plea to Parliament, Hedon retained its right to elect a mayor, the mayor-making ceremony taking place annually within the town hall which was presented to the Corporation in 1696 by Henry Guy, the Member of Parliament for Hedon. After the robing ceremony, the mayor and councillors emerge from the town hall for the traditional 'penny-throwing' much to the delight of the eagerly awaiting youngsters.

The centre of Hedon with its cobbled Market Place is a conservation area with a number of houses and buildings of historical interest. Many of the old street names such as Baxtergate, Souttergate and Fletchergate reflect the past commercial and social interest of the town.

There are a number of objects of interest which are not immediately seen by the visitor to Hedon. In the church of St Augustine are the Royal Arms, the oldest being those of Elizabeth I and dated 1584. There is the Kilnsea Cross, a stone relic situated within the walled garden of Holyrood House, now a home for the elderly in Baxtergate. The stone is said to have been erected at Ravenser Spurn on the site where Henry, Duke of Lancaster landed to be joined by the Earls of Northumberland and Westmorland. They overthrew Richard II and Henry eventually reigned as Henry IV. Hedon also has a rare civic silver collection, renowned for its beauty and antiquity, amongst which is the oldest civic mace in the country.

As in many other areas, a great deal of housing development has taken place over the past 18 years or so and the population now stands at around 6,000. There are two schools catering for primary and junior children, together with a large comprehensive situated between Hedon and Preston.

It is a busy town with a good shopping area including a weekly market held on Wednesdays, and amenities include a post office, library, medical and banking facilities and several public houses, to name but a few. It is adequately served by public transport and the new bypass takes through traffic away from the centre.

A pleasant atmosphere has returned to the bustling town centre now that the new road allows all through traffic to bypass it, but do ensure that you do not pass by without first visiting Hedon, experiencing its charm and meeting its friendly people.

Hollym

The parish of Hollym borders the North Sea, with the village lying about one and a half miles inland from the coast and two miles south of Withernsea.

Hollym is an Anglian derivation of 'homestead near the hollow' and although most of the 400 population is centred on Northside Road (Main Street) and North Leys Road, other homes are well scattered around the parish.

Life in the village revolves around the church of St Nicholas, the Plough inn and the Main Street post office. The church is the main landmark and is now a listed building. It was built some 400 years ago, restored in 1725 and rebuilt in 1814. The walls are of yellow brick with red brick bands and the roof is covered with grey slates. Stained glass windows donated by relatives in memory of their loved ones are part of the lovely interior. Recently, the churchyard walls were rebuilt and the church redecorated. The village also boasted at one time a Wesleyan chapel built in 1860 but closed in 1979. The village school, opened in 1808, was closed in 1963 so children must now attend schools in Withernsea.

Hollym's public house, the Plough, is part of an older building built 400 years ago. One of the pub walls, still in good condition, was built of cow dung and straw and many of the bricks were made at Hollym brickworks which closed many years ago, as did the blacksmith's shop. The only other listed building (at this time) in the village is the pinfold in the Main Street next to the school.

This was a pen for stray cattle until the owners could be found. It is built with large sea boulders and was restored some years ago as a rest area for residents.

Dairy farming, pig breeding and cereal farming are the main occupations of the parish. In addition to these a local farmer has a flourishing herd of deer. There is a well-known 'Gnome Home' which manufactures garden ornaments. Also in the village is a market garden and a recently formed archery centre. However, these industries are not large enough to employ all the working residents, so many villagers must travel to Withernsea or Hull (18 miles) to their daily work.

Nearby Withernsea is a coastal resort with one of the few lighthouses built inland. It ceased working as a lighthouse in 1976 and was recently purchased to be used as a Local History and RNLI Museum and also a memorial to Kay Kendall. The purchase was made by Mrs Rollo Campbell Jnr, the sister of the late Kay Kendall of *Genevieve* film fame. Kay's grandfather, Bob Drewery, helped to build the lighthouse in 1892 and was the last coxswain of the Withernsea deep sea lifeboat, which saved 87 lives between 1862 and 1913. Withernsea is now guarded with an inshore inflatable lifeboat, manned by volunteers.

One of the North's largest outdoor markets is held three days a week on part of the site of the old railway station, which closed in 1964/65. The local hospital is also at Withernsea, built as the Queen's Hotel and designed by the Victorian architect, Cuthbert Broderick. It stands in some three acres of pleasant grounds. The area has much of interest to the discerning visitor, and to the residents also.

Holme upon Spalding Moor

Holme upon Spalding Moor lies at the foot of the Yorkshire Wolds, midway between York and Hull. It is the largest village (in area) in the East Riding of Yorkshire covering over 11,000 acres, mainly agricultural, with a population of 3,000 plus and growing more and more.

The area around the village is very flat apart from a hill on which stands the lovely church of All Saints, which was in existence at the time of the Domesday Survey (1086). It is a real landmark, and alongside the graveyard lies Beacon Field where, in case of invasion, the beacon would be lit. At the foot of the hill stands Holme Hall, which is now a Sue Ryder Home. The old vicarage is also a residential home, and adjoining the Hall is a beautiful Roman Catholic chapel. In the centre of the village is the old school chapel which is used when it snows and parishioners cannot get up the hill to the church, and is also used for Mother's Union and church meetings. Three miles away is a chapel of ease at Bursea, a small hamlet. The Methodist chapel is further along the street, and is a grand building.

The village has grown rapidly in recent years and there are nine new housing estates, 14 shops, six public houses, two banks, three garages, mobile and public libraries, a very modern surgery, a primary school with 263 scholars and a nursery school.

To the west of the village is Dale Farm Foods factory, a very modern and large concern. To the south lies a thriving industrial estate on the site of the old aerodrome, which was a bomber station during the Second World War.

The pride and joy of the community is a magnificent village hall, built by voluntary labour (with the exception of the dance floor) which was opened in 1959 by Professor Norman Feather, son of Mr Samson Feather, a past headmaster of the village school. Norman was a Professor of Natural Philosophy and was one of seven people who first split the atom. A school friend of Norman, Sir Aubrey Burke, was an aeronautical engineer who worked on the construction of the R100 airship and was on board when the airship crossed the Atlantic in 1930.

Mr Geoff Morton, who still does his farm work with horses and lives at Hasholme Carr Farm, has open days when the public can go and see the beautiful animals at work. Hasholme is a small hamlet where the remains of a log boat was recently excavated which had been used by Celtic people 2,000 years ago. It will soon be on display in the Archaeological Museum in Hull after treatment to prevent disintegration.

After the demise of the village's canal and railway line, there seemed something of a decline for a number of years. That is certainly not the case now. However, happily, much of the original character of the place remains – character re-echoed in some of the quaint place names still to be found in the area: Rascal Moor, Duck Nest, Ladies Parlour and Land of Nod among them. Land of Nod is at the end of Lock Lane on the bank of the Market Weighton canal. How it came by the name is left to the imagination.

Holmpton

Holmpton is a village in Holderness, situated right on the east coast. It is unusual for a place which is so close to the sea to have an abundance of trees and it is most likely that this is due to the foresight of lords of the manor in the 19th century. Holmpton village stands on a ridge of boulder clay which ends in steep cliffs overlooking a stony beach. The houses in the village date from the 18th century and later, most being of brick but there are a few buildings of boulders, the boulders laid in a herringbone pattern.

The village is largely unspoilt and without major development. The majority of the village has just been designated a conservation area, to safeguard the character from being spoilt in the future. The lanes round the village are particularly attractive in the summer months when the trees are in full leaf and are quite popular with people who like to park the car and have a walk.

Most of the township of Holmpton lay in the parish of Hollym, a neighbouring village, thus leading to the odd situation that fields and properties even in the centre of the village belonged to Hollym parish. The Hollym part was transferred to Holmpton in 1938 for ecclesiastical purposes.

The church of St Nicholas is a small Gothic structure comprising chancel, with north vestry, nave, and west tower with pinnacle, containing one bell. The tower is of brick and was rebuilt in 1832. The church was restored in 1874, when the boulder-built walls of the chancel and nave were plastered inside and faced outside with pinkish-yellow brick with red brick dressings and the roof raised about ten ft. The stained glass east window was presented by William Parker and his wife Charlotte, the owners of Holmpton Hall in the 19th century. The stained light in the nave was given by Sir Thomas Watson in memory of Rev John Watson of Welwick, who was also the rector of Holmpton in the 19th century.

The rectory was rebuilt in 1821. The rector enjoyed all the tithes of the part of the township of Holmpton parish. Small amounts of glebe land were sold in the 20th century. The rectory was sold in 1964.

Various villagers talk of underground tunnels that exist from certain houses leading to the church. Whether these tunnels were used by smugglers, or were to do with people worshipping certain religions in secret we shall never know. The different theories are certainly intriguing.

The ancient manor of Holmpton was known as Holmetone at the time of the Norman Conquest. It passed through various hands and reverted to Bolton Abbey, in whose hands it stayed until the Dissolution of the Monasteries. The manor was then split into two and one part ended up with William and Charlotte Parker of Holmpton Hall; this was classed as the manorial part of the estate. The other part passed through to the Feaster family in 1811. Anne Feaster sold this to William Parker in 1871. Thus the two parts of the village which were previously split were one again. Holmpton Hall became the chief house on the estate because of this. The Hall, being Queen Anne, was rebuilt in the plain Italian style in 1866.

At Charlotte Parker's death in 1917 most of the estate was sold to J. W. Herd along with Manor Farm and North Farm in 1919. West Farm was acquired by Mr Herd in 1936. He conveyed these three farms to his sons, making the Herds the main farmers in the village.

There has been little non-agricultural employment in the village throughout the centuries; there were usually seven to nine farmers in the parish in the 19th and 20th centuries. Like most villages Holmpton was self sufficient with its blacksmiths, wheelwrights, grocers and tailor and draper. Bricks may have been made east of the village where Brick Close plantation was named in 1852. There was one licensed house in the later 18th century. It was called the Man's Head in 1823 and today it is known as the George and Dragon.

Holmpton also had its own coastguard service by 1841. The rocket house in the village stored the rocket that the coastguards sent up in rough weather to warn ships. The coast line off Holmpton has taken its toll on shipping in the past; the *Baltic* (1868) and *Rapid* (1871), sailing ships, and also the *Canada* (1939), a Danish motor vessel which was hit by a mine. This wreck is still there.

Holmpton school was rebuilt in 1862 and 25–30 pupils were usually in attendance at the school at any one time. The school was closed in 1961. The building is used as a village hall nowadays.

Rysome Garth stands inland from Holmpton and is an ancient manor and estate. The present house dates from the early 19th century and stands on a formerly moated site. It is thought that some unrecorded military engagements took place there because spearheads have been found and in 1889 two cannonballs were disinterred.

Hook

It is well nigh impossible for any stranger looking for Hook to tell when they have found it, for there is no signpost at either end of the village. Hook remains a shy and secret place. It has many secrets well worth keeping but some are of interest to reveal.

The old village of Hook lies on a narrow peninsula, formed by a loop in the river Ouse as it nears Goole, on its way to join the Trent and then to form the great tidal waterway of the Humber.

It is a flat and watery place. Although the banks of the river have been built up in recent years to check the flood tides, the masts of ships can still be seen, slowly gliding across the landscape of fertile, flat, green fields.

In 1213 the Abbot of Selby granted a licence to build a small chantry chapel for the manor house of Baron John de Houke, whose forebears had come over with William the Conqueror. The village takes its name from this Norman family. The manor house can no longer be seen but there are still traces of the moat which surrounded it. The moat acts as a drainage channel and fills up with water on occasions. Wild swans have been seen nesting there and in years gone by, when the moat froze over, tales are told of ice skating and sled races.

The low stone bellcote church of St Mary was consecrated in 1225. It is almost hidden from the road by a screen of fine copper beeches. There are two rows of medieval arches inside and a narrow 13th century doorway leading to the vestry. On the south wall there is a leper squint. The longest surviving register is dated 1673 and burial entries before the 18th century often read 'buried in wool'. This was in accordance with the law to promote the wool trade. In 1832 there was a cholera epidemic and victims buried in the churchyard have their tombstones marked with a 'C'.

The most imposing building in Hook is Hook Hall; a fine red brick Georgian mansion built in 1743 by Admiral Frank Sotheron, said to have sailed with Nelson.

The present vicar of St Mary's is Rev Harry Bagnall, who was the padre in Port Stanley when the Argentinians invaded the Falklands in 1982. His book, *Faith Under Fire*, tells how he and his wife, Iris, coped under armed invasion. He smiles when he compares leafy, quiet Hook, with its medieval church, to the bleak, treeless, windswept landscape of the Falklands and the Christ Church Cathedral of Port Stanley with its corrugated iron roof.

The village today comprises two pubs, the Blacksmith's Arms (previously a smithy needed for the farm horses) and the older Sotheron Arms, formerly a stabling inn for those riders taking the ferry over the Ouse to Howdendyke. There is a post office, a newsagent's and, most importantly for the future strength of the village, a newly built, open-plan church school which has, to date, 104 children on roll. Hook also has a Methodist chapel and there is some mingling of the two congregations.

The Memorial Hall was built in 1925 from proceeds of the Peace Celebration Fund (1914–1918). No drinking or gambling is allowed on the premises (but a blind eye is turned to bingo for the OAPs!)

Hornsea

Hornsea is a small, attractive seaside town with a village atmosphere on the East Yorkshire coast. The approach via the Hull Road is particularly charming, offering a surprise view of the mere and 14th century church. The church is dedicated to St Nicholas, patron saint of sailors, and was built mainly of cobblestones brought up from the beach by pack mules. Many of the old walls and houses of the town were also built of this material. The vault of the church was used by smugglers to conceal goods and in December 1732 they were aided by the parish clerk, who left the door open for that purpose. That night a violent hurricane took the roof off the church, causing the parish clerk to suffer a stroke, from which he never recovered.

A short walk takes you to Back Westgate where some lovely old cottages can be seen. One of these is Quaker Cottage, which was used as a meeting house in the 17th and 18th centuries, and after restoration was reopened as a meeting place for the Society of Friends.

Many of the larger houses in the old part of the town were small farms, and one of these, Burns Farm, which had been in the same family for over 300 years, has been bought by a local doctor. He and his wife have created a most interesting small museum of rural life as it was 200 years ago. This museum has received two prestigious awards, one for the best small museum of the year, and an award for Heritage Education. It provides facilities for visiting groups of school children to partake in such activities as weaving, butter making and washing and to watch old crafts being demonstrated.

The town itself has quite a good shopping centre and a supermarket. There is also a Sunday market which is very popular with holidaymakers. In the centre of the town is Hall Garth Park, with its own golf course, and a corner for the children with swings and roundabouts. A larger golf course is on the outskirts of the town.

Hornsea can be proud of the fine sandy beach (over a mile long) and a good promenade where there is the Floral Hall, mainly used for dances and musical entertainment. Summer events include a carnival, with a procession of coloured and decorated floats through the town. Then there is an annual musical festival which draws competitors from quite a distance and provides several days of good music and evening concerts.

Hornsea has a reputation for being a retirement town and, apart from local builders, tradespeople and shopkeepers, there is no industry, the only exception being Hornsea Pottery, which is well established on the site of a former brickyard.

Started by two West Riding brothers, Desmond and Colin Rawson, Hornsea Pottery soon grew in importance and size. At first it provided an outlet for the sale of good, though 'seconds', pottery items but now the leisure park is an industry on its own, drawing coaches full of visitors who not only look for pottery bargains but also enjoy Butterfly World, birds of prey, a children's playground, a plant centre and other attractions. The latest venture has been to add a permanent display of vintage cars in the appropriate setting.

Several well known people have lived in Hornsea; Joseph Armitage Wade started the railway, the brickworks and the long vanished pier. The railway was closed many years ago but many people remember the cheap trips into Hull, about two shillings and sixpence return in the 1940s, and the fun of meeting friends every day on the 'business special' and playing cards or joining the ladies' knitting carriage. The track is now a pleasant walkway. Among well known visitors, the town recalls that Charlotte Bronte stayed with her former nurse in Swiss Terrace, and occupants of this house have claimed to have seen a small lady in a poke bonnet on the stairs. Truly a ghost to be proud of! The author of *South Riding*, Winifred Holtby, lived here for a time and when this book was made into a TV serial, the camera crew came to Hornsea and many of the sequences were shot here; the local people were eager to appear in crowd scenes as extras. Lawrence of Arabia often stayed here, when as inconspicuous Aircraftsman Shaw he was stationed at Bridlington, some twelve miles north. Brian Rix, actor and producer, and his sister, Sheila Mercier of Emmerdale Farm fame, began their stage careers in the little mission hall, formerly a Congregational church. Their parents lived in Hornsea until their deaths and were both involved in producing plays here.

Hornsea Mere is the largest freshwater lake in Yorkshire, with its own RSPB nature reserve, where many species of geese, swans and other birds and animals can be seen. There is sailing and rowing on the mere, and when there is a yacht race it is a very colourful spectacle on a summer's day.

Hornsea still seems to attract many visitors, although most of them stay at one of the caravan sites. Some of the large boarding houses have become residential homes for the elderly, though there are still one or two old fashioned landladies.

For those who live here, Hornsea is held in great affection, and it is said that people who go away usually return sooner or later. It has that sort of intimacy and charm not always found in larger towns.

Hotham

Although the earliest mention of Hotham only dates from AD 963 there is no doubt that people lived here long before then as flint tools have been found in the fields. Lying beside a beck in the shelter of the Wolds and not far from the Humber, it is not surprising that the name, probably dating from Anglo-Saxon/Danish times, means a sheltered hamlet or farmstead.

When William came from Normandy in 1066, there were already over 650 acres of cultivated land in the village out of a total of some 2,800 acres in all, and about 100 people lived and worked in the village. This was followed by probably the most disastrous time in the village history when within 20 years the population was reduced to 40 and nearly all the land lay waste.

Gradually recovery took place. By 1251 the population was back to 100 although there were '15 ruinous cottages'. Farming was the only source of livelihood, together with work in and around the manor, and remained so until the 17th or 18th century. However the population increased slowly, reaching 250-odd in 1350 (about the same as 1989) and its maximum of 382 in the days of rural prosperity in the late 19th century.

In the last 250 years change has probably been more rapid than in any previous period. Although farming remained the basic economy, the emergence of both Hotham House and Hotham Hall as large estates meant many people were employed as domestic servants, gardeners, grooms, cooks or in other ways. In addition skilled craftsmen and retailers were to be found. There were shopkeepers throughout the 18th and 19th centuries, the last one leaving the village in 1989. There were one or two shoemakers until 1893, a miller until 1872, a tailor until 1921, a clockmaker until 1909, school teachers from at least 1774 until 1955, carriers until 1939, a farrier from 1840 to 1860, a blacksmith from at least 1820 to 1939, a butcher from 1850 to 1872, an innkeeper from 1850, a postmaster/mistress from 1859 to 1989. Now that society has all but disappeared. Some of the older inhabitants are a link with the 19th century social and economic life but for the young there is little or no work in the village itself nor is there anywhere for them to live as the houses and cottages change hands at prices beyond their reach.

The Second World War marked a watershed in the social and economic life of Hotham. The craftsmen and shopkeepers departed, the 'Big House' no longer employed so many people, farming became mechanised, the school closed and in 1989 the last shop and post office closed.

In the latter years, daffodil bulbs have been planted along the approaches to the village, adding beauty to an already attractive little area.

Howden

Howden, a small old market town but with a sense of village community, stands across the river Ouse four miles from Goole, off the M62 in North Humberside, the old East Riding of Yorkshire.

Howden, its medieval name Hovedene, was the centre of a vast ecclesiastical establishment in Howdenshire, belonging to the Prince Bishop of Durham. It is dominated by its minster, the collegiate church of St Peter and St Paul.

The minster leads into the largely undisturbed Georgian town centre, which has taken on a new lease of life under the guidance of the local Civic Society. The society and private individuals have won many awards for the restored cobbled streets and buildings, particularly the Bishop's Manor, the summer palace of the Bishop of Durham.

Howden was renowned for centuries as the site of an important horse fair which lasted six days, beginning on 26th September. In medieval times it was one of the largest in England. The numerous inns providing car parking in their spacious yards and former stables are remaining links with Howden's previous importance.

The Hygena furniture factory is the largest centre of employment, and Howden Dyke on the river Ouse brings trade to Howden. There is a magistrate's court, a newly built health centre, three schools, plus a Roman Catholic church and Methodist chapel.

Howden Marsh, situated on the outskirts of Howden, is a low area of over eleven acres, the habitat of wild flowers, animals and birds, which the parish council is developing as close to nature as possible. The marsh has been drained so the water forms a lake with small islands for birds and wildlife.

Probably the most remarkable native of Howden was the 12th century historian Roger de Hoveden, confidante of King Henry II and friend of Thomas a Becket. Neville Shute, the eminent author, widely known for his book *A Town called Alice*, once resided in

Howden Minster

Howden, along with Barnes Wallis, one of the greatest inventors of the 20th century, who designed and helped to build the airship R100. During the Second World War, Sir Barnes Wallis designed the 'Bouncing Bomb' of Dam Busters fame, which did much to turn the tide of war to victory for Britain.

Near the minster there is the Ashes playing fields which was given to the town by a local benefactor, Charles Briggs. It contains fine old trees and floral displays, and provides facilities for cricket, football, tennis and bowls, with a children's adventure playground. This is also the venue for the annual Howden Agricultural Show, which every year brings friends and visitors together to revel for two days in the old-fashioned atmosphere of an English country fair.

Humbleton

Humbleton is a small country village situated in the heart of Holderness, which is the part of Yorkshire that stretches between Hull and Bridlington southwards to the river Humber.

There has been some form of settlement in Humbleton for at least 900 years and it was mentioned in the Domesday Book in 1086 as Humeltone. The village is surrounded by rich agricultural land and there are five farms all bearing the village name – Humbleton Manor, Humbleton Hall, Humbleton House, Humbleton Moor and Humbleton Grange.

The village school was known as the Herons endowed school. Children travelled from the surrounding villages of Elstronwick, Lelley, Fitling, Flinton and Danthorpe until it was closed in 1960. Since then the building has been used as a village hall for the local community but still belongs to the Herons Trust. The building dates back to the early 1800s and although it was partly rebuilt in the early 1900s it still resembles the original design.

The church was rebuilt in the 13th century and further modifications and restoration were carried out in the 15th century. The oak pews and present pulpit were installed at the turn of this century and hot-water heating was installed in 1899 at a cost of

£75. The 65 ft tower is said to be the best-proportioned tower in Holderness. There are three bells in the belfry dating from 1594 but ringing of the bells ceased in 1935 as the bell rollers became in need of extensive repairs. The clock was installed in 1920 with money raised by the parishioners with the intention of creating a long-lasting memorial to those who served and gave their lives in the First World War. The well-equipped organ has two manuals and was built by T. Hopkins and Sons of York who installed it in 1910; the air was pumped by hand until 1950 when an electric blower was installed.

The Humbleton Recreation Club was founded in 1946, which accommodates a thriving cricket club with two men's teams and two junior teams, a football team, a ladies' hockey team, a snooker room and a tennis court, and a ground which is highly respected throughout the area.

Hutton Cranswick

Hutton Cranswick is two communities, both pleasantly situated and just under one mile apart. They are administered by one parish council, which takes in the hamlets of Sunderlandwick and Rotsea. It is four miles south of Driffield, and skirted by the Driffield–Beverley road. Passing over the parish boundary at Sunderlandwick, the old toll bar is on the right, and Bar Farm opposite. The mill at Hutton is still standing, minus sails, and implies a once thriving community, and a self sufficient one, as were many old villages mentioned in the Domesday Book.

At the present time it is well served by British Rail, so is mainly a dormitory village for commuters to Hull, Beverley and Driffield. It is an agricultural area, growing roots and grain, with milling facilities on the modern industrial estate.

Hutton is the smaller village and stands on higher ground, the very name Hoot meaning 'a hill'. There is much history connected with the area, as it was originally the site of a fortified camp where fierce battles were fought between the Saxons and the Danes. A curiously named farm at the eastern end of the parish, adjacent to the waterway which leads into the river Hull, is Corps Landing, the legend being that corpses were landed here for interment, but this cannot be proved.

The church is situated at Hutton, and serves the combined villages of Hutton and Cranswick. In AD 699, Wilfrid, Bishop of York, built several churches all dedicated to St Andrew, so in later years Hutton Cranswick was rededicated to St Peter. The church is very attractive in a well-treed setting, and fronted by a small village green. The church gates of locally grown oak were fashioned by a local craftsman. Of great interest are the church bells, very fine for a small village church. Campanologists come from far and wide to 'ring the changes'. Six in all, the largest was hung in 1635 and recast in 1949. Tradition says the original three large bells should have gone to Driffield but were delivered to Hutton by mistake.

The vicarage house is a handsome brick building in the Gothic style. It was built in 1874 at the expense of Lord Hotham, who at the time owned much of the parish. It is now privately owned, and in 1967 a new vicarage was built in the extensive grounds.

The Jubilee Methodist chapel at Hutton, 1860, is still used for worship. 'Tween towns' between the two villages is reputed to have a ghost, a lady who crosses the road occasionally.

The focal point of Cranswick is the village green, six and a half acres, believed to be the largest in East Yorkshire. It is surrounded by cottage homes, once thatched. The pond, now landscaped, is fed by underground springs, and was the watering place for horses and cattle in days gone by. In 1976 the green was designated a conservation area. Cottages on Bunkers Hill face directly onto the green, and evidence of a pinfold or pound can be seen by the school wall. There is a refurbished children's playground in one corner of the green. Stately horse chestnut trees guard the green, and that sacred piece of greensward, the cricket pitch, laid down in 1929, is the perfect backdrop for the players in white clothing. Many famous Yorkshiremen have wielded a bat there.

Country lanes, farms and fields have attractive names – Hobman Lane, Howl Lane, Sheepman Lane, Ricklepits, Clay Floors, Scurfe Dyke and Botany Bay. The whole area is criss-crossed with rights of way, used by local people before roads were made, and now used for rambling.

The Methodist chapel, 1861, along with other buildings in the village, is of some architectural interest. John Wesley once passed through on his way to preach in Driffield. The county primary school at the western end of the green is now modernised. An infants school, at the eastern end, was completed in 1850 and closed in 1923. It then reverted to the church, not without some controversy, and it is now known as the church rooms. An interesting donation of £10 to the building of the school was from George Hudson the railway king, who was constructing the Hull to Bridlington line at the time. This line has had many threats of closure, and this would end a vital link to Hutton Cranswick.

Kexby

The small village of Kexby lies about five miles due east of York. It stands at a point where firm ground lies close to the river Derwent, and from olden times has been the site of an important river crossing, first by ferry, later by bridge. For this reason it has always enjoyed a notability out of all relation to its size. The road from Dunnington to Wilberfoss, now part of the York–Hull trunk road, runs through the village.

The ferry across the Derwent, mentioned as early as 1315, was last mentioned in the middle of the 17th century. At the latter time, it crossed near the bridge and belonged to the lord of Kexby. According to some experts, the first bridge, of stone, was built in the early part of the 15th century by a York merchant, but another school of thought suggests an earlier date, declaring that it was mentioned in the reign of Edward III.

In any event, it is certainly the oldest bridge over the Derwent. A lot of work was done to the bridge in the years 1648–50 and an inscription on it states that it was 'built' in 1650. A new bridge was built during the 1960s, bypassing the old one – an attractive structure of three semi-circular arches divided by piers with cut-waters.

Kexby village, strung out along the main road, consists mainly of 19th and 20th century houses, but Manor Farm which stands not far from the bridge is an 18th century building. Formerly it was the Coach and Horses inn, where travellers changed horses, and is said to incorporate some of the features of the inn. Apparently in the old days it was the place where tenant farmers paid their rent to the estate.

The village has a small delightful church in an attractive setting. Dedicated to St Paul, it is stone built in an early Gothic style. It was consecrated in 1852 and consists of chancel, nave, north-west bell turret with spire, and west door with canopy. There is one bell. The chancel ceiling is lavishly decorated in blue, red and gold. An interesting feature of the church is the array of gilded heads high up on the walls of the nave. Though no one seems certain, it has been suggested that they may represent the saints.

In the churchyard a massive rhododendron bush provides a vivid splash of mauve to churchgoers and passers-by during the early summer. The churchyard is said to be the scene of a visitation from a ghost – reputedly a 'young man in black', who caused the frantic barking by a dog one evening and then promptly disappeared! Two more ghosts, two women – also in black – are said to have been seen about the village in days gone by.

At one time there was a mill at Kexby, either a windmill or a horse mill, according to one resident. It stood 'near where the new road is'. A brick and tile works in the village closed in 1974, and a blacksmith's shop was pulled down in 1953. There has been no school in the village since 1906.

Keyingham

Keyingham is properly pronounced 'Kayingham'. Early settlement by Caega and his people gave the village its name. In the Domesday Book it is recorded as Caingeham, and as having a church and a priest.

The Main Street is part of the main A1033 road from Hull, which runs to Withernsea and Easington and to the Spurn peninsula. The houses stand close to the road, with some of the oldest of the village's houses, its two public houses, the post office and the local supermarket all enduring the unremitting throb of the traffic as cars and lorries pound through its narrow confines taking holidaymakers to the coast at the weekend and workers to the British Gas terminal at Easington through the week.

The church, dedicated to St Nicholas, shows clear signs of its growth over the centuries. Its earliest parts were built of large cobbles and later additions in small stones, very early brickwork and dressed stone. It once had a spire which, along with those at Ottringham and Patrington, helped to guide the mariners sailing on the river Humber some two and a half miles to the south. After being severely damaged in a storm, the spire was replaced with a square tower in 1969. Inside, a memorial tablet inscribed in Latin can be found, also an hour-glass timer that ensured that the sermons did not last too long.

The Methodist church has also undergone renovation and modernisation. The cenotaph provides a fitting frontispiece to the chapel and here the memorial garden, cared for by members of the Keyingham Royal British Legion, now houses the remains of the ancient village cross, moved from its site a few yards away where it would have caused an obstruction to modern traffic flow.

The village is punctuated at each end by the tower of a windmill. The Old Mill, at the west end of the village, was still operative until the early years of the Second World War, and the New Mill at the east end, which lost its sails in a gale so severe that parts of them were found in the next village, has been restored in recent years and is now a very attractive dwelling.

As at Domesday, agriculture is still at the heart of the economy of the village. There is a dairy farm and two farmers who keep pigs quite close to the centre of the village, but the larger farms with their pigs and sheep and production of cereal crops are on the outskirts of the village. But by far the greatest employers of local labour in the village itself, at present, are the nurseries with their spreads of greenhouses producing a large proportion of the country's salad crop requirements, and plants for the nursery industry are also produced here.

Other farms that were once situated in the centre of the village have been displaced by extensive house building which began in the early 1960s and continues to the present day. This new housing brought inevitable changes to the life of the village, and many of those who live here now work in the city of Hull or at the nearby installations at Saltend and Easington. The school was extended to accommodate the increased number of children and an additional school was built for the infants.

A meals-on-wheels service was started in Keyingham in 1963, which still operates and serves up to 20 people twice a week. Good Neighbours, Darby and Joan and the day centre at Horrox Court provide regular support and entertainment for the older villagers. The Neighbourhood Watch Committee provides a regular newsletter for the village and has taken over the distribution of Christmas parcels to the pensioners.

Gradually the old has merged with the new and the grandchildren of the 'young couples' who moved into the 'new' houses are now becoming the second generation to attend Keyingham school. It is their village now, just as much as it was for the old village families.

Kilham

From the Iron Age (at least) to the present day, people have found Kilham a good place to settle. Nine roads lead into the village and Celts, Romans, Anglo-Saxons, Vikings and even Daniel Defoe, found their way here. Killum or Killom means 'at the springs' and in a chalky area the presence of surface water is a boon, unless you lived in a house which flooded every time the springs rose. There are today houses with the remains of ingenious devices for channelling away the water.

The village lies in the heart of Winifred Holtby country, between the main Wolds area and the contrasting lowlands of Holderness. It is conveniently near and pleasantly distanced from Hull, Beverley, York and the Yorkshire coast. Evidence of its long lively history is abundant in the village and although some of it is

East End, Kilham

impressively obvious, much of it is tucked away in farmyards and back gardens.

There is a bull ring, now secured in a stone block resting on the verge near the church, which is a reminder of the baiting which entertained our ancestors, and a sun-dial strangely set into the top of a small upright coffin-shaped stone in the churchyard.

Modern building work has revealed Iron Age remains, old almshouses and a Quaker burial ground. The earliest parts of the church date from about 1100, but nonconformist groups have often dominated the religious scene: Methodists, Baptists, Quakers, Salvationists have all left their mark in buildings and street names. The Methodist chapel stands on the site of an 1815 building, and there is at present a vigorous campaign to raise money for the restoration of the church.

The very successful Twydale turkey business began in Kilham. There have been bakers, blacksmiths, carpenters, shoemakers, millers, tailors, bricklayers, glaziers, weavers, booksellers, watchmakers, brewers and rope makers. One of the mill towers still stands as a private house and the old ropery is the base for an antiques shop.

At one time there were six schools in Kilham and a lunatic asylum. The thriving C of E primary school of today is the successor of the National school of 1847. But the modern equivalents of the apothecaries, surgeons, druggists and vets of the past now operate from Driffield, which began to take over from Kilham as the 'Capital of the Wolds' in the late 18th century and through the 19th. The population which had been 1,252 in 1861 fell to 853 in 1921. Now, with the influx of newcomers, the population is rising again and Kilham has the air of an active community which appreciates its roots.

In 1988 the WI produced a village information sheet and it was heartening to list all the trades and professions still being practised in the 20th century in Kilham. At the same time, the Institute worked on a survey of field names and has rescued from oblivion such field names as Strums, Honeypots, Knagsfield and Skitterdale.

Kilham had an honourable war. Crash runways were built nearby for the bombers returning from missions in Europe, and Free French forces were billeted in the village. Kilham also had the distinction of housing the Pigeon Corps which, perhaps surprisingly, played an important part in Second World War communications. Preparations for the Normandy landings took place here because the terrain is similar to that which faced the Allied invasion forces.

Kirby Underdale

Kirby Underdale is a pretty little village, lying in a fold of the Yorkshire Wolds, a mile or so from the busy road between Stamford Bridge and Fridaythorpe. Being part of the Garrowby estate, owned by the Earl of Halifax, it is rather unusual in this day and age as having no privately owned houses or farms, other than the old rectory which was sold several years ago when the parish became part of a joint ministry.

The charm of this village lies not only in the pleasing situation, but in being quite unspoilt by modern buildings, and in still retaining a genuine 'olde worlde' atmosphere. The church of All Saints stands in a hollow and is of great historic interest, dating from the 12th century. The squat tower is almost level with the rectory garden above it. Hills and meadows surround the church, and a gravel path leads from the quiet lane through an iron kissing gate, which is an alternative entrance to the wooden gates, bought to commemorate the Queen's Silver Jubilee. This churchyard is a mass of primroses and daffodils in the spring. An old stone coffin lies near the porch, and beside the path is the 'stone chair'. This is thought to be the base of an old stone cross, and was found in a field higher up the hill which is still known as 'Stone Chair Close'. A steep flight of brick steps leads from the churchyard to the rectory garden, and another long flight in stone connects the churchyard with the street above. This rectory, dating back to 1740 gradually increased in size over the years as large families were accommodated. Rev Monson is known to have had 15 children!

Further up the village is the old school, which is now used as the village hall. The war memorial is near what was once a busy joiner's workshop, manned for many generations by members of the Boyes family. There is a small shop flanked by brick cottages with pantiled roofs, and round the corner near the lane leading to the neighbouring hamlet of Uncleby is the now disused blacksmith's forge, once so busy in the days of working horses.

Cows still meander through the village to pastureland near the stream which runs alongside the graveyard. Behind the church, under the spreading branches of an ancient Spanish chestnut tree, is the burial ground of the Halifax family, where not only the graves of past earls can be seen, but those of much-loved servants too. Royalty, when guests at Garrowby Hall, have attended services in this secluded little church, mixing with the regular congregation with no fuss at all.

A short distance from the village, beside a steep and narrow hill, there is a tall wooden crucifix. This is in the grounds of Painsthorpe Hall, a pleasing manor house built in 1814, once the home of Sir Charles Richardson, who had a brilliant naval career. In 1902, after the Hall had stood empty for some years, Lord Halifax lent it to a small community of Church of England Benedictines under Abbot Aelred Carlyle, the subject of a book *Abbot Extraordinary*. The brothers converted part of the building to make a chapel, and set up an industry in old railway huts which produced exquisite ecclesiastical embroideries, many of which can still be seen in local churches. The brothers were much loved in the village and joined in all activities, until the abbot sought fresh fields.

This area is full of history. Little is known of the inhabitants of the old manor house with its interesting architecture in the centre of the village, but the oddly named Hanging Grimston is within the parish, and here the Bouchier family lived in what must have been a grand castle with cottages nearby, and owned much land.

Nowadays, a gated road leads past scattered farms, and only a few uneven mounds give evidence of the castle. A member of the Bouchier family served under Henry VIII at the Field of the Cloth of Gold, and later in the reign of Charles I, Sir John Bouchier was a member of the Long Parliament and one of those responsible for the King's death.

In this day and age, a few walkers find pleasing footpaths leading through this quiet old village, which was once very much a self-supporting community when access to the world outside the dale was difficult, especially in a hard winter when few travellers braved the snow-blocked lanes between the hills.

Kirkella

Kirkella, Westella, Northella, Southella and Willerby were all originally separate villages and settlements connected by rural pathways and cartroads on the approaches to the Yorkshire wolds. Over the past 60 years these villages have developed into an area of suburbia covering four and a half miles to the west of the city of Hull.

Links with Hull and its river industries brought prosperous merchants to live in their Manors and Halls, some of which still exist as residences, or such as Willerby Old Manor, now converted into flats.

Communication with Hull was maintained by horse-drawn

vehicles, daily local carriers taking anything and everything needed by the villagers. Horse buses gave way to motor transport, and the Hull and Barnsley Railway with stations at Springhead Halt and Willerby village. The rail link has gone and the family firm which provided the public services was absorbed into the East Yorkshire Motor Services, who are still in operation.

The separation of these villages is fast disappearing with the development of land for houses and industry. That magnificent engineering achievement the Humber Bridge is further opening up the area, improving communications and eventually leading to an East Coast motorway, linking up with newly completed roads on the north bank.

The district of Haltemprice is named after the no longer evident Haltemprice Priory. There is also a legendary site containing a Druids Circle in Kerry Pit Way.

Kirkella church, St Andrew's, was mentioned in the Domesday survey. Its registers date from 1558. The vicar of that time had tithes and rights, one consisting of 'pigs, pidgeons and ducks to the value of 16 shillings'. Part of the graveyard was reserved for deceased gipsies, and at the church gate stood the village stocks until about 1880. The church tower, built later than the rest of the building, has a clock, and six bells presented in 1883 by Arthur Egginton Esq in memory of his mother. A daughter church, St Luke's, of recent erection, is situated in North Ella. In the latter part of the 18th century South Ella was the property of Arthur Eggington Esq JP, who kept one of the finest herds of black Aberdeen Angus cattle in England, prize winners at many English and Scottish agricultural shows.

Dairying and arable farms still occupy what open land is left, and one could wish that old and evocative names like Willywire Bottom, High and Low Gillenders, and Folly Flatt could be incorporated into modern developments.

Methodism is represented by a first building dated 1897 and a more recent and well-supported church, both in Willerby Square. Two modern hotels at Willerby offer superior services over a large area, in addition to several public houses dispensing their brands of hospitality. De-La-Pole Hospital, once a mental asylum, has been considerably expanded to deal with general medical and surgical requirements, following the decline in the need for its original purpose.

Langtoft

Nestling in the Wolds, six miles north of Driffield on the B1249 in a valley surrounded by rolling countryside, lies the village of Langtoft. A farming community, existing as a hamlet in ancient times, it probably developed its agricultural resources to fit in with Kilham, which was at one time the chief market town in this part of the East Riding.

One of the earliest of our English poets, Peter de Langtoft, was born in the village in the 13th century, and died a canon of Bridlington Priory in the reign of Edward II. Amongst Peter's works was a five book history of the reign of Edward I, and a chronicle of England from its origin to the reign of Edward II. Although he died around 1307, his memory is preserved on the Langtoft Cross which was erected by the last Sir Tatton Sykes of Sledmere on the small green at the southern end of the village. The cross rises on an octagonal base and depicts on its eight sides the history of the village. Peter is shown on the plinth, being taken by his father to be educated by the monks at Bridlington.

Langtoft is perhaps most notorious for its record of freak weather conditions and violent storms. Many of these are recorded by J. Dennis Hood in his book *Waterspouts on the Yorkshire Wolds* which was published in Driffield in 1892. In May 1853, a terrific thunderstorm broke over the village. Two men were ploughing on one of the hills, and though they escaped with their lives, their ploughs were destroyed and three of their horses struck dead. A waterspout burst over the village in June 1888, washing soil from the surrounding hills and depositing mud and boulders in the streets – 'pots, pans, chairs, stools, mats, and a host of smaller household goods were swept out by the current and deposited in the village pond'. The two 'Great Floods' of 1657 and 1892 are commemorated in the village by plaques showing the height to which the floodwater rose. On 3rd July 1892, a cloud burst on a hill to the west of Langtoft, on almost the same spot where the waterspout of four years earlier had fallen, gouging out two great fissures in the chalk, and rushing along the valley of Briggate towards the village. Mr Bell, schoolmaster at the time of the flood, described the scene: 'The water forced its way across the Nook and made its way down Back Street. It forced in Mr Woodmansey's front window, and in a moment filled his house. It soon forced the back door out, and then took away a great part of his furniture. A joiner's shop belonging to him was washed clean down, and all his tools and stock of wood carried off.'

A modern drainage system means that the village rarely floods these days, but the village green, known locally as 'The Pond' though it was filled in many years ago, shows signs of its former glory whenever there is a heavy rainstorm, and a decent fall of snow, combined with the winds so common to the Wolds, can still cut the village off from the outside world.

Considered in the mid 1970s to be a dying village, with its school in danger of closing, Langtoft's population is now on the increase as property development flourishes. It is the home of light industry, with several small businesses based in the village, and numbers artists, writers and craftsmen amongst its present inhabitants. There is a lively church and chapel community, based around St Peter's church and St Mary's Methodist chapel, and the church rooms, school hall, Methodist school room and the recently renovated British Legion hall, play host to numerous activities including social evenings, jumble sales, whist drives, bingo nights, antiques fairs, coffee afternoons and the like.

The 20th century may have been slow to arrive in Langtoft, but it is all the better for that, and whilst the village has now caught up with modern times, it remains a haven of peace from the mad pace of town and city life.

Laxton

Laxton is situated one mile north of the river Ouse, near Howden. It takes its name from the Norse word 'lax' meaning salmon, which once swam in the river. In days gone by, the village belonged to the Saltmarshe family, from which the railway station takes its name.

The church of St Peter was built in 1875 by public subscription, and contains several fine stained glass windows. A chancel ruin stands in the graveyard opposite, the only remaining part of the original chapel built in the reign of Charles I. The former Wesleyan chapel was closed before the Second World War, and now houses the local garage.

The old village school, which closed in 1968, is now a private house and schoolchildren go by bus to Howden. Further down the street can be found one of the only blacksmiths and farriers in the area, a very busy place, which also doubles as a local meeting place. Other amenities include a post office and general store, and a free house, the Bricklayers' Arms. The village hall, known as the Victory Hall, was an old army hut used in the First World War. It has been much updated and is regularly used by the WI, the youth club, indoor bowls club, and an over 55's club.

Leconfield

The village of Leconfield is to be found approximately three miles north of Beverley on the A154, the main Beverley to Driffield road.

The name Leconfield derives from Llecen-Fylliad, meaning 'the flat stone in the gloomy shade', and its enclosed area was the sacred theatre in which rites of initiation into druidical mysteries were solemnized and in which aspirants performed their probationary noviciates.

At the time of the Domesday survey, Leconfield was held by the Earl of Moreton, William de Percy and the canons of Beverley.

The Percys subsequently appear as lords of Leconfield, who built an 84 roomed castle west of Main Street, the old and original part of Leconfield, surrounded by a wide and deep moat, the remains of which are still to be seen. In 1541 King Henry VIII and his new queen, Catherine Howard, with a 'gallant train of attendants' visited the Earl in his castle.

The magnificent castle was doomed to fall prey to the hand of desolation. The ninth Earl, Henry Percy, was fined £30,000 and imprisoned for 15 years in the Tower of London for omitting to administer the Oath of Supremacy to Thomas Percy of Beverley. This heavy fine so impoverished him that his northern castles fell into decay, and in 1574 the decay was such that all buildings of the castle were demolished and valuable materials removed and used for the repair of Wressil Castle. The estate was ultimately divided into several plots under separate ownerships.

The A164 bisects the village, the old and original parts on the east side, and post-war residential development on the west side. There are three shops in the village, a 'corner shop', a post office and general store, and an electrical goods shop.

Leconfield is the home of the Army School of Mechanical Transport, occupying Normandy Barracks, formerly the RAF station commissioned in 1936, which served in an operational capacity during the Second World War. The east coast Search and Rescue Squadron of the Royal Air Force occupies part of the barracks.

There are two churches in the parish of Leconfield, the church of St Catherine in Leconfield village on the east side of the A164, on the road to Arram, and the church of St Leonard at Scorborough. Both churches are Church of England denomination and services are held each Sunday.

The church of St Catherine holds particular interest. The first church on the site dated from the 7th century. The present church dates from the 11th century, with many fine features, notably the brick tower at the west end, the porch and the pulpit. Records of baptisms and burials date from 1551 and of marriages from 1552.

The population of the parish of Leconfield, which comprises Leconfield, Scorborough and Arram is approximately 2,060.

Together with farming, mainly cereals, it is a mixed community, with those travelling to employment in Beverley and Hull and those employed at the Army School of Mechanical Transport in both a uniformed and civilian capacity. The local school, with a maximum roll of 150, serves both the civilian population of the parish and the children of uniformed staff at Normandy Barracks.

A playing field on the north side of the village caters for the social and recreational needs of the community, and houses a sports pavilion, a private member's club, football, cricket and bowling green facilities, and a children's play area. A new community centre-cum-sports hall is nearing completion.

A parish newsletter, detailing events taking place in the community, other items of interest and a vehicle for expressing points of view, is written, edited and distributed by a group of volunteers to over 400 homes each month.

Leven

Unlike its Scottish namesake, Leven is not by the sea but six miles from it on the main Beverley to Bridlington road, 14 miles from Bridlington and six miles from Hornsea. In the past 25 years the population has trebled due to the building program.

It is one of the few villages that has changed position over the years. Little Leven was once known as Lleven, a name meaning 'smooth' or 'level' a description reasonably applicable to this area. In 1735, Leven was known as 'Rosedale in Leven'.

The church of St Faith, in use from 1350 to 1843, was probably preceded by an earlier wooden church of the same name. Although the church is no longer standing the old graveyard is still there with tombstones which are still readable, on a site one and a quarter miles from the present church. The present Holy Trinity church was consecrated in 1845 on a site on the main road and beside an already established village. A pilgrimage is made each year by villagers from Holy Trinity to St Faith's where a short service is held. Another place of worship is the Methodist chapel situated on East Street. The old rectory, sited on the Beverley road on the outskirts of the village, is now known as Abbeyfield House, a residential home for senior citizens. A settlement of flats and bungalows house about 20 senior citizens, with a resident warden.

Leven Canal is well known for miles around by fishermen. It was built in 1802 at the expense of Mrs Charlotte Bethell, the wife of the then lord of the manor. It stretches for three and a quarter miles from Leven to the river Hull. It was navigable by vessels of up to 90 tons, mostly keels which were used for transporting coal and lime to Leven and took away corn and various commodities made in the village such as candles, rope, and a certain type of brick. At one time there were houseboats on the canal, there are now holiday caravans on the canal bank and the canal is no longer used for transport.

The Church of England school caters for children from the age of five to eleven years, they then attend Hornsea comprehensive. According to old documents, a school appears to have been built in 1796. There were three schools at one time, a dame school, British school and National school. The dame school is now used as a cafe, and is situated on High Stile. The present school, 1862, has been greatly altered and extended over the years. The old police station is now the health centre with four doctors and several community nurses.

Leven has a playing field second to none which is the envy of many villages in the area. Started in 1958, the fund for the purpose of purchasing land was initially raised through various village events. There is a hall for indoor games and social functions, and a large playing field with tennis courts, bowling greens and children's playgrounds. An annual Gala is held on the last Saturday in June. Thriving troops of Scouts, Guides, Brownies, Cubs and Beavers meet in their own purpose-built building in the playing field grounds, and the Youth Club have their own hall in the school grounds.

The recreation hall is another building used by various organisations, renovated over the years from a building of First World War days; it also houses a twice weekly library. A flourishing Horticultural Society is responsible for the flower show, a twice yearly event for classes in vegetables, flowers, handicrafts, cookery and children's classes.

The Wray Education Trust is a fund which benefits young people under 25 years of age who attend further education establishments, also apprentices, and other education activities within the village. It is administered by seven trustees.

There are two public houses, and several shops to supply this large village. A publication of village life compiled by a group of volunteers is issued quarterly and is eagerly looked forward to.

Lockington

The village of Lockington is situated roughly halfway between Beverley and Driffield. It is reached from the A164 by a lane about one mile long with wide verges, or by a lane about one and a half miles long from the B1248. Thus it nestles in a hollow with the Wolds rising to the north. It is thought the name means 'the enclosure of the family of Loca' and the settlement dates from Anglo-Saxon times.

Lockington keeps its appearance of an estate village – it forms part of the estate of Lord Hotham of South Dalton and some of the more modern buildings have kept to the style of the estate cottages with their pointed-roofed upper windows. Some 400 people live in the actual village of Lockington as opposed to the parish. A very small number are employed on the three working farms in the village. Other occupations are of necessity followed in the neighbouring towns so to some extent Lockington is a commuter village. There is a coach business which also does break-down work. The other non-agricultural employment is in the recently refurbished Rockingham Arms. This used to incorporate the shop and post office. The post office is now situated in School Farm.

The church of St Mary the Virgin is not easily found and is approached from Church Lane. It has been there in one form or another since Anglo-Saxon times, probably the first building being of wood. The main restoration of the Norman stone-built church was done in 1893 and remains much the same to this day except for modernisation of lighting and heating, addition of carpets, kneelers etc. There is a fine organ by Prosser of London.

The modern primary Church of England school which caters for about 60 children serves a wide catchment area – in fact at the moment Lockington village provides the smallest number, the rest travelling from Lund, Aike, Wilfholme and surrounding farms. The old school building is now used as a village hall and is in constant use by the community.

A beck runs alongside the main street but due to the vagaries of the rainfall, springs etc it is more often a dry bed. When water is running it enhances the village aspect and in spring flotillas of ducklings can be seen on it. There are many interesting walks around Lockington and from vantage points the pantiled roofs of the village interspersed with some ancient trees (alas, many have succumbed to Dutch elm disease) provide a delightful panorama.

Londesborough

The village is situated about three miles north of Market Weighton, just off the A163. There are 57 dwellings, with another 25 made up of farms and farm cottages in the rest of the parish. The highest part rises to 500 ft on the Wolds which is thin chalk land, the low land is heavy clay with a little sandy gravel.

The first documentary reference is in the Domesday Book of 1086, but there has been evidence of Roman and Saxon occupation.

The Clifford family owned the estate for almost 200 years from 1469, and there is a legend that Henry Clifford was sent into hiding by his mother to Londesborough and brought up as a shepherd. Eventually the estate passed by marriage to the Burlingtons. The most notable member of this family was Richard, the third Earl, who was an architect. A great deal of work was done at that time in enlarging and landscaping the park, creating lakes and the kitchen gardens. The gardener Thomas Knowlton was more of a plantsman and obviously did not really enjoy digging the lakes or 'canals' as he called them. Fortunately many of his letters still exist.

In 1753 the estate again passed by marriage, this time to the Devonshire family, who held it for almost 100 years. It was in this time that the Hall was demolished and farms were built following the enclosure of the open fields. Londesborough was sold to George Hudson, the Railway King, in 1845, who wanted to build the line from York to Market Weighton. His downfall came five years later and the new owners were the Denison family who eventually took the name of the village for their title. They made a great many improvements, built houses, restored the lakes and park and enlarged the mansion house. King Edward visited several times when shooting parties and other entertaining took place on a lavish scale. During the Second World War the house and many other parts of the village were requisitioned. Various regiments were stationed in the village, and visits from former servicemen and women are always a pleasure.

Visitors who knew the village in the past are surprised to find the place little changed. There is an increase in the number of dwellings through careful alteration of old buildings such as the Burlington stable, or the division of large houses.

The school was built by the Duke of Devonshire in 1830, but sadly it closed in 1980. It is now a dwelling. Some sort of a school had existed before, possibly from 1680, and it is thought to be part of the reading room where the WI now meet.

At the west end of the village there are a group of six almshouses, known as Londesborough Hospital. Built by Richard, the first Earl of Burlington about 1679, they were originally for twelve people, but were altered in 1920 to six dwellings of two rooms each. On 6th December 1774, Georgiana, Duchess of Devonshire wrote about visiting the almshouses and taking gifts.

The first reference to the church of All Saints was in the early 12th century, and it seems to be the date when it was built. There are various Norman features, and a number of alterations and restorations have taken place over the centuries. The farming is mainly arable of corn, oil seed rape and peas, with beef, sheep and pigs; there are now no dairy farms. Londesborough is a truly country village with many families having lived there for generations. There is no road going through which makes it fairly quiet and peaceful, though low flying aircraft and farm machinery make up for traffic noise.

Long Riston

Long and straggling, Long Riston stands off the main road from Hull to Bridlington. The traffic problem was solved in 1986 by the building of a bypass, thus keeping the heavy goods vehicles from the main street.

The church, which was built in the 13th century, stands isolated in a field at the north end of the village, and is dedicated to St Margaret. Its position indicates that in the past houses were grouped around this area rather than in the lengthy one-street formation as now. However, over the years this has been augmented by dwellings branching out from the main road. In former days there were in addition the church, a Primitive Methodist chapel and a Wesleyan chapel, these being no longer in use.

The school was built by public subscription as a National school in 1873, and was originally intended to accommodate 100 children; at the present time there are 27 pupils.

A modern village hall was built in 1976 replacing a First World War army hut, originally purchased and maintained over the years by the Women's Institute. There is a post office and general store, a garage, a joiner's shop, various resident builders, and a local inn, the Travellers Rest. In the distant past there was also a cobbler's shop, a tailor's establishment and various carrier's businesses. Whereas Long Riston used to be totally agricultural with ancillary trades, joiner, blacksmith etc (at one time there were three blacksmiths in the village), it is now still agricultural but in the modern way, and most of the population earn their living in Hull, Beverley and elsewhere in the district.

Long Riston has housed many notable characters. Prominent amongst them is Peter Nevill who built Riston Grange and endowed many charities. The Nevill Trust still functions to assist scholars and apprentices financially. Richard Fewson, who taught in the mid 1840s, was a schoolmaster of note. There have been many interesting people amongst the schoolmasters, vicars, land-owners and dignitaries over the years.

For a small village Long Riston is well equipped for sporting and other leisure activities. Adjoining the village hall is an excellent playing field comprising a football pitch, two grass and one hard tennis court, and a functional children's play area and a car park. In abeyance at the moment is a cricket pitch.

Events in the past have included money raising occasions to erect the aforementioned facilities. These included galas, barbecues, dances, concerts, and dramatic productions, a flower festival, social events, coffee mornings, art exhibitions, and sponsored walks for St Margaret's church. No doubt when money is required in the future Long Riston residents will rise to the occasion once more.

Low Catton

The tranquil village of Low Catton lies six miles east of York on the east bank of the river Derwent. Originally an Anglian settlement, the name stems from the Old English personal name 'Catta'.

The village stands along a single street roughly parallel with the river. Its houses and cottages – apart from recent additions – are mainly of the 18th and 19th centuries respectively, the former rectory being perhaps the most noteworthy.

The approach to Low Catton from the direction of Kexby is attractive. A narrow lane, it is bordered for much of its length by an avenue of trees, patches of bluebells along the grass verges beneath them adding a delicately pleasing touch of colour to the scene in springtime.

From the northern end of the village street, a lane runs towards the river and the church. Dedicated to All Saints, the church is tucked away behind mighty trees on a high bank of the river. The external appearance of the building is most unusual, with a sturdy, embattled tower at the west end of the south aisle, and a big chancel much higher than the nave. The imposing chancel is in fact almost as long as the nave, and has four wide steps to the altar.

The original church was Norman and cruciform, and though little of it remains, some interesting detailing of the period is reflected in the north transept, the nave and aisles. A round arch near the pulpit is thought by some authorities to belong to an earlier period. The tower, which houses three bells, is part of the old building; the north arcade is mainly 13th century. The purpose of the opening in the south wall of the choir behind the rector's desk is open to conjecture: is it to give light at the desk, which otherwise would be in deep shadow, or is it a hagioscope (peephole)?

The church has some fine windows. Two are specially worthy of note – the east window and the children's window. The former, the central panel of which depicts the Crucifixion, is said to be one of the finest examples in the North of the noted stained glass expert, William Morris. Beautifully appropriate, the children's window in the transept on the north side of the church, shows Christ holding a child in his arms, a lamb at his feet. It was given by the children of the Sunday school during restoration work in 1908.

The cast-iron lampstands in the lane outside the church commemorate the Diamond Jubilee of Queen Victoria. The manor house stood immediately south of the church. It was apparently moated in 1258–9. The final reference to it in 1577 described it as being 'so utterly ruinated . . . that (it) hardly can be judged where (it) hath stood'.

There was once a small water mill at Low Catton. It stood north of the village, and some experts believe it may have been the fulling mill called Beckmill in 1474.

Low Catton has no school. It closed in 1923 and the children transferred to Stamford Bridge. Temporarily reopened to cater for evacuees in 1939, the building was converted to a village hall in 1955. An unendowed school is recorded at Low Catton as early as 1734. It had 30 children attending.

Lowthorpe

Lowthorpe is a small elongated village, situated five miles north-east of Driffield, which stretches southwards for nearly three and a half miles across the plain of Holderness.

It has a long history and in 1843 twelve Bronze Age artefacts and two portions of a sword were found whilst digging a drain.

Lowthorpe is mentioned four times in the Domesday Book, where it is spelt Logetorp, and in King Edward the Confessor's time it was valued at the princely sum of eight shillings. Some time after 1066, the estate came into the possession of the Heslerton family from whom it passed by marriage in 1336 to the St Quintins and then by marriage again to the Legard family who are the present owners.

It has been said that the name Lowthorpe or Logetorp could have meant 'Law-village' in ancient Norse. It is also believed that the old Scandinavian rulers of the area held their annual 'folk mote' at which the laws were read to the assembled inhabitants at a large circular mound, now overgrown with trees, and known to the local people as Fox Hill, supposedly a corruption of Folks Hill.

A church has stood in Lowthorpe from as early as the Norman Conquest. The present building is supposed to have been erected in 1333, when the church was made collegiate by Sir John de Heslerton and housed six chaplains and three clerks. The college survived until its dissolution in 1579, when it declined in status to a parish church. The church in those days was a large and handsome edifice. The present day building has a small western tower and 12th century nave standing away from the road on the edge of a wood. The chancel is open to the sky. In the 1800s there were two large ash trees growing inside the chancel, these were cut down in 1892 but the stumps are still clearly visible.

Inside the church, the earliest feature is an Anglo-Saxon carved stone cross head which was found in the churchyard in 1934. The font is thought to be medieval. The parish registers begin in 1546 and contain among the memoranda reference to a large gold ring with the inscription 'Obey and Rule' which was given to the church by a Mrs Francis Rokeby on 26th August 1711 for the use, of any who came to the church to be married and were 'unprovided with a ring'. There is a cross in the churchyard which is said to have been brought from Kilham at the time of the plague which decimated that village. On route from Kilham to Lowthorpe, the heavy stone base of the cross fell off at Ruston Parva and embedded itself in the verge side there, from where it was rescued in recent years and now stands on Ruston Parva village green.

In 1826 the Hall, Lowthorpe's ancient manor, was demolished and later replaced by Lowthorpe Lodge which the St Quintin family used mainly as as a shooting lodge, swelling the population of the small village greatly every summer with their visiting shooting parties.

During Lowthorpe's history there has been little in the way of non-agricultural employment. The St Quintin family provided employment for several men not directly concerned with farming, land agent, gamekeepers, water bailiff and woodmen. There was also a water mill in Lowthorpe as early as 1327 but the latest building on the site was said to have been built in the 1700s and was finally demolished in 1959.

During the early 1900s the post office at Lowthorpe was a hive of activity. Mail for villages as far afield as Langtoft and Boynton came by post train from Hull, was dropped at Lowthorpe station at 7 am and then brought by horse and cart to the post office at Lowthorpe. Postmen were waiting there to take it on bicycle to the outlying villages and make the return journey with outgoing mail to be despatched on the 6.20 pm train to Hull. Needless to say this service ended many years ago and the old post office is now a private house, the station is closed and the trains no longer stop at Lowthorpe.

Much of the village housing, including the farms, still belongs to the Legard family, although The Elms, a large 19th century house formerly occupied by the bailiff of the St Quintin estate, is now the offices of a turkey farm.

There are still some inhabitants of the village who work locally in agriculture though not as many as of yore and many of the newer villagers commute further afield to their daily jobs. Village life is therefore not as close knit as it once was, which is common in many villages today, but nevertheless local functions held in nearby Harpham village hall are always well attended proving that there is still a sense of community in the area.

Lund

Lund is a village of some 120 houses on the Wolds between Beverley and Driffield. Though founded by the Vikings a thousand or so years ago it has, like most East Riding villages, very few really ancient buildings. The exceptions are the church and the market cross on the green. The church tower stands out on the skyline in the middle of the village and the church dates from the 14th century, though extensively restored and to some extent rebuilt in Victorian times. It is a large church for what has always been a small village – perhaps the work of some medieval lord of the manor intent on impressing the neighbouring gentry.

The cross is of slightly earlier date in origin and was the centre of a weekly market on Thursdays, for which a charter was granted in the 13th century. It provides its own record of centuries of repairs, using different kinds and shapes of stone from other buildings, each added to fit the current alignment, so that a permanent list is built into the whole edifice. The shaft was probably renewed in the 17th century and was surmounted by an oval ball till it succumbed to schoolboy vandalism some 40 years ago.

Also facing the green at the entrance to the church is the old forge, worked by many generations of the same family of blacksmiths till the 1970s when it was converted to a bus shelter.

To the north of the green, adjoining the Malton road, stands a group of three trees surrounding a small hollow. This was the cockpit, used for cock-fighting in times past.

The 18th century building next to the church is the manor house, built on the site of an earlier building. In front of it is an old wall broken by an imposing 17th century gateway, placed there by the Remington family, lords of the manor, who probably furnished the market cross with its new shaft in the same style and type of stone. The Remingtons emigrated to America in the 18th century, where they founded the great engineering company which bears their name.

Opposite this wall is the Methodist chapel. In the 19th century and into the 20th there were two Methodist chapels in the village and this was for those of the Primitive Methodist persuasion.

The evidence suggests that almost all the village houses in earlier days were built of dried mud with thatched roofs. By about the end of the 18th century they began to be replaced by the brick and pantiles which form the pattern of the present village. There are no outstanding houses but the lines of brick houses grouped around the central green and round smaller greens in other parts of the village form a pleasing composition.

The village is also known for the care it gives to its gardens and grass verges. Apart from several popular Open Gardens events, it has in recent years twice won the North Humberside prize for the Best Kept Village. In the Britain in Bloom competitions it has won the first prize in the Village Section successively for Yorkshire and Humberside (for which it retained the Challenge Shield after winning three times), England and the United Kingdom. It was also invited to compete in the European Entente Floriale.

Like most villages, Lund in past times was much more self-sufficient than it is now, with its own grocers, shoemakers, tailors and the like and, during the 19th century, a second public house, the Speed the Plough. Even in 1949 there were two joiners and a blacksmith, a school, post office and eight shops. Now there is only the Wellington inn.

Yet Lund is by no means a dead village. There is a pleasantly refurbished village hall, centre of a thriving carpet bowl club and many other activities, a newly renovated pub doing good business with a well supported darts club, and smaller church and chapel halls for more intimate meetings.

The recorded history of Lund is scanty. Nothing of national importance has happened there. As far back as can be traced it has been a village of yeomen, small independent farmers, and never since medieval times an estate village ruled by one big landowner, though for a period in the 18th and 19th centuries the Grimston family of Kilnwick and later the Hothams of South Dalton acquired some farms. Perhaps the biggest event in recent times was in the 1950s when a film company made the church the setting for the film *Lease of Life* with Robert Donat. Many villagers took part in the film as extras.

Mappleton

Mappleton is situated on the coast of East Yorkshire in the Holderness district. The name Mappleton is said to have evolved from the Saxon 'Moe pel tun', the farmstead by the maple tree. It is mentioned in the Domesday Book of 1086; indeed evidence seems to indicate that it was one of the oldest and largest settlements at the time of Domesday. At the time of the Armada in the reign of Elizabeth I, Mappleton had three beacons to light to give warning of invasion.

The village is mainly given to agriculture, though tourism will play an increasing part in the future. A farmer's wife of Middle Farm has over the years developed a very attractive plant and shrub centre with success. A retail milk business is run by the owners of the post office and general store which also delivers newspapers and magazines. The largest employer in the village is Maple Garage, employing 19 people. As there is no access to the shore there have never been any businesses based on the sea. There are six farmsteads, 25 houses and approximately 100 residents in the village. There is now no school. The school built in 1872 closed many years ago and the school building and school house are now two very attractive residences. All children attend school in nearby Hornsea. The Wesleyan Methodist chapel likewise closed a number of years ago, but serves the village well in its present capacity as the village hall.

All Saints' church stands on a high mound of land in the centre of the village – one might say it is the guardian of all it surveys. The church originally had a square tower at its western end, but in

1855 when it underwent considerable restoration, a tall spire was added, built of stone from a ship wrecked on Mappleton sands. This is a landmark visible for miles along the coast; indeed there was a protest from seafarers when in recent years it was feared the spire might need to be dismantled. However, it was found only necessary for repairs to be made and the spire remains in place as a valuable landmark for passing shipping.

The village has one main street, the B1242 coastal road which runs south from Hornsea to Withernsea. A by-road branches west to Hatfield village. Next to the church there is a crossroads. Church lane leads westwards to a row of council houses, Church Mount, the old vicarage (no longer used as a residence for the vicar) and Mill Farm, now empty.

The walls of the mill, first mentioned in 1343, are still intact. Eastwards, Cliff Lane goes past the old school, the post office and a row of cottages to the cliff top, where it is demonstrated why Mappleton has recently achieved tremendous publicity as it is the next English village in danger of being swept into the North Sea. The soft clay cliffs on this coast have been eroded by the sea since Roman times and 29 villages have been lost to the sea. Mappleton is at the cliff edge, indeed at the northern end of the village the main road is only 50 metres from the cliff top. In February 1988 the parish council launched a campaign for the provision of sea defences. Holderness Borough Council has accepted a design for three groynes and an access ramp to be constructed off Mappleton cliffs, but this cannot go forward without government financial aid. Residents are now anxiously awaiting the decision which will either give Mappleton a future or condemn it to perish in the North Sea.

One other place of interest, outside the village limits but within Mappleton parish, is Rolston Hall. It is said that Paul Jones, the American privateer, fired a salvo at Rolston Hall to mark his hatred of the then owner, William Brough, Marshall of High Court of Admiralty, who was entitled to hang Paul Jones as a pirate if he was captured. One of the cannon balls was said to be in the Hall in 1840.

Nafferton

Situated at the foot of the Yorkshire Wolds, the village of Nafferton is one of the largest in the East Riding. The village itself stretches for about a mile southwards from the Driffield-Bridlington road. Evolving over centuries, the fabric of the Nafferton which stands today bears witness to a continuous process of both change and continuity. The population in 1981 was 1,640 but housing development since then has substantially increased this number.

As in so many villages, the parish church is the oldest building, the earliest parts of which date from the 13th century. It dominates the centre of the village from its elevated site where the four main village roads converge. A former vicar here was Francis Orpen Morris, who, besides making many alterations to the church, wrote a standard book on British birds.

A workaday village, Nafferton has no pretentions to 'prettiness' although there are many attractive features. near the church, the mere, a large expanse of water fed by natural springs and formerly a mill pond, is a picturesque area attracting many birds to overwinter, whilst in summer whole families are to be seen feeding the ducks.

Due to the varied types of building, and its historial features, most of Nafferton was designated a conservation area some years ago. Although many of the houses were originally built earlier, development in the 18th century is marked by the numerous date stones on property about the village, the earliest being 1746.

Nafferton supports many organisations from toddler groups to clubs for senior citizens. Sports and hobbies are also well catered for. The recreation club has its own sports field, whilst some club meetings and classes are held in the school or the village hall. This hall was built in 1861 by the Loyal Order of Ancient Shepherds, a Friendly Society, but presented to the village in 1946.

Nafferton is very much a self contained village, having a school, doctor's surgery, post office and newsagent, two small supermarkets, a greengrocer, a fish and chip restaurant, four public houses and several mobile tradesmen including a library, besides many small businesses. Fortunately it has retained road and rail links with Hull, Scarborough and the historic town of Beverley. The seaside town of Bridlington, with its bracing air and good shops, is only ten miles away.

That Nafferton is a pleasant place to live is shown by the rapid sale of new houses, both to local people and those from further afield.

Newbald

Newbald (North and South) lies in a hollow, sheltered to the north and east by the Wolds, which rise to about 150 metres, with a good water supply from clusters of springs. The site has been occupied by man for thousands of years. Prehistoric tools and pottery, and the remains of a Roman villa, have been found. The Roman road from Brough to York passed to the west of the village.

The 'new building' was an Anglian settlement, the name first recorded in the 10th century. In AD 963 the Saxon King Edgar granted 30 'casati' of land to Earldorman Gunner, which he bestowed on St Peter's church at York. It would appear that the Danes then occupied the area. Ulphus, son-in-law of King Canute, dedicated his lands, including Newbald, to God and St Peter. His hunting horn, title to his estate, is still in York Minster. Thus the lands of Newbald remained in the possession of the Church for nearly 1,000 years. The income of the lands was divided among the canons of the minster, and they built their respective manors to the north and south of the church. The canon for North Newbald became the rector.

Domesday Book records land for 16 ploughs at Newbald, and a church. The present building, dedicated to St Nicholas, dates from 1125. It is recognised as one of the finest Norman churches in East Yorkshire. It is cruciform and aisleless, built of locally quarried ashlar stone. It stands on a small mound at the junction of the 'two' villages. A small carving on one of the capitals of the south door arch depicts the Hound of Heaven, straining to gain admittance to the church. The lovely font is 700 years old. The iron handle on the vestry door is reputed to be the original 'sanctuary' handle. Made in the shape of two serpents, it is said to represent sin, and also the fact that there are two sides to every dispute!

Newbald possesses a spacious green. A charter to hold a market and an annual fair was granted in 1348, but it is not known when the use was discontinued. A large circular flat stone on the green is said to be the remains of the market cross. It may have had a more sinister purpose later, as it is now known as The Whipping Stone. A record is said to exist of a whipping which took place in 1624, when a man was whipped to death.

The main occupation of the village throughout the centuries was obviously agriculture, but three quarries have been worked since Roman times, and the oolitic limestone is found in many local churches, including Beverley minster. Four mills were located along the beck, the last one being demolished in 1954.

The Civil War did not pass Newbald by, as the Monkton family of South Newbald were Royalists, and the parish registers of 1643/45 recorded 30 soldiers being buried in the churchyard.

The enclosure of the open fields was completed in 1783 and brought prosperity. All the medieval buildings were torn down and replaced by stone built ones, with red pantiled roofs. With few exceptions the cottages and houses opened directly onto the street with no front gardens. A terrace of visually pleasing stone cottages facing the neat village green are dated 1846. The stream is fascinating, disappearing from view from time to time, to re-emerge from beneath road or path in an ever delightful manner. For much of its length it is bordered by sloping lawns, and sometimes edged with stones and flowers in a most attractive display.

A school for 150 children was built on the green, and remained in use until 1914 when a new school was built in Beverley Road. The old building is now a storeroom. The medieval street names were retained, and there is still East-gate, West-gate, Burgate, Galegate and Trundlegate, though the 'Rabbit Warren' in South Newbald, known as 'The Coney Clappers', has gone.

Newbald did not have a railway and remained very self contained. In the late 19th century, besides the usual rural trades, it could boast ten grocers and drapers, eight tailors, a tea vendor and 14 dressmakers. There were four public houses. This for a population of 627 in North Newbald, and 172 in South Newbald. There were also four nonconformist chapels. There are now only two village shops and two public houses. Three of the chapels were demolished, the remaining one is converted to a house.

The 'twin' villages were officially united in 1935 as Newbald civil parish. This would not have pleased the old 19th century residents who took care to have the information 'of South Newbald' or 'of North Newbald' recorded on their tombstones.

The depression years of the 1920s and 1930s hit the village hard. As a result many of the buildings fell into disrepair and were eventually demolished. After the war, 60 council houses were built, and two small private estates. The centre of Newbald was made a conservation area in an attempt to preserve some of the more attractive features of the village. The Council for the Protection of Rural England commissioned a village study in 1974. Sadly, few of the recommendations were acted upon. Two more private estates have been built and the proportion of commuters has risen sharply. Many of the old village families still work in the area, in agriculture, or in the thriving haulage industry.

Surprisingly, the village still retains its compact 'cosy' atmosphere with plenty of activity going on during the day, but any large scale development could reduce it to just another dormitory for Hull.

North Cave

North Cave is an extensive village situated in the foothills of the Wolds in the East Riding of Yorkshire, with Hull 14 miles to the east and York 25 miles north-west. The population is around 1,200 and the main occupations are in agriculture and, in more recent years, industry.

The ancient and beautiful church of All Saints is the oldest building in the village, newly built in 1318, although an unendowed building probably stood on the same site from 1086 when the Domesday Book was compiled. The Georgian vicarage, built in 1823, stands south of the church, where the north wing was demolished in 1950 after the vicar's wife fell through the floorboards!

North Cave beck, where trout may be seen, meanders pleasantly through the village, in earlier days providing the water for three mills, where corn was milled until earlier this century.

From the 1740s North Cave was the meeting place for Quakers in the area, and Quaker Cottage on Church Street was built in 1892 on the site of the old Friends' meeting house; the cottage garden once was their burial ground.

The Primitive Methodist chapel on Westgate was built in 1871 to replace a smaller chapel on Quaker Lane, and a campaign is in progress at the present time to raise funds for its refurbishment. The Wesleyan Centenary chapel was built on Church Street in 1839, but is now used as a warehouse and the Young Farmers' Club meets in the original schoolroom. John Wesley preached at North Cave in 1761, probably in a barn or in the open air.

North Cave boasts two public houses: the White Hart on Westgate, built in 1776, but much altered at the front, was one of the main coaching inns in the mid 19th century; and the Black Swan on Church Street, rebuilt in 1813, where ladies could buy bonnets and trimmings in a little shop in the small single-storied part at the far end.

The old church school, situated near to the church and now a private dwelling, was built in 1833 and extended in 1870. The school moved to a new building in Station Road in 1974.

The village playing field stands opposite the old school and occupies the old titheyard where tithes were paid to the church up to the early 19th century. A children's adventure playground has been built in recent years, and the field is well used by the village football and cricket teams.

North Cave is a very pleasant place in which to live, with a thriving Women's Institute, Pensioners' Club, Mothers' Union and playgroup. There is a real sense of community, and the village hall provides a focus for many activities. The village has a post office, newsagent and two general stores, a butcher, florist, bank and building society/estate agent and a garage, as well as a restaurant, two antiques shops and hairdressers. Other facilities include a doctor's surgery, a joiner and funeral director, and building and electrical businesses. The shopping facilities of Beverley are only nine miles to the east and the M62 motorway starts at the western end of the village. The surrounding countryside, with many fine old trees, is ideal for walking.

North & South Cliffe

There are only some 40 dwellings in North and South Cliffe, and most are widely scattered. Six farms, one shooting lodge, one private house and eight cottages are all built of a white brick which was brought from Derbyshire.

St John's church, North Cliffe, was built in 1873 by Mr Samuel Fox, and the deed of consecration was signed in October of that year by the Archbishop of York, Dr William Thomson. The church cost £2,000 at the time. The architect was the first Lord Grimthorpe, who also designed Big Ben. The church is a neat stone building, lined with white brick, and consists of chancel, nave and organ. The chancel fittings are of oak, and the pulpit is carved stone. A rent of £50 was paid yearly, and this is still the same today.

Samuel Fox Esq was born in 1815, and when he died in 1887 he was the first person to be buried in the cemetery attached to the church. A massive, handsome monument of granite is placed over the grave. He was a prominent Victorian industrialist with extensive ironworks in West Yorkshire. He was the inventor of the first reliable light steel umbrella frame, and early in his business life purchased the Cliffe estate from Sir William Worsley. In 1844 he bought Hotham Hall where his wife and son principally lived, until another estate was purchased at Bradwell in Oxfordshire.

However, Mr Fox made frequent visits to his estate in Cliffe, staying at his house, The Lodge. He took a close interest in his adopted village and urged Canon Jarrat, who was the vicar of nearby North Cave from 1830 to 1891, to have a school built. A portrait of Canon Jarrat and his wife hangs in the church today.

Canon Jarrat offered to build the school if Mr Fox would build the church, and so the two buildings were constructed, immediately adjacent to each other. The school ceased to function as such many years ago, and now serves as a village hall.

St John's church cannot claim to have any outstanding architectural merit, but it can boast two unusual features. Firstly, the altar faces north and not west, as in most churches, and secondly, the tower is most attractive and in perfect proportion to the intimate size of the church.

Mr Fox planned to build himself a home very near the village, of which he had plans ready, but unfortunately he passed away before it was built.

North Dalton

This picturesque village is situated in a delph valley on the Yorkshire Wolds and centres around the mere and church with an extension eastwards along Main Street. Two council house estates have been introduced to the south and west. The village is six miles from Driffield and ten miles from Beverley. It houses approximately 200 residents in 115 dwellings.

The first documentary reference to the village occurs in the Domesday Book of 1086, but most of the buildings, with the exception of the church, date from after 1780.

Originally North Dalton was a self-supporting agricultural village with farming being the only means of employment. Before the Second World War it boasted a church, two chapels, a school, three shops, a post office, two joiners, two tailors, a ladies dressmaker (specialising in high quality garments!), a cobbler, a slaughter-house and butcher, a fish and chip shop and two public houses. Today, all of this is reduced to a church, a public house and a small shop-cum-post office. The school was the last to close in 1968 and now primary school children have to make a four mile

North Dalton Village

return journey to Middleton-on-the-Wolds. Secondary schooling is in Driffield.

The mere is the large village pond surrounded on three sides by a dense bank of elm and sycamore, and is closely associated visually with the churchyard. It is a very attractive feature and has only been known to dry up once in the summer of 1826. Wildlife is abundant in fish, ducks and water hens, and it is a great joy in springtime to see mother ducks bring their families down the steep church embankment, across the road and onto the pond.

All Saint's church stands on a conical mound of earth in the village and is an ancient edifice. It has a nave, chancel and low embattled tower. The south door is Norman with clustered cylindrical jambs and the north door, although much plainer, is of the same style. The arch between the nave and the chancel is also Norman with zig-zag ornaments. At the west end is a beautiful pointed window, and at the east end three lancet windows. The font is circular. In the not so distant past, North Dalton's church was well supported. It held regular services, ran a Sunday school and was involved in numerous village activities. Indeed the vicar was the most important figure, taking an active part in village life. He was also on parish councils and acted as the school's manager.

In fact, sometimes the vicar was inspired by the village, like the Rev Baring-Gould, who wrote *Onward Christian Soldiers* amongst other hymns during his time as vicar of the parish.

Today the church is no longer 'active' in the village as it once was, and sadly the congregation rarely has more than 15 worshippers. There is no Sunday school, and the vicar is 'shared' by four parishes and no longer lives in the village.

Today developers are trying hard to increase the size of North Dalton, wanting to build houses on every spare piece of land. Indeed eight such houses have already been built. Consequently the few younger inhabitants of the village are being driven away. Fortunately the village is in a conservation area and hopefully little more development will be permitted.

North Ferriby

The village of North Ferriby is situated on gently rising ground on the north bank of the river Humber, about seven miles west of the city of Hull.

As the name suggests, there was once a ferry crossing the river from here to the village of South Ferriby on the south bank, probably from Viking times – about AD 876 until 1300. In recent years, even the paddle steamers linking Hull and Barton have been made obsolete by the building of the magnificent single span Humber Bridge, completed in 1980 – the north bank approach of which is just three miles east of North Ferriby.

Between 1937 and 1963, the Wright brothers discovered the well-preserved remains of three oak-planked boats embedded in mud and clay at the water's edge. They were successfully raised and after being carefully examined and analysed with carbon dating techniques, they appear to have been under construction around 1500 BC – that was at the same time as Stonehenge was built. They are now thought to be the oldest planked boats built anywhere in the world outside Egypt. One boat is in the Hull Museum and the other two are in the National Maritime Museum, Greenwich.

Although like most villages North Ferriby has increased greatly in size, especially since the Second World War, there are still some very pleasant walks in the area, and the Wolds Way walk actually starts at the foreshore car park. Standing on the south bank and looking across the river at the village, one can see that it is still well-wooded with only the church spire and a small number of houses visible through the trees.

The village school comprises one old building dating back to 1868 and two modern buildings with ample playing field facilities. There are now 160 children under the age of twelve and ten teachers. Most of the older children go on to South Hunsley school – approximately two miles to the west in the village of Melton.

There is a railway station served by trains running from Hull to Doncaster, Leeds, Manchester and York, and a fairly frequent bus service to Hull.

In the Domesday Book (1086) a church is recorded and most likely the present building is on the same site. Until St Mary's, Lowgate, Hull, was built, North Ferriby was the parish church for a large area stretching from the river Hull westwards. In 1844 the church was declared unsafe, so money was raised from the rates and voluntary subscriptions and a new church was consecrated in 1848, which is the building one can still see today.

The Methodists first established a chapel for worship in 1828, in a small building later converted into the Oddfellows Hall, and so named until a couple of years ago when it became a private residence. The present larger chapel in High Street was opened in 1878 and provision was made for a Sunday school behind it in 1883.

When, in the 18th century, Hull became a prosperous port, rich merchants began to look westwards for clean Wolds air and scenic views. Ferriby saw the erection of stately homes and mansions, notably in the High Street, and some still remain today. An outstanding example is Ferriby house, which dates from circa 1775, and was built by Sir Henry Etherington. This is now used as a private residential home for the elderly. The manor house and Ferriby Hall are still extant and remind one of the former grandeur of the High Street. Aston Hall, which sadly was demolished in

1970, was built and occupied in the 1740s by William Wilberforce – grandfather of the William Wilberforce famous for his anti-Slavery Bill in Parliament.

North Ferriby is an extremely pleasant place in which to live and property is keenly sought after by those wishing to join this village community.

North Frodingham

North Frodingham is predominantly an agricultural village, conveniently located between the principal towns of the area, being situated on the B1249 ten miles from Bridlington, eleven from Hornsea, 13 from Beverley and six miles from Driffield. In addition to several arable and livestock farms, there is extensive pig and turkey breeding in the area. The current population is over 600, the great majority being involved in agriculture and local trades.

The village is a typical 'street' type of community, with the original single line of houses having been augmented in recent years with additional housing developing along the back lanes, behind the Main Street. This development has not yet however spoilt the essentially rural nature of the village. The church is outside the village at the west end, on high, safe, ground and doubtless on the site of the original village.

That pre-Conquest village is mentioned in the Domesday Book of 1086. Even then there was a church, indicating some importance in those times. Until the last century the bridge at Frodingham was only one of two across the river Hull. Originally a ford, this crossing made Frodingham an important crossroads in medieval times and even earlier was part of the southern Viking route from Flamborough to York.

After the Conquest the village and manor was given by William I to the lord of Holderness who later bestowed it on the newly founded Thornton Abbey, in Lincolnshire. It remained with the abbey until the Dissolution in 1539, when it reverted to the Crown. Church Farm, close to the church on the outskirts of the village, was the rectory when Thornton Abbey held the manor.

Charles I sold the manor to the City of London in 1628 to raise finance, after which it changed hands several times until the Bethell family of Rise held it through most of the 17th and 18th centuries. The open fields in the parish were enclosed in 1808.

The village possessed a charter to hold a fair twice a year, on 10th July and 2nd October, and a market was held every week in the Market Place, near to the cross, until Driffield developed to become the principal market town in the area, after which it was transferred there. The village reached its peak in the middle of the 19th century when the population reached 846 and the occupations listed in the census of the time show it to have been totally self-sufficient. There was also consideration for two railways, one from Beverley and one from Bridlington, neither of which came to fruition.

The village cross, in the Market Place, is believed to be the second cross, the current one being erected in 1811 after the original was destroyed by workers on the Hull drainage scheme. This second cross has suffered the effects of today's traffic pollution and is being replaced with a replica.

The church, uniquely dedicated to St Elgin, was largely renovated in the 19th century, although a Norman font remains and also the remains of a 10th century Viking cross of unusual detail, found in the churchyard.

The nonconformist movement built their first chapel in 1821, with four having been erected over the years for the Primitive, Congregational, Baptist and Methodist movements, only the latter still regularly meeting.

The primary school serving the village and the surrounding area celebrated its 75th anniversary in its current building in 1990, having been established in 1845. There is a sub post office and general store, and two public houses, the Star inn and the Blue Post inn.

The village has an active community with several local organisations, including a branch of the Yorkshire Countrywomen's Association. There has been a social centre since 1964, used regularly by various groups, young and old. Football and cricket teams in the village play in the local leagues.

The free landing place, by the bridge, is frequently used by pleasure boats, particularly in the summer, with a gala being held there each year.

In the current commuting age, when there are diverse calls on people's time and energies and the countryside is constantly under pressure from urban development, the village community is anxious to retain the village's rural character, whilst acknowledging the need to attract and maintain a balanced community.

Ottringham

A rural community of approximately 200 houses, Ottringham is situated in the area of East Yorkshire called Holderness. The village is 14 miles from Hull and eight miles from Withernsea on the east coast. The small village centre is surrounded by arable farms. An unclassified road to the south leads to Sunk Island, an area of reclaimed Crown farmland.

The village has one general store, an antiques shop, a garage, two public houses and a post office which was opened in 1851 and has been run by the same family since that date. A mobile library visits once a fortnight. Older members in the village remember the days when there were two general stores, a butcher, baker, sweet shop, tailor, draper, three blacksmiths, a carrier and a wheelwright.

The fine church of St Wilfrid dates back to the 12th century, although there is mention of a church in the Domesday Book. The slender 102 ft spire was once a landmark for ships sailing up the river Humber to Hull. Three interesting features inside are the box pews, the semi-circular altar rail, and the stone lectern dating from Norman times. There is no longer a resident priest, the vicarage has been sold and the parish is now one third of a united benefice. It is interesting to note that during renovations to an old house in the village dated 1638, a priest hole was uncovered under the fourth step of a spiral staircase.

The Methodist chapel was built in 1856, replacing an earlier building which was then used as a day school. This has now been demolished to make way for new houses. The village school was closed in 1948 and the children are taken by bus to other schools in the area.

The railway line between Hull and Withernsea was axed in 1965 by Dr Beeching, though the station was a good distance from the village centre. There is now an hourly bus service.

Two annual events which are popular in the village are the Handicraft and Produce Show in the summer, and a party in the winter for the senior citizens. These are organised by the WI for everyone to enjoy. A village gala is held in July, a very popular day with visitors from a wide area. Various fund-raising events throughout the year finance a Christmas party, and give a gift, such a box of groceries or a basket of fruit to every pensioner in the village. The village supports a church hall and a village institute. There are plenty of social activities, a football club, children's play area on the playing field, and a well-equipped snooker room in a building once known as the reading room.

The free monthly village newsletter is called 'The Beacon'. It takes the name from the Ottringham beacon, a radar transmitter on the outskirts of the village which is a vital communication link for all civil and military aircraft. During the Second World War Ottringham was chosen as a site for a BBC station from which European broadcasts were relayed. The eight 500 ft masts are no longer in existence but the rest of the station remains with its 18 inch thick walls and three ft thick concrete floor, beneath which the vital equipment was housed. The site has been bought for use by a local builder who plans to make a feature of its earlier history.

There have been some new houses built in the last few years, but Ottringham is one of the few villages in Holderness which has not seen large housing developments taking place.

Patrington

Patrington was one of the 'towns' recorded in the Domesday Book and has the earliest recorded evidence of any settlement in Holder-

Bleak House, Patrington (by kind permission of Mr P. Garvey)

ness. Today it would be classed as a large village. A charter in 1033, granting the manor of Patrington to the Archbishop of York, describes the boundaries of the manor which, except on the south where changes have taken place along the river Humber, appear to coincide with the present boundaries of the parish.

Despite its age there are few of the early features of Patrington remaining. The church dates back to the 14th century, and in the grass fields to the south of Station Road can still be seen the ridge and furrow of the open field arable strips which probably originated before the charter. The basic street pattern is no doubt as old as the village itself and the street names are mostly of ancient origin. Otherwise, what can be seen of Patrington today is of the 18th century or later.

The manor passed out of the hands of the Archbishop and into the hands of the Crown in 1545. Eventually, in 1739, it passed to the Maisters, a family of Hull merchants. The second half of the

18th century began to see some big changes in the parish and it is from this period, which was one of expansion and moderate prosperity, that the present houses and buildings begin to date. One such, the manor house, has the date of erection and the name of the first owner on the tablet over the front door, inscribed 'Elinor Ellis 1743'. After falling into decay this century, the house, gardens and outbuildings were extensively and sympathetically restored by the present owner in the 1980s.

In the 1760s improvements were made to Patrington Haven, a small port on the river Humber in the days before much of the land was reclaimed, and this facilitated the export of corn from South Holderness to places like the growing towns of the West Riding. At the same time the road through to Hull was improved by turnpiking, making the markets of Hull more accessible to the farmers of Patrington and the surrounding area. A flax processing mill was built in the 19th century and some workers were brought over from Ireland. This closed in 1881.

The new houses of the 18th and earlier 19th centuries were built of small rough bricks made in Patrington's own brickyards.

Many of the old houses have been enlarged or improved, but historically are very interesting. Rushton House with its grey brick, fine bow windows and elegant Doric porch was built for Robert Clifford, surgeon, about 1810–1820. The rear of the house is 18th century and belonged to Robert Rushton who died in 1783. Bleak House, remodelled in Tudor style by Dr D. W. Coates who bought the property in 1894, originated about a century earlier. This house has recently been converted into a home for the handicapped.

Dunedin House was built by the surgeon J. S. Land in the mid 19th century, and lived in for over 50 years this century by the late Dr Cripps, Medical Officer of Health for the Holderness area.

Linsdall's Hospital was a row of almshouses built in 1843 with money left by Pheobe Linsdall of Winestead. The cottages were originally intended to house 'four poor widows' who each received four shillings a week out of Pheobe's endowment. The cottages have recently been modernised and windows have replaced the old front doors.

The old red brick police station was the site of the village lock-up until 1849, when it was enlarged and used for the monthly petty sessions until 1899. The cells of the station were removed in the 1950s and the building is now a private house.

The workhouse, erected with its fine boardroom in 1838 at a cost of £2,000, was built to accommodate 170 inmates. It was also the meeting place of the Board of Guardians, whose duty it was to look after the poor, and the Patrington Union which was responsible for 27 parishes. The building was closed when the National Health Bill became law, and was used as a potato crisp factory. It was eventually demolished and is now the site for a small housing estate.

The twelve licensed premises of the 18th century have dwindled to four. In the 1830s a corn market was held regularly by three merchants who had a room each at the Hildyard Arms, still there in the market place. The usual group of shops occupies the market place today, with a new up-to-date health centre. The Roll of Honour, dedicated to the men of Patrington who served in the First World War, stands in the middle of the village. The cricket club have very attractive grounds south of the church, and there are playing fields and football pitches on the Welwick road.

The Meridian Line runs just east of the village, hence the naming of the monthly church magazine, 'The Meridian'.

The pride of Patrington is the nationally known St Patrick's church, often said to be the most beautiful parish church in England, and locally known as 'the Queen of Holderness'. Sir John Betjeman wrote 'There is no doubt that, inside and out, the parish church of Patrington is one of the great buildings of England. It sails like a galleon over the wide, flat expanse of Holderness, its symmetry and many pinnacles lead the eye up to its perfectly proportioned spire which crowns the central tower'. The structure has suffered little at the hand of man, or from the lapse of time, so that without much imagination it is possible to picture it as the builders left it about the year 1410.

The village is also well served by two well attended Methodist churches. This is an agricultural area still, as it has been through the centuries, and most of the residents are employed in the district, with some commuting to Hull, the nearest city. There has not been too much building to spoil the village, and the population has not greatly altered over the years, so it is a pleasant village in which to live.

Patrington Haven today is a compact hamlet. Until the formation of Sunk Island, it was a small port and most heavy goods were transported through the 'Haven'. This is now grassed over and just one old warehouse still stands. The hamlet has a Methodist church and a public house, but no shops. A former RAF site nearby is now a large caravan leisure park.

Paull

Paull is a small village lying beside the river Humber some seven miles from Hull and three and a half miles south-west of Hedon.

Once important for shipbuilding, ships carrying 74 guns have been launched from here, including the *Anson* of 1,741 tons built in 1812. It has now reverted back to a quiet village, disturbed only at weekends by visitors from surrounding areas who come to fish, walk the frontage and watch the departure or arrival of passenger ferries and other shipping.

The most notable feature of the river frontage is the 'L' shaped tidal defence wall built in 1986 to prevent flooding from tidal surges on the Humber estuary, at a cost of nearly £3 million. Before the new wall was built, serious flooding occurred in the village under surge tides in 1969, 1976, 1978 and 1983, so the new wall came as a welcome relief.

Another feature of the river frontage includes the old lighthouse with the coastguard cottages adjoining, which was built in 1836 by Trinity House. The lighthouse and cottages are still lived in and command extensive views of Hull waterfront and the Humber Bridge. Also on the eastern frontages Paull Battery which saw service in the Civil War when Charles I attempted to blockade Hull, the first city to turn against him. It later saw service in the Napoleonic wars and as an anti-aircraft point in this century. The whole battery site is now earmarked to become a country park or war museum, but as yet still remains untouched, used now and again for playing war games and a place to stable locally owned horses.

Main Street consists of 19th century cottages which back onto the river frontage and mid 20th century terraced houses on the other side. There are three licensed houses in Main Street. The Humber Tavern, built 1808, was where the landlord used to try to attract visitors from Hull with a bathing machine. The second is called the Royal Oak, built in 1823, and there is also the Crown, opened in 1865. All three are still serving good ale.

The village has only one shop which is the post office and general store. Up to 1980, there were two and before that a number of riverside cottages at different times were shops. Also, the fish and chip shop remains.

Other features of Main Street include the village school, the Wesleyan chapel and the shipyard. The school was built in 1868 on a site given by St John's College, Cambridge and opened a year later. The building has twice been enlarged and now has temporary accommodation. The average attendance in the 121 years of its existence has been 60–80 pupils. The school also suffered war damage in 1942.

The shipyard was opened in 1940 and rebuilt in 1986 along with the tidal wall. It is a very busy yard and employs 20 workers, mostly from the village.

The Wesleyan chapel built in 1805 and restored in 1912 is still in use today. The Primitive Methodist chapel built in 1871 and closed in 1915 is now used as a house. The whole of the Main Street and the river frontage has been made into a conservation area. Until the mid 20th century, Paull village consisted of a single riverside street (Main Street) connected to a back lane by Town End Road. Many houses have since been built in and near Back Lane. There are 82 council houses and 120 private homes. The population in 1961 was 629 but has now risen to just over 800 and will probably remain at this due to the closeness of BP Chemicals which dominates the skyline at Saltend.

The church of St Andrew stands just outside the village. Building started about 1355 and consists of chancel with north vestry, crossing tower with transepts and aisled nave. The church was burnt during the siege of Hull in 1643. Work done in 1881 included the addition of a gallery and the church was restored in 1879 and an addition to the churchyard was consecrated in 1901.

When Hull was a major fishing port, all the trawlers passed by Paull on their way to Iceland and other fishing grounds. The Humber was a very busy river and even before the large trawlers, eleven shrimp boats sailed out of Paull along with ferries to Hull and Lincolnshire.

Maybe when the river runs blue again, shrimp boats will return to Paul, which has been described as a village unique in Holderness.

Pocklington

Pocklington is a small market town with all the characteristics of a village. Situated as it is approximately one mile from the Hull/York road, it has grown gradually, and yet not been subjected to heavy traffic apart from distribution and collection purposes. From an aerial view one can still trace the travellers' ways it had in 1245 when a market grant was made. There is still a Tuesday market with many stalls, the market place and Market Street being closed to traffic on this day only.

The church dominates the commercial centre with its clock tower visible from the housing developments on the outskirts.

Pocklington beck, which played a large part in the 13th and 14th centuries, though no longer used for the running of mills or for carrot washing, is a favourite place for youngsters who paddle in it or catch tiddlers. The beck runs from fields via springs, down London Street, hides under the road, emerges again round Bridge Street flats, underground again until it appears in the churchyard, then under the road and into West Green where it runs beside an avenue of stately chestnut trees, out of Pocklington and on to the river Derwent.

There are many attractive buildings. The Roman Catholic church was built in 1807 and enlarged in 1863; the Grecian-style

Methodist chapel, 1864, is of red brick with a large portico supported by six Doric pillars; 1807 is the original date of the Pentecostal church. Dwellings of note have inspiring names such as Eden Place, Ingledene, Bloomsbury Plate, York View, Alexandra Terrace and Waterloo Buildings. Attractive modern housing developments have names such as Sherbuttgate, Algarth, Mile End Park, Chapel Hill Estate, Oval, Burnby Lane Estate and West Green, rather like the outer ring on a dartboard.

Street names are unusual too like Chapmangate and Grape Lane. Railway Street is a name retained as a fond memory for a public transport system axed by Beeching in 1966. Pen Lane, now widened for parking, was one of the original short cuts around the church. Brass Castle Hill is the site of a dwelling, a few small shops, the post office and the First World War memorial.

The Feathers Hotel is the principal inn, and was used on hiring days, as were most of the other original public houses, this being an agricultural area. It is an 18th century building with alterations from a coaching house with stables to an AA listed hotel and motel. All the remaining public houses do bar meals and meals.

Apart from the local authority-run schools, Pocklington has an independent public school. First founded in 1514, the most famous pupil to date has been William Wilberforce, the slave law reformer.

The church is of 13th century construction with a 15th century tower. It has had modest restoration, but fortunately with no drastic alterations to the basic fabric. On the east wall of the chancel is the inscription to Thomas Pelling, the 'flying man' from Lincolnshire, who fell to his death from the battlements when the rope went slack as he was descending from the church tower to the Old Star inn in April 1733.

There have been two benefactors of note. Francis Scaife died in the 1920s and left to Pocklington monies towards the building of a swimming pool, which turned from a dream into a reality in the 1960s through the legacy and much fundraising.

Percy Marlborough Stewart left to the people of Pocklington his collection of water-lilies, one of the finest in Europe, and the Stewart collection containing illustrations and objects of the many countries of the world which he visited on his hunting expeditions. These gardens attract many visitors by car and coach, being listed in the tourist books as gardens to visit. During the summer, once a month, the Pocklington council arrange band concerts. Major Stewart also made it possible for many sports clubs to have their own ground so all sport is catered for.

Does Pocklington have a ghost? Yes, so it is said. A young girl who haunts the Feathers Hotel, a one time serving wench, and only seen by a very few.

The small market town becomes a village when people say 'good morning' to all they meet, thus making it a friendly place in which to live.

Preston

Preston was founded during the later stages of the Anglo-Saxon invasions and the name means 'Priest Town'. The village was mentioned in the Domesday Book and the entry indicates village life was thriving and there was a population of at least 250.

The village developed gradually, and although road communications were poor there was a stage coach going through the village from Hull to Patrington Haven.

Today Preston is a large village and still expanding. Once mainly agricultural, it is now a dormitory village for commuters to the city of Hull seven miles away, and for workers at one of Europe's largest chemical plants at Saltend on the river Humber, barely two miles distant.

It was during the 1800s that Preston became one of the principal pig producing areas of East Yorkshire. There were then five butchers in the village. In 1859 Thomas Storey is listed as a 'Pig Jobber'. In 1921 Earnest Fletcher was noted as being one of the biggest pork butchers in the area and his abbatoir provided work for 50 people.

The village also had two corn mills during the 1800s, although no remains can be seen today. Other interesting trades of the time were shoemakers, a weaver, a straw-hat maker, a druggist and a castrator, plus the more usual ones. In the early 20th century the village was flourishing with shopkeepers, tailors, boot-repairers, and others. Although the population has gradually increased the number of tradespeople has dwindled. There are two grocery stores, a post office plus groceries, butchers, hairdresser, two garages, estate agent, fashion shop, three public houses, and a blacksmith. The sound of the forge echoes around the village now as it did in the 19th century. The village blacksmith was re-established three years ago and makes hand-forged articles to the customer's requirements.

The church of All Saints has traces of Norman architecture, but most of the building is in Early English or Decorated style, so was probably enlarged in the 13th century. The chancel was rebuilt in 1870, and the rest of the church thoroughly restored in 1882 by public subscription. The large rectory in Staithes Road is now a private house.

A board school was built in 1887 and was used until the new primary school was built adjacent to the South Holderness secondary school which caters for pupils from a wide area. The schools are situated along Station Road, as is the fire station for the area. The railway station was shared by Preston and Hedon, and when the line was axed the track became a pleasant country walk. The old school site has now been developed for housing, but the name School Road remains.

The main problem in Preston today is the traffic, especially along the Main Street, and the church's foundations must be suffering, as the tower is only a few feet from a sharp bend in the street. The Methodist chapel is also in a vulnerable spot, standing as it does at the crossroads. Some people would say that the most exciting pastime in Preston is to watch the traffic lights change, but others would strongly disagree! Many are happy to live in the village of Preston – not Lancashire, but Yorkshire.

Rawcliffe

Rawcliffe can trace its history back to 1078, the name of the village undergoing many changes in that time.

Rawcliffe is 'The Queen of Yorkshire Villages' and with its picture-postcard prettiness it well deserves the name. Situated on a wide bend of the river Aire, it was once a thriving port. River boats brought wool to Rawcliffe from the West Riding, transferring their cargoes to the sea-going vessels that took the wool abroad. The once bustling riverside is now a quiet street, with many of the old buildings well preserved.

The heart of the village, now a conservation area, is the large green, with many old beech and chestnut trees adding beauty throughout the year. The parish church of St James, dating from the 18th century, dominates the green and has many associations with the lords of the manor, the Creyke family. The Creykes lived in Rawcliffe Hall until 1924, when it became a hospital for the mentally handicapped. One of the six (yes, six) village pubs bears the name Creyke Arms.

Rawcliffe's most infamous son is James Hirst, known as Jemmy (1738–1839). He was an eccentric who, amongst other exploits rode a bull named Jupiter to the hunt and attracted the attention of George III. Jemmy then rode to London to visit the King, in a carriage pulled by four mules. He made money by charging people to look at his coffins. He kept two in the house, one equipped with a bell so that he could ring should he want anything in the grave! In his will he left £12 to be given to twelve old maids who were to act as pall bearers. When twelve women who professed to be virgins were found, only two would swear an oath to that effect, but the executors decided to take the women's word for it. Rawcliffe Women's Institute once depicted the scene of Jemmy's funeral in the float procession of the annual Rawcliffe Festival. A coffin, complete with 'corpse' and bell, was pushed through the streets by twelve suitably dressed members (who wouldn't swear an oath either!) to great cheers and hilarity.

Rawcliffe's good communications systems serve the local industries in agriculture and manufacturing. Paper packaging and chemicals are made in the area, and the international headquarters of the Croda Chemical Company are nearby at beautiful Cowick Hall.

The former boys school is thought to have been founded about 1670 by a member of the Boynton family. There has been a school on the site ever since. The building is administered for the Charity Commissioners by a Board of Trustees, all resident in Rawcliffe. Besides the Women's Institute, there are over a dozen other active groups in the village, which cater for a variety of ages and interests.

There are many long established local families, one member tracing her family back to the time of Jemmy Hirst. A growing number have moved into the village, attracted by the serenity of village life.

Rimswell

The civic parish of Rimswell is made up of three villages – Rimswell, South Frodingham and Waxholme. Altogether there is a population of only about 190, who live in a scattered community, largely agricultural. Most of the families in Rimswell, especially those concerned in agriculture, have lived there for some generations.

Rimswell's most marked characteristic is isolation. The nearest town of any size is Hull, 18 miles away, to which there are two buses a week.

Rimswell is part of the ecclesiastical parish of Owthorne, which is now combined with Withernsea. In 1816 the old church at Owthorne finally succumbed to the coastal erosion and its remnants disappeared into the sea. The church authorities decided to play safe and built its replacement at Rimswell, one and a half miles from the sea, the sturdy, unpretentious but pleasing little church of St Mary. This was erected in 1801 at about the same time as some of the farmhouses in the parish.

There was also a Methodist chapel in Rimswell, built in 1899 not far from the church, until 1966 when it was imaginatively converted into a comfortable home.

There is no school in the parish, no shops and no public houses. There used to be a public house, the Rugged World, but this is now a most attractive private house. Rimswell children go to school in Withernsea on the school bus.

The village hall is run by an energetic committee who have raised sufficient money over the past few years to convert it from a wooden building to a brick one, and to refurbish the interior. It is the only meeting place in the parish, and local residents have happy memories of such occasions there as Coronation parties, Jubilee teas, wedding receptions, dances, whist drives etc.

Rimswell was mentioned in the Domesday Book, but there are no really old buildings left, although some are of interest. The most distinctive land-mark in the parish is the Rimswell water tower, built in 1916 to serve South Holderness with water. The two tanks hold 400,000 gallons of water, which was sufficient in 1916 to last South Holderness for two days but would now last only about two and a half hours. The tower is now a listed building.

The deeds of Hall Farm, Rimswell (originally Manor Farm) go back to the early 18th century although there was probably a house on the site before that date. The originally thatched building was extensively altered and enlarged about the middle of the 19th century, as were several farms in the parish. The house is as interesting inside as out, having a collection of about 70 stuffed birds.

Waxholme is on the coast and suffers badly from coastal erosion. A landmark on the Waxholme/Withernsea road is the old Black Mill, and has been so for many generations. It was marked on a map dated 1648 and according to local reports was a working mill until 1900. It is interesting to note on the old maps how many bridlepaths and footpaths radiate from the mill – it was obviously used constantly by the farmers of the area. Black Mill also served a useful purpose during the two world wars, when it was used as a look-out by the army.

It is said that Renish Farm at Waxholme was once used as a

Quaker meeting house. This is another site on which there has been a farm for hundreds of years.

South Frodingham is two or three miles further inland. The names of two of its farms, Great Newsome and Little Newsome, indicate, to historians anyway, that these settlements were newly colonised, probably in the 13th century.

Frodingham Hall was first recorded in 1240 when it was the home of the Frodingham, or Frothingham family. The present moated Hall was rebuilt during the 16th century and altered in the early 19th century but the house preserves the plan of the 16th century building.

The Frodingham family emigrated to America soon after the Pilgrim Fathers, and at different times since the Hall has been owned by Sir John Lister the Hull merchant, and the Sykes family.

As well as the above, several other houses and farmhouses have character and charm. Some have remnants of 18th and 19th century buildings constructed in the local fashion using small boulders from the beach.

During the past ten to 15 years a few new bungalows have been built, and with the eight council houses built in the 1930s, there is a pleasing variety of architectural styles. There are also many very attractive gardens.

Although it will probably never be a picture postcard village, during the last two or three years some farmers have started to replace the hedges that were removed a generation ago, and to plant trees, so perhaps in years to come the parish will again look something like the pictures of it in days gone by, less bleak and windswept than it does today.

Rise

'Rise is a pleasant village and parish, six miles south-west of Hornsea, and twelve miles north-east of Hull, contains 164 souls, and 1,920 acres of fertile land, nearly all the property of the lord of the manor, Richard Bethell Esq.' This extract from an 1830 North and East Riding Gazette still holds good today, with the exception of the population, which numbers around 120, and the parish now covers nearly 4,500 acres.

Rise Hall, a large and handsome stone edifice, forms the centre of the village with a small but beautiful park. This fine and little known house has a number of features of interest, and is by far the most important neo-classical house in the area. The principal entrance to the park near the church is ornamented with two stone lodges, the drawings for which date back to 1818. The place anciently belonged to the Fauconbergs, but has been for many generations the seat of the Bethells. The present Mr Richard Bethell now lives in the rectory sited behind the church, overlooking the park. He is the Lord Lieutenant of Humberside, a member of the Jockey Club and well-known in racing circles, serving as a Steward at many racecourses in the area.

Rise Hall was rebuilt by the Bethell family in 1815–20, and designed by the architect Robert Abraham, a relation of the family. It is now occupied by an order of nuns, Canonesses of St Augustine, who have been in residence since 1946, and who run religious retreats, holidays, weekend courses and meetings. The Hall was used as a convent school from 1946 until 1989. The Hall stables and coach house are all listed buildings, along with a Round House a short distance away, and South Lodge Cottage on the western side of the woodlands.

The church of All Saints is a humble edifice with a bell turret at the west end. It has three bells cast by a London foundry in 1865. Tradition says the church was once much larger than it is today. The style of the building is that of the 14th century, and it holds many monuments to previous rectors and the Bethell family, including a reference to Christopher Bethell who was one of the first whites to be killed in the Mafeking riots in July 1884.

To this day a few of the fields around the village tell of its past history. Black Hall Close contains the moot-hill for Mid Holderness, as well as the foundations of the Black Hall, in which the Fauconberg family once lived. Farnton, a high piece of ground in the parish, is a training track for racehorses. A horse bred at Rise and trained on the track won the St Leger in 1779.

Throughout the years, celebrations have been held to commemorate Coronations, Jubilees, and Royal marriages. Special church services were held, sports days organized for both adults and children, and parish teas were served in the village hall, which was once the village school.

Before the coming of mains water to rural areas, the water for Rise Hall and stable yard was supplied from a very deep well under a sawmill floor, a full quarter of a mile away. It was pumped by steam up to tanks at the top of a high brick-built tower, a landmark for miles around, then gravity-fed to the Hall.

Gas was also manufactured, and Rise had its own gas works. The gas was piped over a quarter of a mile to the Hall and stables. Later on in the 1920s the Bethell family installed their own plant for providing electricity. This was done by using a huge oil engine as a generator. Even horse clippers were powered by this system, but this was replaced by mains electricity.

Steam ploughing was another area where the Bethell family and Rise were in the forefront of development at the turn of the century. This is one reason why the fields around Rise, in particular on Park Farm, were so large. At least one brick-built open well remains, where these steam ploughing machines drew their water.

During the Second World War, Rise had a large military camp. This army unit was the headquarters of all searchlight detachments scattered throughout the area of Holderness, and they were all supplied and maintained from Rise.

Little has changed over the centuries, the main difference being the changing shape of the woodlands surrounding the Park and the village. There are several footpaths around the village, which during the summer months provide a rich variety of flora and fauna. It is difficult to realise when walking around the area that you are only twelve miles away from Hull, the surrounding woodlands creating a block to the sights and sounds of modern living.

Although a small village, Rise has tradition, and a love of its history, which will result in it always being remembered by the people who live within its boundaries.

Roos

Roos is a small village lying on the plain of Holderness, 15 miles east of Hull and four miles north-west of the seaside town of Withernsea. This is a farming area with open fields on all sides. Its roads are often narrow and usually circuitous, following dykes and field boundaries from one community to the next. Two miles away at its closest point, the North Sea annually gnaws five or six ft from the clay coastline. Roos itself is far from any risk of erosion but a private garden in the village contains a sad relic: the rebuilt east windows of the church of Owthorne, one of many coastal parishes swept away over the centuries.

Public transport to Roos is poor: without a private car, residents are as isolated as their forefathers were. Yet the village has become a favoured home for commuters. By car Hull is only half an hour away. There, the North Sea Ferry makes travel to the Continent easy, and to the west of the city the M62 provides the rapid access to the whole motorway system.

There were settlements in Holderness long before the Romans came. Friesian place-names survive from that time, including that of Roos itself: it is a Friesian word meaning 'watery land'. The carrs of low-lying land must often have been water-logged before the complex system of drainage ditches was dug. There was certainly a settlement in Roos well before the Norman Conquest. The Domesday Book records that Roos had 'a priest and a church and 30 acres of meadow'. King William granted the Seignory of Holderness to Drogo, a Flemish knight. One of his vassals, Fulk, became lord of the manor of Roos and adopted 'de Ros' as his title. The foundations of his manor house, Roos Castle, can still be seen as regular contours in a field south of the church. No walls remain. The stones were probably pilfered for other building.

Fulk's great-grandson married into the Trusbut family who had a seat at Warter village. He adopted his father-in-law's coat of arms, which shows three 'bougets' or 'bouts', which are double water bottles of animal skin such as were slung across a rider's saddle during campaigns in Palestine. As often in heraldry, the Trusbut device involved a pun – three water bottles, or 'trois bouts de Wartre'. for 'Trusbuts of Warter'. It is still used as a sign at one of the two public houses, the Roos Arms.

In the 1700s, the Roos and Sledmere estates came into the Sykes family, who still live at Sledmere House, on the Yorkshire Wolds. Two rectors were members of the family and another was an in-law. There is a Sykes memorial in the churchyard and a family vault north-east of the sanctuary.

The present church dates from the 13th century and has many interesting later additions, both structural and decorative. There are also reminders of church life in earlier times. For example, the south chancel wall has scratch dials that are probably Anglo-Saxon. Also known as 'mass clocks' they offered a means of telling the time for church services: an appropriately placed stick cast a shadow on the hour-scale. The Wallis window in the south aisle also reflects early church history: it represents 7th century missionaries converging in East Yorkshire.

For the modern visitor, the main approach to the church leads through an avenue of yew trees and up an impressive flight of stone steps to the west door. In spring, the churchyard is carpeted with snowdrops and primroses.

Roos today is a friendly village where older residents and newcomers mix very well. New housing is being built and the community is growing steadily. At one time villages had to be more self-sufficient and the village used to have more shops and trades than there are now. There is still a grocer/newsagent's (with a petrol pump) and a butcher's shop selling savouries and cakes.

Owing to the projected increase in population a new school was opened in 1982. The old school, built when state education first came to Roos, has been tastefully renovated as a private house, as have other local buildings, some no longer needed for farming. Land for the playing field was acquired on lease some years ago and an energetic committee have worked ever since to maintain and develop it. Since the 1940s the Roos and District Horticultural Society has attracted impressive entries in its Annual Shows. The village hall was built after the First World War and serves the community's needs. Recently refurbished and extended, it provides a meeting room, a smaller games room with snooker table, and a kitchen, and is well used for all the activities that make up village life.

Rudston

Rudston is a very pretty little village in East Yorkshire of some 350 inhabitants. It nestles on the edge of the Yorkshire Wolds about five miles west of Bridlington along the A1253 Bridlington to York road. Driffield, said to be the 'Capital of the Wolds', an attractive market town, is eight miles south-west of Rudston and 17 miles away, a little higher up the coast, is Scarborough.

Rudston's history goes back a very long way to Neolithic times and it is believed to be the oldest inhabited village in England. It has been the site of a number of archaeological explorations in recent years which have yielded valuable information about earlier settlements, with discoveries of bronze spears, remains of chariots, and graves of several warriors. These and earlier relics are now in museums in London and York. There were until about 20 years ago, mosaic pavements from Roman times displayed in their original positions where they had been discovered during field work, together with one unearthed some little distance away at a later excavation. All have since been removed and installed in a museum in Hull.

There is a truly beautiful church, with a 12th century chancel arch and a Norman tower, which is visited and admired by people from all over the world. Close by, in the churchyard, is the famous Rudston monolith or rood-stone from which the village takes its name. It is 25 ft four inches high, six ft wide and two ft three inches thick at its base; how far it is sunk into the ground is not known. It is of a rock type not common to the immediate area, the nearest appears to be found at Cayton and Cornelian Bays, ten miles distant, and is believed to have been brought to Rudston for religious reasons, since it was there long before the church. It stands at the meeting place of four Neolithic ditches which enter the village from the four points of the compass. Its origin is probably similar to Stonehenge which has the biggest ditch, a single one, and many stones, where Rudston has four ditches but only one stone, which is larger than any at Stonehenge.

Another claim to fame by the village is that it is the birthplace of authoress Winifred Holtby, who sadly died in 1935 at the age of 37 and is buried in the churchyard here. She is perhaps best known for her book *South Riding* which was based locally.

Unfortunately there is no longer a village school. Since 1967 the children have travelled to Boynton school three miles away, then transferred to Bridlington for secondary education. The former school building is now converted to a lovely house.

There is a very well-stocked general store incorporating the post office, a public house, the Bosville Arms, which stands on the site of a previous public house of several centuries ago, and a petrol station and garage. Rudston is basically a farming community, but mechanisation and modernisation have resulted in much less employment than of old and the majority of people now travel out of the village to work.

The village hall was a disused chapel bought for the use of the village by Sir Godfrey MacDonald, the local squire at the time, to replace an earlier public hall which was destroyed during the war. It overlooks the Gypsey Race, known locally as 'The Beck', which winds its way through several villages from its source at Wharram, high on the Yorkshire Wolds, before finally flowing into the sea through Bridlington Harbour. As it leaves Rudston, it runs through the grounds of Thorpe Hall on the outskirts of the village which is the home of Sir Ian and Lady Juliet MacDonald of Sleat, descendants of Sir Godfrey, whose family, originally the Bosvilles, arrived in the community in the 1770s. As the Gypsey Race meanders through the estate it encourages and supports much wildlife and some quite rare birds.

The great community spirit has enabled a children's play park to be established close by the village hall, and more recently a sports field which has a beautiful pavilion and caters for football, cricket, tennis, bowls, and a floodlit area for football training and five-a-side tournaments throughout the winter. Most of the work of creating this field and pavilion was done voluntarily and funded mainly by money raised from various village functions. The land is rented to the village by Sir Ian MacDonald for the annual rent of one white rose. Volunteer labour was also responsible for recent alterations and improvements to the village hall, which is now able to accommodate indoor bowling throughout the winter. Villagers are proud and fortunate to be living here in this peaceful little village, surrounded by beautiful countryside.

Sancton

The village of Sancton lies about eight miles west of Beverley on the Market Weighton to Brough road. It sits in a hollow of the steep western slope of the Wolds, and the slopes above the village are the location of the largest known pagan Anglian burial grounds north of the Humber. It is recorded that found in one of the graves were the bones of a man with his sword and spear, his wife with her work-basket, and a child with its toys.

The Romans were here too, for the road on which the village stands follows the line of the Roman road from Brough to Malton. Many of the houses stand in two side roads on either side of this road, sometimes referred to as King Street.

In a commanding position high on a hill overlooking the village stands the church of All Saints. The tower is particularly striking. Added in the 15th century, this three-stage tower is octagonal for its full height and has slender buttresses and a lantern top. It is surely one of the most beautiful church towers on the whole of the Wolds. The only similar tower in the area is at Coxwold in North Yorkshire.

All Saints is built of ashlar and rubble and consists of the chancel, nave with north and south porches, and west tower. The chancel has a 13th century priest's doorway and a 13th century lancet with a low window at its foot. Other noteworthy features are, respectively, the carved capitals of the chancel arch, fragments of the old window tracery, and a stoop inside the doorway.

With the exception of the tower, the church was rebuilt in 1869–71 in the Early English style to designs by J. B. and William Atkinson of York. Records show there was a church at Sancton as early as 1086.

A free school was built in Sancton before 1609 by the local benefactor Sir Marmaduke Langdale, renowned for his bravery while fighting in the Civil War for Charles Stuart's cause.

The school stood in the churchyard. It was rebuilt on the same site in 1870 and united with the National Society. Typically Victorian in style, the school remained in use until recent times.

The brick-built Methodist chapel stands in one of the side lanes of the village. It was built in 1803 and enlarged in 1840. Two of Sancton's early dissenters earned the highest honour which Methodism has to confer on its preachers: Thomas and Samuel Jackson both became presidents of the Wesleyan Conference. They were the sons of Thomas Jackson, a humble farm labourer who brought up ten children in a thatched cottage. His grave is in the churchyard.

Many of the gravestones record deaths at early ages. A brother and sister, for instance, died within a month of each other in 1861 – one of them 16, the other 18. Could there have been an epidemic of some kind in the village around this time? It would be interesting to know.

Almost entirely agricultural in the past, records show few references to other occupations, but a brickmaker lived in Sancton in 1851. There was a windmill in the village in 1583 – the only early mention of milling there, but a miller was recorded from 1913 to 1931.

The name Sancton, in common with many English place names, refers to the nature of the soil or ground, ie Sancton – 'sandy'.

Sandholme & Hive

Sandholme and Hive are two hamlets side by side, where many years ago the inhabitants must have lived in blissful seclusion amid a farming community. Progress and time have wrought many changes, some good, some not so good. At one time there were two or three inns, and a little shop in Hive, but 'the old order changeth', they no longer exist. There are several smart new dwellings here, no doubt built upon the old closes and orchards where at one time the Anabaptists were buried.

The village hall has seen many activities, including Fur and Feather Whist Drives at Christmas, when the prizes were often brought very much alive in sacks! Meetings, rallies, dances and wedding receptions all brought the small communities together. It is now in need of complete renovation. The new meeting place is to be the day centre at Gilberdyke House, cosy and warm, but the villagers feel a sadness to have had to finally abandon Sandholme village hall.

Sadly, the dear little chapel also was demolished some years ago, and the demise of the railway took place about 30 years ago.

The invading motorway, the M62, sliced and slashed its way across the peaceful countryside, separating the lovely old Quaker Farm from some of its pastureland, which is now at the other side of the flyover which almost marks the boundary between Sandholme and Gilberdyke.

Seaton

Seaton is a small village three miles from the coast, on the main Hornsea to Beverley road. Though lacking in prominent features, it is an interesting and lively place including two working farms in the centre of the village.

There are two village greens; both were levelled, and the pond was reclaimed on one of them about ten years ago. Trees were planted and picnic seats were purchased, so this now makes a popular place for children and visitors in the summer. There is a small Methodist chapel which is over 100 years old and still used every Sunday.

One rather unusual feature is the Whin Common, which lies about half a mile to the north of the village. To get to it there is a right of way through fields. The common is a piece of land of just over two acres, where the poor of the village could collect firewood, as much as they can carry, 'whin' meaning a gorse bush.

An infant school built in 1840 served both Seaton and Sigglesthorne. This closed in 1923, and is now a snooker club. Opposite the Swan inn is the recreation hall. Built in the 1930s this is still well supported and is used practically every day. The village Horticultural Show is over 50 years old, and is still a very popular event.

Seaton has not grown much over the years due to lack of building land, though there are now new terrace-type cottages in the centre of the village. These have brought young families into the community, which is good for the continuity of village life.

Seaton Ross

The sundial on a cottage in North End was made in the 1840s and is said to be the largest in England with its twelve ft diameter. Its maker was William Watson, farmer and surveyor, who made the similar one on nearby Dial Farm, his family home, and another above the church door.

Still to be seen are the remains of two windmills, the Old Mill and the New Mill. Old Mill, which had its sails removed in 1952, was the last five-sailed mill in the district.

The older houses and the village church are of local red brick. Most of the original dwellings were built or rebuilt under the aegis of the Everingham estate, owned by the Constables who married into the Norfolk family. They are solid foursquare houses with solid names like Cross Farm, Green Farm, Manor Farm, Rose Farm and Seaton Old Hall, as well as Old and New Mills. They are well spread out down the long narrow winding village, built originally along the edge of marshland, hence the 'Sea-ton'. The flat open spaces also explain the presence of the mills. There is plenty of wind!

The church is a plain red brick building, dedicated to St Edmund, and 1989 saw the celebration of the bicentenary of the rebuilding of the church. Many new houses are being built, infilling between the older houses.

Every spring the village looks very pretty, the aconites, snowdrops and crocuses flower in abundance in gardens and on the grass verges. The village is well known for its flowers, and has been rewarded several times with a place in the Britain in Bloom Competition. It is especially colourful at showtime.

The Seaton Ross Show is a two day event. It has flourished for well over 100 years and is always held on the first weekend in July. It began life as a village feast and is now an agricultural and country sports show attracting entries from all over the North of England.

The village has bought its own playing field and children's play equipment. Various events and an annual Family Fun Day in August help the finances. The village hall is used as a venue for all village meetings and activities. It was formerly the village school, sadly closed in 1961. Since then village children have gone by bus to the primary school in neighbouring Melbourne. Carollers, originally from the church, have sung around the village every Christmas for very many years, and the WI is keeping the tradition alive. There is even Seaton Ross's own special carol *Welcome Christmas*.

Seaton Ross is a thriving, growing village. Council workmen have had to tidy footpaths and repair roads and curbs, partly in response to the number of heavy lorries passing through. There are at least seven haulage firms or drivers operating from the village. There is also a builder, a repairer of aircraft parts and a small industrial area on part of the old wartime airfield, with a seed merchant's, the maker of agribuggies, an explosives firm, another haulier, and a repairs garage. The village boasts a general store, a butcher's shop, a community post office and two public houses. One of these, the Blacksmith's Arms, is familiarly known as the Bombers, from its wartime associations with Melbourne airfield, built partly on Seaton Ross Common. The pub has a bar commemorating No 10 Squadron, which was based at the aerodrome. Outside the Bombers is a seat funded partly by the No 10 Squadron Association in appreciation of the villagers' support during the war. There is also a permanent memorial to the fliers, erected in 1986 by the Association and the Seaton Ross and

Melbourne Parish Councils.

The number of farmers is decreasing, 16 at the last count, but agriculture is still the dominant industry in this corner of East Yorkshire.

Sewerby

The village of Sewerby is situated between the popular holiday resort of Bridlington and Flamborough Head, a massive outcrop of chalk cliffs which juts into the North Sea and protects Bridlington Bay from the northern winds.

The Danes gave Sewerby its name, which has been spelt in many different ways – Sywardby, Sewardby and Suerby – but its history goes back much further. Iron Age man built a massive earthwork here, now known as Danes Dyke, and the early settlers also found a ready supply of flints in the chalk cliffs from which they made many of their primitive tools. The Romans and Danes had settlements here too and the village became permanent in Norman times when William the Conqueror's brother Robert, Count of Mortain, built a manor house. Later the de Sewardby family, who took their name from the village, owned the estate.

John Greame built Sewerby Hall on the site of the old manor house in 1715 and the property was gradually extended over the years, being completed by the adding of the conservatory in Victorian times. The threat of invasion too continued into more modern times, for the occupants of the Hall fled to York in great panic in 1779 when the battle of Flamborough Head took place and the Americans under John Paul Jones won a decisive victory.

Danes Dyke farm, which was originally part of the Sewerby estate, found its place in literary history as Anerley Farm in R. D. Blackmore's romantic novel *Mary Anerley*. This tale of smugglers, murder and romance was set on this piece of coast and many of the places and people from the book have been commemorated in the names of streets and new houses built in the area.

Being close to Bridlington, Sewerby has lost some of its village atmosphere but life still revolves round the church and, of course, the Hall which is now a museum visited by thousands of people every year. The grounds of the Hall are very attractive with mature trees, colourful gardens and quiet areas for those who simply wish to sit and rest. There is a cricket pitch in a village green setting and small zoo for the children. Not far away is a miniature village; a 'Noddy' train takes visitors back to the outskirts of Bridlington.

Sewerby Hall museum has a fine collection of Anglo-Saxon jewellery, clothing, pottery and weapons excavated from the burial site at nearby Home Farm which was also part of the estate, but the most interesting exhibits in the museum are to be found in the Amy Johnson collection.

Amy Johnson was a Hull girl who found fame as a pilot in the early days of aviation. After going to Sheffield University she worked in a London store and trained to be a pilot in her spare time. In 1930 she set off on her first solo long distance flight and broke the record from England to Australia. The difficulties were considerable for aircraft were still primitive with open cockpits, and airfields were very few and far between. She set many long distance records over the next few years, culminating in the England to Capetown and return record in 1936 in the Percival New Gull. There are many mementoes of her life in the collection – everywhere she went she was feted and given souvenirs of her visits to distant parts of the world. Many of these souvenirs are in the museum. When the Second World War started she joined the Air Transport Auxiliary and spent her time ferrying new aircraft from the factories to their airforce bases. In 1941 the aircraft she was flying disappeared without trace, crashing in the sea near to the Thames estuary and neither she nor her aeroplane were ever found.

Flamborough Head was defined as a 'Heritage Coast' by the Countryside Commission in 1979 and in 1982 the Flamborough Headland Heritage Coast Project was launched to promote and encourage interest in the area. The twelve mile coastline has magnificent scenery and a wealth of bird life, wild flowers, marine life and features of geological and historical interest. The project employs a full-time warden and has support from voluntary helpers. An MSC workforce carries out essential maintenance work and provides guides and information points.

Shiptonthorpe

The village of Shiptonthorpe lies a short distance west of Market Weighton on the main York to Hull road. Until the year 1876 it was known as Shipton, it then amalgamated with Thorpe Le Street. Thorpe was used in the sense of 'a secondary settlement' or 'outlying farm'. For centuries agriculture was the main industry together with self-employed small businesses giving support, blacksmiths, cobblers, tailors, and village stores.

A village of some attractive properties, Town Street alone contains four Grade II listed buildings. A charming white house, originally thatched, but now with a red, pantiled roof, is at least 400 years old, and said to contain some fine old beams.

The church is 12th century, and until 1876 was a chapelry under Market Weighton. It has a narrow Norman tower, the battlements of which were added at a later date. A fine south doorway has some strange looking beak heads in the richly moulded arch. Of particular interest and speculation is a carving over the archway of the modern porch, a small, quaint, skirted figure, one hand clasping a crook, the other raised as though in blessing. It is believed to have been carved some eight centuries ago. Points of interest inside the church are the finely carved pulpit, the stained glass windows, the ancient corbel heads, and the carving of two creatures in the jaws of a monster.

There are two gates to the church, a lychgate from the main road side, the other on Town Street. These are referred to by some of the local people as the 'funeral gate' and the 'wedding gate', respectively.

In contrast to the ancient church, the small Methodist chapel fairly close by in Town Street, is modern. It was built in the late 1960s. It is of interest that the altar table was made by the minister of the time.

In times past, Shiptonthorpe has not been lacking in interesting characters. Legend has it that Mother Shipton of Knaresborough, 1488–1561, whose real name was Ursula Sonthell, lived in Shiptonthorpe during some period in her life. It is also recorded that in the early 18th century 'Edwin Calvert, gentleman, apparently died of alcohol poisoning at the age of 17'. It is said that his height at the time of his death was only 39 inches.

The village school, built in 1870, is now closed and used for the village hall. The children now attend schools in Market Weighton. With machinery being used more and more on the farms, the village has seen the number of people employed on the land drastically fall, and is now one of many with commuters travelling further afield to their place of employment. The population has remained between 300 to 400, as the village has never been designated for large residential development.

Sigglesthorne

Sigglesthorne is in Holderness, about three miles inland from the coastal town of Hornsea, and ten miles east-north-east of Beverley – the county town of the former East Riding of Yorkshire.

The name is believed to be derived from a personal name Sighel or Signup, and the second part from the thorn bushes which grew in abundance at the time, and dates possibly from the 7th century. The first written evidence of its existence as Siglestorne was in the Domesday Book, although recent archaeological excavations on Spring Field revealed the existence of a previous settlement which dated back to Roman times or earlier.

Sigglesthorne has a twin village – Seaton – which is about a mile distant. The Methodist chapel, the inn and the post office are at Seaton, whilst Sigglesthorne has St Laurence's church and the school. There was an ale house on the outskirts of the village kept by John Skaling – this is now a dwelling house, with a renovation plaque dated 1818; it is known as Skaling House.

The present church of St Laurence dates from the late 12th century although the tower is probably of 15th century addition, being built from ashlar and cobble and various types of old bricks. There are three bells in the tower – age unknown – but they were mentioned in the churchwarden's accounts in the 17th century.

At the rear of the church was an old girls school erected in 1818 by a former rector, Archdeacon William Henry Edward Bentinck. This has fallen into disuse, having been used as a military hospital and to sleep troops in transit in the First World War, a Sunday school, a library, and up until five years ago a store for the church gardening equipment. With the arrival, in 1984, of the present rector, Canon Gerald Pearce, who set about its renovation with the aid of the YTS and other helpers, it is now a useful little hall for church meetings, play groups etc. Archdeacon Bentinck also provided the present school and schoolhouse.

Sigglesthorne Hall has housed most of the well-known members of the community. The Bethells bought the house in 1890. They were Deputy Lieutenants, High Sheriffs and joint lords of the manor. They provided seats around three old elm trees, which were named Bass, Alto and Tenor. The trees stood at intervals down the Main Street and provided a meeting place for the villagers and presumably a resting place whilst they journeyed to Lowry Field at the bottom of the village, which had the communal St Laurence Well and provided water when all the house and farm wells were dry. Tenor tree was only felled in the last ten years – and the stump can still be seen planted with pansies.

Sir William Wright followed the Bethells; he was Chairman of the Hull Dock Company and has one of the docks named after him. In 1920 David Christian Smith, head of Horsley Smith Timber Merchants, lived there. The present owner is John Townend, a Hull wine merchant, who is presently the Conservative Member of Parliament for the Bridlington constituency. There are very few new buildings so the village is largely unspoiled.

Skelton

The village of Skelton lies on the east bank of the river Ouse, near Goole, and has a population of just over 100 people. The Romans were early settlers here, and the village was thriving during the survey for the Domesday Book. In 1379, when Richard II levied poll tax to pay for his wars with the French, Skelton was recorded as having 137 people over the age of 15 years.

One mile to the south of the village lies Sand Hall, a large brick building erected in 1774. It was once a hunting lodge of the Kings of England. The estate belongs to the Schofield family. The late Mrs Schofield was a past President of Skelton W.I. and she allowed the grounds to be used for various events. Until the 1950s the village had a chapel, a school, two shops and a public house. At the present time there is only the public house left.

The children travel by school bus to Howden, and social events are held in the old school. It is no longer a farming community. People travel outside the village to work, so turning it into a dormitory village.

Skerne

Skerne is mentioned in the Domesday Book as a small village and seems to have changed little ever since! It was a fairly important village, the church having possible connections with Meaux Abbey. Certainly the Abbey were known to be large landowners in the area.

The Norman church was much larger than its present day form, having a north transept of which the arches leading to it can still be seen. The entrance porch on the south side and the bell tower were probably 15th century additions, and it is obvious from the stone benches in the porch that as well as church, civil business was also conducted there! The church seems to be slightly set away from the village, and is very elusive as you drive through, being only reached either through a farmyard or down a lane off the road to Wansford.

In more recent times the village was part of Lord Burlington's estate at Londesborough, and was eventually sold off at the beginning of this century. At that time it was a thriving community with a blacksmith's shop, bakery, joiner and tailor's, to name a few. The blacksmith's shop can still be seen near the bus stop but the bakery is now Southlands and the tailor's Holly Bank. The joiner's buildings are still used as stables. There is still Londesborough Lodge on the road to Driffield where the 'gentry' used to stay whilst on shooting expeditions. Further along the village another house used to be the 'cookhouse' and game room for them – the meals must have been cold by the time they arrived at the table of Londesborough Lodge!

The school was built in 1877 and is now the village hall. Local inhabitants recall that thistles used to be placed down the outside school toilets before the unsuspecting used them!

The local meeting place for the young people 'out of school' was at one Mrs Ances's, whose house is now part of Lilleygarth Farm. She was known to regularly have to cook Sunday lunch with all the village youths lounging around her kitchen – times do not change.

The last shop, the post office stores, closed about seven years ago – even that was once a chapel no longer in use, but there is still the pub, the Eagle. This hostelry has a county-wide following and is one of the few pubs in England that still has no bar and serves its wonderful beer straight from the barrels in the cellar.

Skerne is now expanding with new houses, as are a lot of rural communities, but it still retains the farming background with familiar names still resident, Dixon and Bean to name but two.

There are still old rural traditions retained and newer ones introduced, like auctioning produce from the church harvest at the pub with a small prayer whilst drinking your beer, or taking a stroll through the churchyard on a summer evening to the lane beyond.

Skidby

The village of Skidby is situated to the west of the A164 (the road linking the Humber Bridge to Beverley) about five miles south of Beverley. The parish of Skidby includes the hamlets of Eppleworth and Raywell.

The village has a long history. It is believed to be of Danish origin founded about AD 890 when Danish raiders began to settle in the area. In the Domesday Book the village is recorded as

Schitebi, a berewick or manor cultivated by the monks or canons of Beverley. At the Dissolution of the Monasteries, Henry VIII gave the manor to Trinity College, Cambridge. For a period of the late 16th century it appears to have come into the possession of the Earls of Leicester but eventually came back into the full possession of Trinity College, which remained lord of the manor until quite recent times.

Little physical evidence of the village's long history remains. The parish church of St Michael dates back to the 13th century. The present porch was added in 1777 and the small tower in 1827. It is a charming building and is listed as a building of Architectural or Historic Interest.

Another listed building is the fine windmill which stands on the hill above the village and makes an outstanding local landmark. The mill was built in 1821 and is one of the few surviving working tower mills in the country. It is also considered by many to be the best surviving example of a tower mill. The mill is now owned and maintained by Beverley Borough Council and is open to the public at certain times of the year. On occasion it is put into operation producing stone-ground flour for sale to visitors. The mill buildings house a museum of old implements and materials associated with corn production and milling.

Other protected buildings in the parish are Braffords Hall on Eppleworth Road, Raywell House, West Cottage at Grange Farm, Eppleworth and 44 Main Street. The present Methodist chapel was built in 1902, the former chapel now being part of the village hall.

The population of about 1,250 is served by two shops and a well appointed inn. There is a Church of England primary school in the village and many flourishing social and community organisations. Among these are a Women's Institute, a village hall and institute and a Darby and Joan Club as well as Scouts, Guides, youth clubs and football clubs for the younger members of the community. The parish council has recently provided a playing field which, in addition to cricket and football pitches, is being provided with children's play equipment, a pavilion and club room.

Skipsea

The village of Skipsea lies close to the North Sea, which gnaws voraciously on winter nights at its cliffs of boulder clay. It is flanked to the north, west and south by the villages of Ulrome, Beeford and Atwick, which nestle under the wide open skies and clean air of this piece of East Yorkshire.

Travel the B1249 however, and even in the height of summer, the whole scene can be transformed by the mist which rolls in from the sea, shrouding the landscape in mystery. Travel back into those mists of time and you will meet many who have gone before and who also may have experienced these sudden sea frets, for that is what these mists are. Peer back to the time of William the Conqueror who gave the Isle of Holderness to a knight 'well tried in feats of arms', Drogo de Bevere. Drogo built his castle high upon the mound at Skipsea Brough surrounded by ditches and earthworks. Drogo's wife was a relative of the king himself yet, 'in an evil hour', Drogo killed her. Could she be the 'White Lady' who is said to haunt the district? No one knows for sure. Nor do they know why for many years, almost to this day, footprints were to be found in a field near to the earthworks of the castle where a famous duel was said to have been fought between two brothers during the Civil War and where no seed would grow. Now they no longer remain except in the memories of people native to this village. The third mystery concerns another ghost known as 'Old Moll' who at times walks around the churchyard, the legend being connected with a horse which threw its rider when it reared at the sight of something supernatural coming down the hill at Skipsea Brough. Take care then in the mist!

What of Skipsea now? In daylight the mound is still to be seen and is worth the climb for views of the sea, the plain of Holderness, and the village itself with the church standing proudly at the west end of the village.

The church is dedicated to All Saints and is an ancient building of stone. One chapel still remains, and the village is well served with a modern school, a public house, the Board inn, a post office/ grocer's, hairdresser's, grocery shop/cafe, pet shop and craft shops. There is also a fish and chip shop, betting shop and a selling centre.

Many of the older houses and walls are built of cobbles from the sea shore, and there is a fair amount of new building to accommodate young people and those who wish to retire here. Farming thrives as it has done down the years and now with the swallows come the caravans to the clifftop with people in search of sea, sand and serenity. For a time the villagers must share their breezes, shops and sunshine with the leisure seekers. Harmony prevails, and friendships are made.

One thread which binds the years and the community together is the WI, 1990 saw its diamond jubilee. To celebrate their 50 years a commemorative wooden seat was given to the village. The oldest member, Miss Doris Statters, at 83 years old can conjure up many colourful happenings from her years in the village. Picture then the annual visit through the village of the 'Plough Lads' – local lads who appeared with blackened faces. The travelling bear with its master on their journey through the local villages. The Temperance Society meeting on the village green in the hope of turning the local ungodly into Christians and freeing them from the 'demon drink'. The annual fair on the green with swings, roundabouts, coconut shy and the brandy snap stall. The circus held on the field near the old school. The annual feast when the 'men only' members wearing blue sashes and white gloves marched with a band to the church for a service followed by a dull dinner in the Board inn clubroom, then in the afternoon there were sports for the whole village. A day when nearly every home in the village was open house to anyone for a cup of tea and something to eat. In later years the villagers have celebrated Queen Elizabeth's Silver Jubilee, and the wedding of Prince Charles. What will future travellers remember as they look back through the mist of time? Who knows? But, Skipsea hopefully will be as now, a green and pleasant land.

Skirlaugh

Skirlaugh was mentioned in the Domesday Book in 1086 when it was known as Schireslair or Schylake; 'scyre' – to divide or cut, 'lake' – a dyke or sewer. As North and South Skirlaugh were divided by the Lamworth stream, it was well named. The population of South Skirlaugh in 1891 was 261 and in the North 289, including the officers and inmates of the workhouse. It is nine miles from Hull and Beverley, 20 miles south of Bridlington and seven miles from Hornsea.

The railway station, built in 1876, was actually in Ellerby one and a half miles away. It had a station house and station master. It was closed and pulled down around 1965.

In the late 19th century businesses were varied – tailor and insurance agent, saddler and parish clerk, carrier, shoemaker, wheelwright, pig jobber, taxidermist, doctor, grocer, miller, blacksmith, bricklayer, butcher, cattle dealer, five farms, market garden and three public houses. The lord of the manor for South Skirlaugh was Sir F. A. Clifford Constable and for the North it was William Bethell.

Skirlaugh church (St Augustine's), built in 1401–1405 by Walter Skirlaw (then Bishop of Durham), is one of the finest examples of early Perpendicular architecture in the county of York. The register dates from 1719. Walter Skirlaw was born sometime during the middle of the 14th century, the son of a basket maker – his coat of arms had an interwoven pattern (by 1656 the windows painted and set with his coat of arms were nearly gone). The interior of Skirlaugh church was thoroughly repaired between 1813–19 and it was at this time that a screen, fine pulpit, pews and a wainscot gallery were finally removed. In 1967 repairs were carried out, namely rewiring, new roof and ceiling, some windows replaced and belfry woodwork repaired. The part of the churchyard which was closed in 1883 has been levelled and re-seeded with grass and is now able to be mown and kept generally tidy. More repairs have been carried out over the years – the most recent and probably most rewarding is the cleaning, repointing and replacing of stonework – all done by one of the parishioners.

The vicarage was a gift of the Archbishop of York and was built 1869/70. William Wilberforce and Marmaduke Langdale were patrons of the church and set up the Langdale Charity. They gave £20 annually for the maintenance of the church and £100 annually for grants towards the marriages of peasants and servants. The charity is still in force today, but is used for grants for students and apprentices for books and any equipment they may need to help them in their careers.

The Methodist chapel was built in 1892 at a cost of £800. It had a pipe organ installed in 1924 which cost £400. The chapel has some fine coloured glass windows. It has now been sold and is a private dwelling and pottery workshop. The Methodists have joined St Augustine's as a shared church for worship.

Skirlaugh church school was built in 1861 at a cost of £1,000 and was originally supported by the Langdale Charity. It was in use until 1968 when a new school was built. This held 200 pupils, but had to be extended in 1980 to hold 250. A nursery unit was built in 1977 and has two teachers. The old school has been converted into the village hall and is in regular use.

Millhouse Cottage, built in 1640, was one of the oldest buildings, adjoined by a windmill built in 1250. This windmill was the last of the Dutch barn type left in England and was in use until 1930, but had to be pulled down in 1945 as it was in danger of collapse.

The Poor Amendment Act of 1834 grouped parishes together into Poor Law Unions. Skirlaugh was given a workhouse, built in 1838, housing 132 inmates drawn from 66,898 acres of Holderness parishes. It remained a workhouse until 1916, when it was used as billets for the army. It was later taken over by Holderness RDC and used as offices. It is still used as offices for Holderness Borough Council.

There are some old buildings left apart from the ones mentioned, however most of the existing buildings are post-war. There are three housing developments and a housing estate. The old post office, doctor's surgery, saddler's and butcher's were demolished during the mid-1970s. There is an antiques shop, blacksmith, village store, post office, old established builder's, old established joiner and builder, agricultural machinery firm, pottery and reading room, and many people from the village are employed in these businesses. There are also thriving rugby, cricket and football teams, a playing field (also equipped with swings, slide, etc) and a pavilion.

Skirpenbeck

Secluded from the old Roman road running eastward from Stamford Bridge, Skirpenbeck is a small, quiet village with some charming properties, several of which are listed buildings.

In the 18th century – and perhaps earlier – Skirpenbeck had a corn mill which served the village. It is said that there are surviving accounts of repair work done to the mill both in 1744–5 and 1751–3. It seems the brick and tile building consisted of two storeys and a loft, and that the wheel was fed from a dam which is now dry. There is mention of a miller as late as 1937, and evidence that the mill was in use for several years after that date.

The village church, tucked away at the very end of a winding, leafy lane, is dedicated to St Mary. From the outside, the most striking aspect of the building is the tall, slender tower, constructed entirely of brick in contrast to the stone of the rest of the structure. Inside, the church has cream-washed walls, a brick floor and green painted pews. A list of past rectors of the parish goes back to the year 1274.

The church's Norman story is illustrated by the doorway, the simple arch connecting nave and chancel, and the massive tub font. A carved chair close by the altar, a small ancient-looking chest, and an ornately-carved table which looks for all the world like a chest on legs, may well be Jacobean.

A wall monument of 1636 is detailed and of much interest. It depicts Richard Paget, in court dress, complete with ruff, and his wife – her hair arranged in immaculate tight curls, her wrists and fingers adorned with bracelets and rings respectively. Their two children are beside their parents, and all four appear to be looking up into Heaven. Since two of the past rectors bore the name Paget, it seems likely that there were family connections between them and Richard.

Quiet, secluded places often attract ghost stories. Skirpenbeck is no exception. A child seen at the window of a house where no child then resided, for instance, and a 'strange feeling' felt about a particular area of the village.

Sledmere

Sledmere is a farming estate village on the top of the Yorkshire Wolds, twelve miles from Malton to the north, and eight miles from Driffield to the south. Its country folk are very much at one with the land. There used to be two small hamlets just outside but part of the village, known as Mill Cottages and Pry Cottages. They both made a contribution to the village and the school, but sadly of late these have been demolished, so shrinking village life. The population is diminishing due to the advancement of the machine on the farm, so very few men are needed on the land, and many of the young folk have to go elsewhere to find work.

The village is in a beautiful situation, and attracts great numbers of visitors and sightseers during the summer when Sledmere House and grounds are open.

The house was begun in 1751, a magnificent mansion set in 2,000 acres of parkland and gardens landscaped by Capability Brown. In the grounds the village church of St Mary is one of the most attractive in East Yorkshire with a wealth of detail in the Gothic Revival style. A Roman Catholic chapel adjoins the house, and the village has a Methodist chapel.

Many interesting architectural features are to be observed in the village, including the stables and carriage house, built at the end of the 18th century just after the house. Triton Cottage, dating from around 1700, is the earliest house remaining in the village. The Triton inn was formerly a coaching inn, and is still providing meals and accommodation. The village post office is in one of the estate houses designed by John Birch in Queen Anne style, and has a George IV post box incorporated in the left-hand window. He also designed the school and schoolmaster's house. The vicarage is the only house not owned by the estate. There is still the village well, now covered, with a monument above it to the memory of Sir Christopher Sykes, second baronet, in 1840.

In the village are two remarkable monuments. The first on the village green is in the style of an Eleanor Cross, and dedicated to men from the estate who died during the First World War. The second is a structure, unique in its figures and inscription, in memory of the Waggoners' Reserve, a volunteer corps of 1,000 local farmworkers, paid only £1 a year, who provided horse-drawn transport carrying vital supplies to the trenches in Europe during the First World War.

There is a third monument on the outskirts of the village, a 120 ft tall Gothic spire, paid for by subscription and dedicated to Sir Tatton Sykes, fourth baronet, who died in 1863, much loved and respected by all his villagers.

The village cottages have been modernised, with lock-up garages and car parking. There is a sports field second to none, a good village hall with stage, dressing rooms and billiard room, and above all a friendly atmosphere.

Everyone is the same in an estate village, and here estate workers are much in evidence. There is friendly gossip and fun in conversation, and above all a sense of caring and looking after each other.

Snaith

Snaith is a busy thriving village and lies between Selby, Goole and Doncaster. To 'off-comed 'uns' it is not even a large village, with only 2,080 inhabitants, but to the native it is a town because it has held a market charter since 1223 and although no market has been held for many years, the charter was read once a year in the market place until 1939. Because the market has lapsed, the Court of Pie-Powder, which allowed the market to right any wronged there, has also lapsed.

The name Snaith is thought to mean 'enclosed by water' and the area is known locally as the Three Rivers area. The river Aire, which is tidal, runs through the centre of the town and in medieval times Snaith was a busy port with a harbour and ferry across the river to Selby, one of the few Aire crossings in the area. The actual founding of the town is obscure, but it was well established as part of the Royal hunting lodge before 1066 and so has no separate entry in the Domesday Book, since Snaith was a royal manor held by the King 'for the support of his table', and therefore already documented. It is, however, mentioned three times as having jurisdiction over the manors of Birkin, Whitley and Hensall. Today it is still a convenient centre, being close to the M1, M18, M180 and the A1 and A19, and within 20 miles of York, Leeds and Doncaster. There is little industry except the old dog mill which now makes plastic chairs and the new brewery which brews real ale, but being surrounded by the power stations of Drax, Eggborough, Ferrybridge and Thorpe Marsh, it makes a good base for power station workers, who can move for promotion without uprooting their families. There is a new primary school and a modern comprehensive school in the village. There is also work at the modern pit at Kellingley or the new Snaith pit.

In its hey-day Snaith had twelve pubs and four tailors, and although there is no tailor and the pubs are reduced to five, it is still a busy little shopping centre. There are no big stores but 'one of everything' and the old pattern of Snaith, the centre serving about ten villages, has returned. Parking is a problem but the parish council are working to get a proper car park to give off-street parking. The railway runs to Leeds and to Hull, and a bus from Leeds to Goole comes through Snaith giving limited access on public transport.

In 1777, in response to a public petition, Thomas Stapleton of Carlton Towers (the family home of the present Duke of Norfolk), built a bridge to encourage the flax trade and to ease the difficulty of transporting bodies from Carlton by ferry to be buried in Snaith churchyard. With the advent of motor traffic the New Bridge was

Priory Church of St Lawrence, Snaith

built in 1928. During the Second world War the centre span of the old swing bridge was removed by the Royal Engineers so that they could practise making Bailey bridges against the tide. Snaith was on the eastern fringe of the West Riding of Yorkshire but since the 1974 boundary reorganisation, it is on the western fringe of Britain's newest county, North Humberside.

The priory church of St Lawrence at Snaith is a Saxon foundation, though very little of the Saxon church remains. The present building dates from 1086 and the report of its state in 1275 lists among its treasures four tropers (the Anglo-Saxon service book) and several part tropers, so it was a rich church. There is a rood-loft stair enclosed in a pillar but the rood screen where the priest stood to preach on Good Friday, or to make special announcements, has been removed. In the Stapleton chapel is a memorial carving of Lady Elizabeth Stapleton, whose husband was the General of HM Horse at the battle of Edgehill in 1642. In the Dawnay chapel on the south side is a statue of Viscount Downe made by Chantry and an Easter sepulchre. The east window of this chapel contains the only remaining fragments of 14th century glass.

Near the chancel arch is a niche dedicated to St Sitha – her only claim to fame, according to local tradition, is that she was martyred, her head was cut off 'and she picked it up and ran three miles to the nearby (sic!) church to warn the other Christians.' Not surprisingly the only other shrine to her is in Bradford Cathedral. Some say Sitha is a corruption of Etheldreds, sister to the Abbess Hilda of Whitby, but this seems to be wishful thinking. Certainly Snaith Priory was a staging post for pilgrims travelling from Lincoln to York, as recorded on the altar kneelers.

Snaith was a Peculiar, ie it had its own ecclesiastical court and in many ways it was exempt from the jurisdiction of the Bishop, which may explain the fact that the Bishop's inspectors came to interview the brothers at Snaith for reported 'indiscretions' and were unable to carry out their inspection because the brothers had summoned the ferry to the Snaith bank so they could not cross the river! At the back of the church is the Consistory court, part of the church building but not consecrated and now housing the creche. It was used to try ecclesiastical matters and to settle disputed wills and land settlements. Because it was a Peculiar, the priory church had four wardens – one of their duties was to enforce the wearing of woolly hats on Sundays: failure to comply brought a fine of fourpence.

Adjoining the churchyard is the Buttermarket, but only in name now. The butter booths and the fire station have been removed but the local branch of the Heritage Society has restored the old town lock-up, known as the penny cells. Men who were drunk at market were put in these cells till sober, and then had to pay a penny to get out. There were two tiny windows, each with one bar across originally, but friends of the prisoners delayed the sobering up process by passing jugs of ale through the windows, so two bars were fitted. Nothing daunted, the bearers of comfort brought a flagon of ale and a long clay pipe. They put the bowl in the ale and the stem through between the bars – perhaps Snaith invented drinking straws. Exhibitions are held there from time to time and there is an art and craft gallery in the old vicarage opposite the church.

The population of Snaith has doubled in the past 25 years but it is still small enough to 'know everybody'; ask for people by name, rather than by their address! There is much modern housing and many restored buildings. Bed and breakfast is readily available and there is much to see in the area.

South Cave

South Cave was first and foremost an agricultural settlement. Its name came from Jordan De Cave who owned a large amount of land here many years ago. South Cave is situated twelve miles west of Hull.

Although classed as a village it has a town hall in the market place. By the late 18th century it was a thriving corn market, which resulted in the town hall being built in 1796. It is a very interesting two-storeyed building with an open arcade facing the street. It was first known as the market cross and part of it was a boys school. In bygone days all proclamations were made on the market cross steps, and the hiring of labour was carried out there too. The corn trade in the village gradually died out due to the arrival of the railways in the 1840s. This new form of transport gave easier access to larger markets and towns.

Opposite the town hall is 'the Copper Shop', an antiques shop. The name originated from the days when this house belonged to the local policeman. At the back of the house was a lock-up gaol and if any one caused any trouble they were locked up for the night, then transported the next morning by the local 'taxi', which was a horse and cart, to the police station at Brough to be tried.

The Market Place has a very interesting history. In 1291 King Edward I granted a charter which gave the villagers the right to hold a market every Monday, and a fair every year on Trinity Monday and Tuesday. As a local market centre there was a large variety of trades and crafts. In the 18th century there was a pedlar, furrier, weaver, millwright, maltster, and an apothecary. One of the 18th century bylaws was 'that no person corrupt the town beck by letting into it stinking or hurtful water or washing

Cave Castle

unwholesome things in the same.' The beck trickles into the main street in the Market Place. Also the parish stocks stood in the Market Place. In 1664 Thomas Burton was fined the sum of one shilling for letting his wife wash puddings in the town beck. Not even the lord of the manor was exempt, L. U. Boldere Esq was fined one shilling for his beck being 'undressed'.

At one time there were nine inns in the village, now there are two. The Fox and Coney was built in 1739. When it was first recorded it was known as the Fox, named by its first owner who was a furrier. The Bear inn, also 18th century, got its name from the crest of the Barnard family.

South Cave is divided into two distinct parts, separated since the 18th century by the grounds of the Barnard family house, now known as Cave Castle Golf Hotel. A stone over the rear door bears the initials of Sir Thomas Danby, dated 1586. It is said that tunnels once used by escapers from the castle still exist beneath the grounds. The grounds were laid out in 1787. The castle was built in the late 18th century then extensively restored and altered in

1872–1875. It was reduced in size and modernised after its sale in 1937. The castle was taken over by the Hull Brewery Company in 1961. At one time it was a Country club, now it is an hotel and a very popular venue for wedding receptions and other festive occasions. The castle ponds attract various species of ducks and geese, waterhens and coots. A large amount of the surrounding land has recently been made into a golf course. Wooded areas are being planted and new ponds created in the hope of attracting more wildlife to the area.

There are three churches in the village including All Saints, parts of which date back to the 15th century. A large Family Centre being built next to the church will cater for various activities. Many years ago opposite the church was the Bay Horse inn. This inn was combined with a blacksmith's shop. The blacksmith was a lady by the name of Rachael Levitt.

The United reformed church was founded in 1662 and rebuilt in 1873. The Primitive Methodist chapel was built in 1837 and then rebuilt on the same site in 1877. Near the chapel stands the church institute, a Gothic-style building built in 1844. Years ago it housed all the village activities including lantern slides, then moving pictures when they came into being. Now it is used by the local playgroup and various other events take place there too.

South Cave school was opened in 1967, further extensions including a sports hall were completed in 1978. This hall caters for many sporting activities and social events. The area round the school houses the library, tennis courts, a children's play area, and a bowling green. At one time South Cave had a water mill, and a windmill. The windmill was sited near the school, but it had disappeared by the second half of the 18th century. The water mill was sited at Mill beck and it continued in use until the 1860s.

Like many other rural areas, South Cave is rapidly losing many acres of its lovely open spaces due to expansion, nevertheless it is still a very pleasant village to live in. South Cave has 18th century houses, an ancient castle and churches, but amongst all this antiquity it is very much alive. Its inhabitants have the future of the village very much at heart as well as the past.

Sproatley

The name Sproatley originated from two words and means a clearing in a forest. A glacier stone in the churchyard is also mentioned in the Domesday Book and is believed to have come down during the Ice Age.

With Holderness being very flat land it was often swampy and wet, so people originally tended to build their homes somewhere on a hill. Sproatley is between 74 and 85.7 ft above sea level, so was an ideal site. The church stands on the highest point in the village. On the north-west corner of the tower is an ordnance survey mark (approximately level with the key-hole) which is said to indicate the height of the tower of Holy Trinity church at Kingston-upon-Hull. There were many wells in the area and almost all the houses had their own water pumps.

Over the years Sproatley passed into the hands of many people, until 1840 when the principal landowner was Sir Talbot Constable of Burton Constable Hall. One of the late owners, one Mr Raines, planted about 1,000 trees and was a generous benefactor to the school.

On the 5th January 1733, Mrs Bridget Briggs in her will left certain properties in the vicinity of Sheffield, two thirds of the rent of which were to build a schoolhouse and school to educate ten poor boys and ten poor girls of Sproatley; other children were to be educated there, but to pay for their instruction. Any surplus monies could be used to put the boys to an apprenticeship, or the girls into service. Sometimes clothing was provided also for them to be suitably clad to take up their work. About 1868 a new school was built but this has now been replaced by a modern and forward thinking school for five to eleven year olds. The charity still continues but as well as maintaining and providing extras for the school, grants are given for further education or books.

The church in AD 837 was named St Swithin's after the Bishop of Winchester. The old Norman church was taken down in 1819 and another built on the site. In 1885 this church was taken down to the window sills and rebuilt. There are two bells hung from a stout beam, thought to be from the old church, and eight tubular bells given in 1888. Hymn tunes were played on these to call people to worship; unfortunately these can no longer be used due to the weak state of the tower. The organ is perhaps the main feature of the building. It was built by Father Smith and brought from Temple Newsam, Leeds. It is unique in that the keys are black, and black and white striped, and thought to be the only one still in use in the country. The approach to the church is through a lychgate erected in 1889 to commemorate the long and successful reign of Queen Victoria.

In the churchyard stands the remains of the old village cross, also the graves of Joseph Rank and his wife (of the Rank Organisation family). He was the great uncle of Joseph Rank, the miller. Joseph Rank had his first mill in Sproatley and the house where he lived is still outwardly the same, but the mill foundation was removed about 20 years ago when a modern housing estate was built.

There is still a village shop with newsagency, and a post office. The post office was started by David Pickering in 1838, two years before the penny post was introduced. He had to walk about three miles to collect the mail and carry it back to the village, for which a charge of sixpence per missive was made. He died in 1876 at the age of 93, and his son John took up the duties. He also founded the Burton Constable lodge of the United Ancient Order of Druids. After his death in 1896 his sister Edith became the sub-postmistress for 33 years. A niece took over the post office when she married, and it was moved to the present premises. Telegraph came to the village in 1901 and messages were sent by morse code. The family connection was finally broken in 1974 on the retirement of the sub-postmistress, who was a great niece of the said Edith Pickering.

There are two public houses, a butcher's shop, a chapel, and a court house. At one time there was a police inspector and a police constable at the police station. It was complete with cells and used regularly. Now it is used for the hearing of court cases only.

The village hall, built in 1912, is a busy and thriving place. Land and some money was given by the family of Rev Howard-Hall, who was the rector at that time, for the erection of a building for the use of the people of Sproatley, of any denomination, for their education and recreation. The WI hold their meetings there, as do many other organisations, and it is in use every day. Rents are kept to a reasonable level to enable as many people as possible to benefit, and the maintenance is in the hands of a committee who hold regular fund-raising events.

Standing in front of the hall is a war memorial, which records the names of 13 men who served and/or lost their lives during the First World War. Thankfully all men and women returned safely from the Second World War, so a sum of money was given to the hall and a brass plaque erected declaring it to be a memorial village hall. There is a playing field with equipment for the younger members of the community, and a football and cricket pitch.

When the WI was formed in 1937, Sproatley was a village with about 100 houses and plenty of grass fields and open spaces. There are now about 550 dwellings with a population in the region of 1,400.

Stamford Bridge

Stamford Bridge played an important part in the history of England. In September 1066, King Harold defeated his brother Tostig, who was attempting to regain the earldom of Northumbria with the help of the King of Norway, in a fierce and bloody battle on the banks of the river Derwent. Harold then heard of the landing of William of Normandy and had to force march a weary army to Hastings where he was defeated and William became King of England. On a rise near the corn mill is a stone that commemorates the battle of Stamford Bridge with an inscription in English and Danish. Up until 1878, the first Sunday after 19th September was 'feast day' in Stamford Bridge, commemorating 'the battle'. On this day boatshaped pies were made bearing the impression of the fatal spear, in memory of the Englishman in his boat who slew the Norseman defending the bridge. The day was called Spear Pie Feast. These early times are commemorated in the names of some of the roads in the village: Haroldsway, Tostig Close, Danesway, Viking Road and Battleflats.

Though always an important crossing place, the village remained relatively small until the 19th century, when the population rose from 170 in 1801 to 417 in 1861. The western half of the village over the river Derwent was the scene of the annual fair from about 1200 until the early 20th century. Stamford Bridge, meaning a 'stone-paved ford' across the river Derwent, is now a conservation area and a thriving attractive village. It is a popular stopping place for those en route to the Wolds and coast. The river draws many visitors who delight in the beautiful scenery, the majestic old corn mill, now a restaurant, and the fierce and powerful weir.

The riverside has been landscaped and is home to many ducks and geese, a big attraction to children and adults alike, though sometimes a traffic hazard. The closing of the railway line was regretted but the station has been made into a club and the old engine shed into a sports hall. A room in the old station is available for meetings and classes, and the village holds many attractions for all age groups. There is a well-used village hall, the usual sports clubs, and the school swimming pool is available for hire in the summer months.

The Church of England and Methodist church are active, with large Sunday schools and youth groups. There is a council home for the elderly and three private homes as well. A well-run caravan site beside the river brings holidaymakers to the village, which is well served by the shops, three public houses, two tea-rooms and two restaurants, and the best fish and chip shop in the area. Stamford Bridge is an expanding village with much to offer, both to those living within its boundaries, or just passing through.

Sunk Island

The parish of Sunk Island lies in remote countryside east of Hull, where the great plain of South Holderness meets the north Humber foreshore. Reminiscent of Canada, or the American mid-west, it is landscape drawn large; huge skies and wide river prospects, acre on acre of golden wheatlands dotted with ancient stone churches and large prosperous farmsteads of red brick and orange pantile.

Sunk Island itself pushes its great productive belly out into the Humber, protected from the North Sea by the encircling arm of the Spurn peninsula. It is hard to believe that this 8,000 acre agricultural estate owned by the Crown was once a small mid-river sandbank often submerged by spring tides. The Island's strange evocative name takes a little explaining. In fact Sunk Island is a kind of water-logged 'phoenix' thrown up by the rides of the Humber, resting on the submerged remains of low-lying medieval farmlands overflown by a series of great storms combined with exceptionally high tides that engulfed the area in 1399, the site of a number of drowned villages.

These lost lands are named on old charts as 'Sunke Sands' and it must have been a logical progression to name the risen sandbank 'Sunk Sand Island', eventually over the centuries to be shortened to today's Sunk Island.

The growth of Sunk Island is intimately linked with the Gylby family who, for almost 200 years leased it from the Crown, embanking it as it increased in size.

The Gylbys' story reads like a historical novel. Col Anthony Gylby was the first lessee from 1668, he was Lieutenant of Hull Fort and an ardent Cavalier who died under something of a cloud accused of misappropriation of the fort's materials for use on his solitary island mansion. Next comes grandson William Gylby, wealthy London lawyer who made great strides, increasing the size of the island to over 1,500 acres by his death in 1744, and having the dubious distinction of attempting to reduce the troublesome rat population by having them killed, dressed and offered up to his tenants and workmen to eat.

The next lessee, for just one year, was to be Captain Lovelace Gylby, another flamboyant character credited with temporarily losing the island in a card game. His widow Margaret held on for another 45 years, beset on all sides by warring local landowners who claimed parts of the island, as its boundaries grew ever-closer to the Holderness mainland. When Margaret died in 1790, she bequeathed Sunk Island in the form of shares to a bewildering number of relatives, and as she died childless, here the name 'Gylby' dies out.

The main beneficiary became Rev John Lonsdale, whose great embankment of 1800 in effect joined 'Sunk' to Holderness creating a total of 4,389 acres of embanked productive farmland. It was Rev Lonsdale's son, also John, eventually to become the Bishop of Lichfield, who relinquished the lease on the island in 1834, leaving the way open for his sub-tenants, the real Sunk Island farmers, to take up individual leases on their land.

The parish church of Holy Trinity was declared redundant in 1983 and now houses the Humber Bank Heritage Centre, that plots the island's history and places of interest, including Stone creek with its panoramic views across the busy Humber estuary, and Fisherman's channel, a wildlife sanctuary created by the South Holderness Countryside Society.

The Heritage Centre, a registered charity, plays host to small prearranged groups of visitors from June until September, and is happy to provide both a short guided tour of the island and excellent afternoon teas for the refreshment of the weary traveller in Sunk Island's village hall close by.

Today's Sunk Island is a fascinating spot unspoiled by modern development. The farmhouses, many of them listed buildings, mostly date from 1855–7 and proudly bear on their outer walls plaques commemorating the year of their erection and the fact that their owner was Queen Victoria.

Sutton on Hull

The ancient village of Sutton in Holderness lies about three miles from the city of Kingston upon Hull. Originally named Sudtone, or South town, it was a thriving community long before the city of Hull was in existence. In very early times water and marshland covered much of the area. Boats were able to sail from the river Humber into the village carrying fish and other commodities. There are still wells in the area which were in use until recently. A true story is told that the steeple of Hull's Holy Trinity church, is on a level with the road in Church Street, Sutton.

The church of St James, dedicated September 1349, and the daughter church of St Peter's, Wawne, played an important part in the life of the village. The first building was a chapel of ease. The clergy officiating at both Sutton and Wawne were drawn from the abbey at Meaux, which was close to both. Relations between the two churches were often strained, partly because of the question of status of the various monks working in the area. A serious controversy arose when the Wawne clergy decided that all the burials from Sutton should take place at Wawne. This meant that the Sutton monks would lose a large part of their income, and the four mile trek carrying the coffin was arduous, especially in bad weather. A stone which was used to rest the coffin on along the way is now in the Memorial gardens in Sutton. Sutton people became so enraged about this, that the Pope eventually became involved. Letters went to and fro from Wawne to Rome with no result, until eventually the Pope sent an indignant letter ordering the Wawne clergy to stop the practice or risk punishment. This ended the controversy and at last the Sutton villagers were able to be buried in their own churchyard.

During the Middle Ages rich merchants came, and built large houses around and in Sutton, letting the land out for farming. The village became surrounded by fields and pasture land. During this time several charities were set up to help the poor. Some of these are still in existence, and have resulted in flats being built for the elderly of the parish, and also housing for widows and daughters of clergymen.

Before the closing of the railway from Hull to the coastal town of Hornsea, Sutton was a station on the way. Hornsea became a favourite resort for day and evening visits. The track has been converted into a cycle and pedestrian walkway, and people with energy can walk the eleven miles to the coast.

In the early 1960s the Hull City Council purchased most of the farming land round the village, and it is surrounded by housing estates, one of which is Bransholme, one of the biggest in the country. All the large houses have been pulled down, or taken over as nursing homes. The many village shops have closed and reopened as video or betting shops, or estate agents. There is still a post office.

Sutton has been designated a conservation area and the local committee are able to keep a check on the plans of any new building proposals. The village atmosphere is kept alive by an annual May Day event and tree and bulb planting schemes. Several organisations are active, and aim to keep the village character, which is still there despite the many changes, not always welcome ones, which have taken place in recent times.

Sutton upon Derwent

The village of Sutton upon Derwent is situated on the east bank of the river Derwent, which is now the county boundary. The village lies on the B1228 and is an equal distance from York and Pocklington.

From York a bridge crosses into the village. A bridge has been on this site from the 14th century. Before then it was served with a ford, and a ferry when the tide was high. Nowadays the river Derwent is non-tidal due to the flood barrier at Barmby marsh. Also the first lockgates are at Sutton. Originally The Ings behind the village was the natural flood basin of the river. As the road, at this point, was frequently flooded a raised causeway or footpath was built to give access.

The old watermill was demolished a few years ago, but was active until 1960. Across the river the remains of a salmon leap can be seen. When the lampreys were on the 'run' it was a very lucrative business for the local fishermen. Today, two angling clubs share the fishing on the banks of the river Derwent. There is not a public pathway along the river to the south, but if there was, the bridges built for the barge houses could be seen over the drainage dykes.

The church of St Michael and all Angels is on a ridge overlooking the river and the old water mill. It is the fourth church to be built on the site. Remains of the chancel are said to be of the 12th century, and the tower was rebuilt in the 15th century and has three bells. Like many churches it is in need of restoration, but it is very pretty and well worth a visit. In 1135, Robert de Percy is named as donor of the church, and the churchyard contains gravestones belonging to the Percy family, who originally owned the village and had Sutton Hall as a hunting lodge. The village was much more wooded in those days. The patronage of the living and estates passed from Robert de Percy to Whitby Abbey, then through the years to several different families, eventually being sold in 1947 to the Crown estates who are still the owners.

The manor house is a Grade II listed building and stands next to the church. In the manor yard there was a chalybeate (impregnated with iron salts) spring called Monk's Well. The Sutton rectory was sold and is now an hotel and restaurant.

On the corner of the road leading to Woodhouse, a hamlet within the parish, is the village hall. Built by voluntary labour, under the direction and enthusiasm of its then rector, M. H. Pimm, it was completed in 1931. It is a meeting room for the youth club and other sections within the community, such as the indoor bowls, and is also used as 'the dining room' for the local school. There is also a tennis and badminton club.

Nearby are two public houses. The Vincent Arms is an old building with pseudo black beams made from railway sleepers. It is a popular meeting and eating place. The other, Turpins Tavern, is a new building replacing the old Cross Keys, and provides accommodation, food and entertainment – especially at weekends.

The local school was established in 1824, rebuilt in 1844, added to in 1873 and enlarged in 1906. Along the road, and opposite the junction to Whynham lane was the Wesleyan chapel. It was a temporary iron structure erected in 1882, and stood until 1937 within the gardens of Wheelwright House. When it was sold it became the village hall at Bishop Wilton. Down Whynham Lane is the village play area, in a safe place off the main road, well used and very well kept. Nearby is the local shop/post office, a busy establishment with a very helpful owner. Here day tickets can be bought for fishing in the river Derwent. Opposite, unmarked, is the site of the pinfold of the village, in the garden of Blacksmith's Cottage. The village continues for a further half mile to the turn-off for Sutton Hall, a small Georgian residence, now privately owned.

The boundary to the parish is Hagg Bridge, which spans the Pocklington Canal and Blackfoss beck. The population of the village is around 360. The housing has followed a linear type of development, which has made the village about one and a half miles long. There are a few small estates, and a council estate was built in the 1950s. At the present time some of the old Airey houses are being demolished and rebuilt.

In the past agriculture provided work for the inhabitants, but with its decline, and with modernisation, the mill, wheelwright, blacksmith and breweries have disappeared. Small cottage industries, an hotel, the two public houses and the shop provide the only additional work to the farming industry now. Small blocks of land and infilling have provided homes for commuters. In spite of this the village remains a village. It is an attractive, friendly, and appealing place in which to live.

Swanland

The village of Swanland, approximately seven miles west of the city of Kingston-upon-Hull, has since the 19th century been considered one of the most attractive areas in North Humberside, or East Yorkshire as many would prefer. When the East coast enjoyed its mighty fishing fleets, many of the skippers had their imposing homes built in the tranquillity of Swanland. The village has changed somewhat now, being within easy reach of the M62 motorway and, nearby, having the added attraction of the largest single-span bridge in the world across the river Humber. This impressive sight attracts the camera enthusiast to Swanland from where excellent photographs of the bridge can be taken. Many of the larger houses have been demolished to make way for more modern houses and bungalows. Agriculture was the main occupation for many years but now unhappily few farms remain, due to building development.

The centre of the village is still much as it has always been, with an attractive pond, complete with swans, surrounded by the school, chapel and public house (named appropriately the Swan and Cygnet). It has only been there (altered from a house) since 1980 because Sir James Reckitt (of Reckitt and Colman fame) who bought Swanland manor in 1884, was a devout Quaker and would not allow a pub in the village. It is now a popular meeting place. Sir James Reckitt was a great benefactor though, providing money for the library, tennis courts and bowling green. There are other organisations well supported in the village involving people of all ages, like the Wine Guild and Women's Institute.

Of the few remaining large houses, Mere House which faces the pond is possibly the oldest, thought to be Elizabethan and reputed to have been visited by the ghost of a monk. The floors throughout the house are made of stone, including upstairs! It is a house of character and adds beauty to the centre of the village. Close by is the chapel, now known as Christ church (United Reformed), built in 1803 on the site of a previous one founded in 1693, then known as the Independent chapel.

Another place of worship was built in 1828 for the Methodists but as attendances dwindled in the 1970s it was decided to share with Christ church, a facility which made economic sense. The last place of worship to be built, in 1899, and known as St Barnabas', was for the Church of England. It does not hold such a prominent place in the village as Christ church near the pond, but nevertheless it is now too small for the congregation, so after years of searching a place has at last been found to build a new larger church on the outskirts of the village.

The earliest place of worship would appear to have been the chantry, constructed, it is said, as early as 1332 and rumoured to have had a secret passage running to Mere House. Sir James Reckitt did some amateur excavating when he lived at the manor and some stones, which could have formed church windows, can still be seen in the gardens of houses since built on the site. Another interesting discovery was made in 1942 near the site of the chantry; a leaden bulla of Pope Clement III (1187–1191). The bulla was a seal attached to Papal documents issued from the Vatican. The oldest 'object' in the village stands outside the post office, which incidently has a date stone above its door inscribed 1721. The 'object' is a lump of granite, with a plaque above stating that it was brought down on ice from Westmorland during the Ice Age 300,000 years ago.

Not so old is the village show, now held in the James Reckitt Memorial Hall every September. It is on a much smaller scale than those held just after the Second World War when animals and livestock were included and a show ring was erected for the horse and pony events. Very few horses are seen around the village these days but Swanland was a self-sufficient village, catering for all needs, with a blacksmith, shoemaker, tailor, wheelwright and undertaker. The old craftsmen may have disappeared but in their place there is a bank, chemist, butcher, grocers, and many more essential services, trading in the same cottages built more than a hundred years ago, so not destroying the character and heritage of the village.

Swine

The village of Swine in Holderness is steeped in history, both ancient and modern. The very name of this comely and quite small village which is situated to the east of Kingston upon Hull attracts attention. When Kingston was a mere spot on the map, Swine was a place of great importance, with a flourishing pig market. The old cross is situated in the garden of one of the local cottages.

The ancient church of St Mary, with its beautiful east window, was at one time the parish church of Drypool. The parish extended to Ellerby, Skirlaugh, Bilton, Burton Constable, Coniston, Thirtleby and Benninghome. It was built in the 12th century (1150). The church in those days was cruciform with a magnificent tower (now pulled down) in the centre. The present church is the chancel of the original church with Norman-style pillars. In 1154 a Cistercian nunnery existed in Swine; this was destroyed by Henry VIII when he gave orders to dissolve all monasteries. The first listed vicar was Rev John Haitfield, dated 6th July 1323. In more recent times Rev William Cobby was the vicar from August 1875 and died here in 1930 aged 83 years, after ministering to the parish for 55 years.

The tombs of the Hilton family, who were the lords of the manor, are dated 1393–1431 and can be seen in the church, where there is the Hilton chapel. Until recent times cobbles ran down the main street. There is evidence of a Roman settlement as quite a number of coins have been ploughed up relating to this period in history. A feature of much interest is a large mound named Giants Hill, now planted with trees. Some historians believe this to be the burial place of the Saxon king, Swaine, from whom the name of the village is reputed to have been derived.

At one time the village was owned by the Wilberforce family and during this period it was a thriving community. There was a public house named the Black Bull, a butcher's, saddler's and a shoemaker's. The present blacksmith's shop was built around 1840 and has a unique entrance in the shape of a horseshoe. The village became the property of the Crown Commissioners around 1850. The Hull and Hornsea Railway was opened around 1864 and closed in 1965. A school was opened in 1868 and closed in 1968, after 100 years of use. The school is now a private house.

Now sad to say all the little businesses have gone, leaving us with the beautiful church and small post office. The post office was started in 1860; the first postmaster was Mr Robert Harker and it stayed in this family for 100 years. The post office has a very interesting sign in the shape of a black and white pig hanging at the entrance. The Swine parish Council was formed in 1894 and the meetings are now held in the church vestry every four months. Every year in August there is a Village Fayre down the main street, with a different theme each year. This event is very well attended and all the local people run the stalls and dress in different attire to suit the theme. The money raised at this event is put towards the running of the church and things needed for the village to keep it looking attractive.

Thorngumbald

Thorngumbald is situated on a busy main road, which is used by both industry and coast-line traffic. It lies between the city of Hull and Withernsea and is built on the heavy clays of South Holderness. First heard of in the Domesday Book, listed as Torne, eventually a Baron Gumald settled in the area, adding his title to the original, and thus emerged its present name.

What was a traditional farming and market garden community of some 290 population, has now developed into a large sprawling suburban area of over 3,000, the majority employed in the city of Hull. This process swallowed land and buildings for four central farms, though one attractive farmhouse survived, converted into a public house.

Still serving the village well are the church and chapel, both modest buildings, yet well maintained despite depleted congregations.

An imposing large house stands back from the main road, known as Thorne Hall, dated 1881. It is now divided for an old people's residential home and private residence, yet much the same in appearance as the original. Central to Thorngumbald was the blacksmith's shop, hub of working activity for a large area, now rebuilt as a modern garage but still owned by the fourth generation of Willinghams.

Children are well catered for with new infant and primary schools, also a health clinic nearby and a play school. A useful set of shops supplying basic needs is central too, all within easy reach of the estates. The old school serves as a village hall while the church institute, once a hive of activity, is little in demand.

A popular Darby and Joan Club was formed by the WI members in the 1970s, also an Entertainment Group. Eventually this became independent; now it produces sought after family shows to entertain the elderly and to raise funds for charity.

Thorngumbald was once renowned for its Agriculture and Flower Show until costs and age overtook its original helpers. A worthy successor has emerged with the Annual Gala, raising funds to help village projects and renovations.

Old and new have integrated quite well, though few of the true Thorngumbald villagers are left to recall the transformation.

Thornholme

The hamlet of Thornholme has been part of Burton Agnes parish since time immemorial. Strung out along the Bridlington road, Thornholme is about half a mile from Burton Agnes. Earthworks in the area suggest that the village was once larger than it is today.

For a long time the lords of the manor of Thornholme were the St Quintins of Harpham, an early St Quintin having married into the de Stuteville family. The estate descended in the St Quintin family until the death of Violet St Quintin in 1943. It then consisted of 1,174 acres. It was sold by Violet's trustees to Marcus Wickham Boynton who in 1948 sold 154 acres to the Air Ministry for Carnaby airfield. Most of the remainder was sold in separate lots in 1949. Smaller portions of Thornholme land have been variously held over the years by members of the Griffith, Somerville and Boynton families, and changed hands within these families.

Court papers relating to the St Quintin manor at Thornholme show that two bylaw men, a pinder, and one or two constables were being appointed there in the 19th century.

A Primitive Methodist chapel was built at Thornholme in 1892. This was demolished in the mid 1980s, the congregation attending the chapel at Haisthorpe.

Thwing

Opinions are divided as to the meaning of 'Thwing', but most historians agree that it is derived from the Scandinavian and could mean a 'strip of high land'.

Thwing is a small village on the eastern end of the Wolds of East Yorkshire. Together with its associated hamlet of Octon-cum-Octon Grange, it forms a parish four miles long covering 4,024 acres and situated between 300 and 500 ft above sea level.

The parish is aligned from the tumulus known as Willy Howe in the east to a prehistoric earthwork in the south-west, and bounded by the Gypsey Race valley in the north and a Roman road (the High Street) in the south.

Over recent years, the parish has been of great interest archaeologically and excavations have revealed signs of occupation from neolithic man to the Middle Ages. The 'dig' carried out in 1984 brought to light what could have been the main centre of administration in Anglo-Saxon times and could well have been the site for the ancient 'Dic Ring' from which Dickering got its name. Some 130 skeletons removed for histological examination have been ceremoniously re-interred in the presence of the Archbishop of York.

Although reported as poor in the Domesday Book, Thwing could well have been an important place in medieval times, the prosperity of the village being a direct reflection of the influence and affluence of the Thwing baronial family, who were amongst the most distinguished and prosperous families in northern England.

One of the most illustrious members of the Thwing family was John de Thwenge, born at the manor in Thwing in 1320. After education at Oxford, he became the greatest of all the priors at Bridlington. Known as St John of Bridlington, he was the last English saint to be canonised in 1401 prior to the Reformation.

All Saints' church is a 12th century building which retains several features of the original Norman construction, notably the fine chancel arch and the south doorway with its carved tympanum of the Paschal Lamb. One of its more unusual features is a very long 'squint'. The communal plate of silver gilt was presented to the church by Thomas Lamplugh in 1689. Lamplugh was born in Octon in 1615 and became Archbishop of York in 1688. His name lives on today in the title of Lamplugh House, once the rectory of Thwing and opened as a Christian conference centre for young people in 1973. Today, it continues its ministry of spiritual renewal of the church, attracting both clergy and laymen from home and abroad.

There is a listed monument to the north of the parish, an obelisk erected in 1799 to commemorate December 1795 when a huge meteorite, weighing approximately 56 lbs, fell on that spot near Wold Cottage Farm.

Thwing and Octon, with a total population of some 200 souls, is completely rural in character with no intrusive housing schemes to mar the landscape of rolling wold. A century ago, there were some 400 to 500 people in the village, a fairly self-sufficient community with farmers, grocers, shoemakers, blacksmith and joiner. Today, however, the village has gradually succumbed to the advent of the motorcar and modern day living. Types of occupation have altered, although farming is the predominant industry, and more people are commuting from the parish. With no village shop, bus service or school, the village church and public house are now the focus of activity in the parish, with little to mar the tranquillity of the quiet backwater.

Tibthorpe

Continuing north along the B1248 road from the Bainton roundabout, the road rises and falls as Tibthorpe (Tibetorp in the Domesday Book) is approached, flanked by avenues of trees. High Wood and Low Wood, favourite walks for local people and visitors, are a haven for wildlife. In recent years deer have arrived. These shy creatures may sometimes be seen and have been known to stray onto the road, startling passing motorists. Another surprise for passers-by at the entrance to High Wood may be the ghostly figure of a woman! She has caused motorists to slow down, only to disappear before their eyes.

Approximately 150 people make up the population of Tibthorpe; their homes with beautiful views over the surrounding countryside. It is said that centuries ago monks from Watton Abbey roamed these pastures with their sheep and were able to rest in a chapel of ease which was situated in the village.

Butts Lane takes its name from the medieval archers who practised their skills close by. The lane has also been known as Thornton Street, when an inn – Thornton's inn – was located there. In present times Tibthorpe is a 'dry' village, with the nearest public house a couple of miles away. Another point of interest is that a family of Huguenots (persecuted French Protestants, who escaped to north-east England in the 1680s) occupied a house in Butts Lane.

Many years ago several small businesses flourished, besides farming; a cobbler, fishmonger, fruiterer, village store and butcher. Today a well stocked shop/post office and a market garden are the sole suppliers. There is no church or chapel here, the Methodist chapel was demolished some years ago when road improvements were being carried out. It is said that there is an ancient burial ground on one of the farms – supposedly haunted!

As there is no school for Tibthorpe children they had to walk to nearby Kirkburn, but today the school bus provides a more convenient form of transport. Those wishing to attend church services also have to make their way to Kirkburn.

The water supply used to be drawn from an ancient well, remembered still by one or two of the older residents. Its memory lives on by the lane in which it existed – Well Lane.

In 1990 a group of children took part in 'Operation Lifestyle' – a scheme organised by the Humberside police to involve young people in worthwhile activities during the summer. They chose for their project the task of landscaping an area of waste land, turning it into a very pleasant garden with flowers, trees and shrubs for the benefit of the village. For their hard work these youngsters received an award.

Tickton

The village of Tickton in East Yorkshire is situated on the Beverley to Bridlington road about two and a half miles north-east of Beverley and separated from it by the river Hull.

It has historical connections going back many centuries, as early as the reign of Athelstan (AD 925–940); it was the property of the church of St John of Beverley. Athelstan is known to have endowed the church with lands following his success against the Scots and Danes at the battle of Brunanburg consequent upon his pilgrimage to the shrine of St John.

At one time the village was known as Ticketone, said to be called after a bishop of that time. Along with many other villages of later times, Ticketone was mentioned in the Domesday Book of 1086 and was still at this time the property of the church of St John.

The intervening years must have rolled away uneventfully and only much nearer our time do records appear of the development of village life.

In 1828 a Wesleyan chapel was built, followed in the early 1840s by a chapel of ease to Beverley Minster known as the church of St Paul. Its influence on village life, along with marriages and other services performed by the church, can be demonstrated by an entry in the records of baptism; 'November 25th 1880. Joseph and Hannah Redshaw, shepherds, has their children baptised in Tickton church. Their ages were one month, one year, two yrs, five, seven, eight, ten, twelve and 13 years'. Around this time also Tickton got its first school.

In 1948 a group of volunteers from the village started to build a village hall. It was opened in 1951, by which time the men had moved 400 tons of rubble, 154 tons of gravel and laid 44,000 bricks. Village functions are mostly held in the hall and today it accommodates a play group, a Darby and Joan club and other social and recreational activities.

In recent years a bypass was built, considerably lessening the load of traffic which passed through the village, and a period of comparative peace was enjoyed. But development is going on apace and many new houses appear where once stood fields and open spaces. The original school has been replaced by a modern one with spacious play areas, and the old one has been converted into a home for the elderly. The population recorded in the late 19th century was 305 and today has grown to 2,370.

Tunstall

Tunstall is a hamlet rather than a village. It has some 70 inhabitants and it has no shop and no public house. Yet once it sported a blacksmith's, joiner's and a public house, all situated in the main street – Town Street. By the 1980s these had all gone.

There are now six farmsteads and a few cottages together with a number of modern bungalows. The only building of note is All Saints' church, standing on what is for Holderness an eminence. This together with the oldest farmsteads and cottages is built in whole or part of cobbles.

The earliest mention of the church is in 1115 when the church and titles were given to the Abbey of St Martin in York. There is no mention of the church in the Domesday Book.

Being situated within such a short distance of the coast (about half a mile) Tunstall suffers the threat of coastal erosion. At a point on the coast called Sand-le-Mere is a small area of dune which has always been a danger point from incursion from the sea. Sand-le-Mere now gives its name to a large caravan site which is nearby.

Tunstall does have a village hall where whist drives and an annual coffee evening are held. Tunstall is also now a favourite venue for fishermen.

Walkington

It is true that there was a settlement at Walkington as far back as the Bronze Age – recent excavations of burial sites prove this. Yet, paradoxically, most of the real history of the village has unfolded during the past 30 years or so.

Let us take a look at the Walkington of some 50 years ago. It was a quiet farming village. Whilst it is true that there was a bus service to Beverley, three miles away, Walkington was nevertheless an isolated, self-contained community. A day trip to Hull, or the annual Sunday school trip to Bridlington, were events to which the villagers looked forward with eager anticipation. The ancient church overlooked the village. Then, as now, little was known about its history, but few people really cared. The fact that the modern village had been shaped by the Fergusons who, father and son, had occupied the rectory for virtually the whole of the 19th century, was of little concern to most folk. Far more villagers remembered Rev Michael Dawe, who had succeeded Douglas Ferguson as rector at the turn of the century. Even then, they remembered not the words of wisdom which had emanated from the pulpit, but rather the unecclesiastical words which used to be uttered by Marcus, his old parrot of doubtful gender. The other village potentate was the schoolmaster, who got on with his work almost unchallenged, and who ruled his charges with his favourite cane. One event which was still widely talked about was the sacking in 1911 of a much respected schoolmaster, James Truscott. Officially this was because Truscott liked a pint at the Dog and Duck; unofficially it was because Truscott was a staunch Methodist, and was at loggerheads with Mr Dawe, the rector. Whatever the reason, on the day of their departure, the Truscotts were accompanied to Beverley station by the whole school, who then sang protest songs outside County Hall before their sad return to Walkington.

By the outbreak of the Second World War Walkington was still a self-contained village. Rotsey Lawson, the joiner, made everything from coffins to farm waggons. Across the road, Tom Bailey the blacksmith was kept busy meeting the needs of the local farmers. The butcher, the tailor, the cobbler, and the shopkeeper were all within a hundred yards of the centre of the village. In terms of recreation, there was very little. There were enthusiastic cricket and football teams. A new parish hall had been built in the 1920s. Here the WI held sway, and the occasional dance was held. But the Dog and Duck crossroads formed the real hub of village life. Here the menfolk gathered of an evening to chew over the latest village gossip and to catch up with events in the world at large. Yes, Walkington was a typical sleepy East Riding village, with three pubs, a pond, and an abundance of old characters, whose memories stretched back into the Victorian era.

By the end of the war, Walkington was poised to undergo significant changes. The village water carrier had already been made redundant since mains water had arrived: the standpipes scattered along the village street were the pride and joy of the parish council. Electricity had also arrived, though many houses stuck for several years to their paraffin lamps. Walkington was at last in touch with the outside world. Council houses sprang up in Autherd Garth – the first real development ever to appear in Walkington. Prior to that, Lythes the builders had put up the odd house when it pleased them – each was embellished in true Lythe fashion with redundant relics salvaged from churches in the neighbourhood.

As the 1950s dawned, Walkington was destined never to be the same again. The wider use of the internal combustion engine meant that travel became so much easier. The sons of the village soil moved away to earn their living. Only a few of the old village characters remained. But those few are still remembered with affection. Supreme among them was Oliver Cromwell. Oliver – an unusual name for an unusual person. He had left the village at the turn of the century to travel, as a railroad builder, across the United States. His tales of the American Wild West, related in a rich East Yorkshire accent, were a joy to the ear. 'Crommy' Oliver and many of his friends had spent their youth as labourers on Yorkshire farms, then they had served in the trenches during the

First World War. They had so much to tell, and they told it well, especially under the influence of a few pints of beer in the Dog and Duck.

By the mid century there were signs that things in Walkington were changing. A group of villagers, in which the young new rector, Tony Lawrance, and the schoolmaster, Bethel Taylor, featured strongly, decided, for example, that the new Walkington would need a playing field. Much to the consternation of the residents, £200 was spent to purchase the field on which cricket had been played for as long as anyone could remember. What foresight!

Whilst many had left the village in the post-war years, others had arrived. One such new arrival was destined to lead the village towards its greatest hour. Ernie Teal, an ex-Coldstream Guardsman and a Beverlonian, decided that he would do his best to make his newly adopted village a happy place in which to live. At first, the newcomer was regarded with suspicion by the natives, but he was a born leader of men and had the charisma of a pied piper. His first innovation was a seemingly trivial one: monthly general knowledge quizzes to raise funds for local organisations. Amazingly, 30 years later, they are more popular than ever. The reason is simple: an evening of good, home-made entertainment (for only 30p!)

Meanwhile, up at the church, churchwarden Norman Castle decided in 1960 to produce a monthly news sheet through which to communicate church news to the village. General news was soon included and the publication became a village newsletter. That monthly newsletter is still going strong; it is still produced voluntarily; it is still delivered free of charge to every house in the village. The church approached the 1960s with an appeal for £1,500 to provide a new ring of bells. The village responded magnificently, just as it did in later years when appeals went out to provide a new east window and to restore the organ. Also in the early 1960s, the Methodists were busily carrying out a massive renovation of their chapel.

The dawn of the 1960s marked the beginning of the end of Walkington as a small rural village. Large tracts of farmland were sold for private housing development: first the Crake Wells estate;

then All Hallows; then Manor Park; more recently Red Gates. Broadgate Hospital – once a flourishing psychiatric hospital – has now closed, and will soon be razed to the ground to make way for yet more houses. Houses, houses everywhere! The orchards and the pleasant lanes that were the very essence of old Walkington are now covered in tarmac. Heavy lorries roar through the village on their way to the M62.

The number of people who were born and bred in Walkington is in sharp decline, but whilst old Yorkshire characters like Eva Boynton and Dick Grantham are still around, memories of old Walkington will linger on. The 'new' Walkington is still a splendid place in which to live; it is still bustling with activity; there are events by the dozen to prepare for and to anticipate; each year there are new innovations, new challenges, and new friends to make. They say that what Walkington does today, Ambridge will do tomorrow. The Walkington Song – always sung at the end of the village pantomime, and on other special occasions – sums up our feelings: 'Happy, oh happy, oh happy are we: living in Walkington, you and me! Of this pretty village, we're all very fond: three pubs and a church and a mucky old pond'.

Ernie Teal, the architect of modern Walkington, could not have foreseen how the village would change. Nevertheless, he must be quietly proud of the way in which he has guided it through the years of change. His fruitful mind has dreamed up idea after idea for events which would both raise money and provide entertainment. Every Christmas, carols are sung round the pond to the accompaniment of a steam organ, then Father Christmas crosses the pond in a boat and gives out free sweets to the crowds of eagerly awaiting children. The money raised ensuring that the pond remains an attractive centrepiece to the village. He had always toyed with the idea of recreating a Victorian hayride, in which an army of horse-drawn wagons, accompanied by a multitude of villagers in Victorian costume would descend on Beverley to raise money for charity.

In June 1991, the 24th hayride set off Beverley. The villagers are very proud that Ernie was awarded the MBE in 1990 for his services to the community. Never was a medal more richly deserved!

Wansford

'Wansford is a picturesque old world village on the banks of the Driffield Navigation and river Hull, two and a half and one and half miles respectively from the Driffield and Nafferton stations – North Eastern Railway. The houses are mostly modern, the farm buildings are ample in size, and both are excellently planned and most substantially built, and are in first rate order. The water supply is good and abundant.'

Thus Wansford was described when the village went under the hammer of auctioneers Hornby and Wilberfoss on Wednesday, 3 July 1918 when it was sold at the Bell Hotel, Driffield, along with Brigham and Rotsea, by Sir Mark Sykes, owner of the Sledmere estate, to raise money for death duties. The 16 lots included five farms – all still going strong today; a water mill; a 'gentleman's residence' – Park House, now known as Manor House and home of the Butterell family for nearly 100 years; a detached house and joiner's shop – now the Gatehouse; a smallholding; two new cottages; the Row of eleven cottages; Ireland Square in two lots of six cottages; and the Trout inn – 'a modern, well-built, well accustomed, free and fully licensed public house.'

The village stands much the same today – with the addition of the council houses, old peoples' bungalows and a large handful of other private dwellings. (The building boom as experienced in and radically altering many villages has yet to hit hard in Wansford.) The Square may still be recognisable to Sir Mark, but it is doubtful whether he would know the Row, where only four homes stand where once there were eleven cottages. Legend has it that Sir Tatton Sykes, a forebear of Sir Mark, ordered that every other front door of the Row be bricked up to stop village wives idling away their time by employing their tongues and gossiping over garden hedges.

Life in the village would, for hundreds of years, have been almost solely based on agriculture until the building of the Driffield Navigation brought the world to Wansford.

Five cottages were built on land between the canal and West beck, south of what would have been the swing bridge, to house the 'navvies' working on the waterway. When the canal was finished a carpet mill was built on its west bank.

The cottages, the foundations of which, according to one elderly native, can still be seen today, were then used as homes for orphans who worked in the mill and were taught their trade by a Bradford couple, Charles and Bettie Bentley. And so the name Orphan Cottages came into use.

The carpet mill burnt down in 1816 but the canal continued to ensure Wansford's place on the map as boats and barges plied their trade between Driffield and Hull until as late as 1944 when the waterway became unnavigable. In the canal's heyday it is said the village boasted at least two pubs, one at Manor Farm and another at the Gatehouse.

Many of the village's farmhouses and homes also date, like the canal, back to the 1700s. Not so St Mary's church – built by the Sykes family in 1868, the vicarage – an early 20th century addition to the village, the former school (the Finishing Post) which closed in the late 1960s, and the schoolhouse.

Immediately prior to 1868 it is doubtful whether the village – variously named throughout the ages as Wandesford, Wandesforth, Wandysford and Wandsworth, had its own place of worship. But records indicate that it certainly had in 1330. There was then a chapel dedicated to St Mary and St Nicholas, probably sited in what is now called the Wansford Parks, which stretches from the rear of the council houses and behind Park (or Manor) House and is bordered by the Nafferton beck. It was founded by one Elyas de Wandesford, on the site of a previous chapel and was a dependant of the parish church of Nafferton.

The chapel, as was Nafferton church, was overseen by the Abbot of Meaux. An interesting record dated 25 January 1354 perhaps casts a little light on village folklore that Wansford has its ghosts – monks. 'At the instance of the Abbot and Convent of Meaux the inhabitants of Wandesford were inhibited from burying their dead in the chapel or chapelyard of Wandesford which before by reason of the plague they had licence granted them to do by Archbishop Zouch'.

Imaginative talk has it that mysterious hunched and hooded figures can sometimes be seen making their solemn way into the village from the direction of Nafferton and then into Wansford parks. When expanded the tale goes on to talk of monks from Nafferton using the Wansford chapelyard as an overspill graveyard during the time of the Great Plague and making a sorry progress from Nafferton church, along Priestage and on to Wansford bearing their sad burdens. The record just might bear this old tale out. Whether you believe in the ghosts or not – that's another story.

Warter

Warter, a village pleasing in every aspect except in the meaning of its name. The name is puzzling and somewhat gruesome in origin. According to William Thurlow's book, *Yorkshire Place Names*, the name Warter is a compound of the Old English 'treow' – tree, and 'wearg' – felon, and means 'gallows'.

Nestling in a green hollow of the Wolds, Warter is a village of rare delight. The approach from Pocklington is like a green tunnel, with shady embanked roads bordered by lofty trees of the 300 acre park in which Warter Priory, the 'great house', stood until it was pulled down some years ago.

There was an Augustinian priory founded at Warter some 800 or more years ago. It stood, not in the park, but on the site of the present village church. A 19th century structure, rebuilt in 14th century style by Lord Muncaster, the church occupies a commanding position on a high bank overlooking the triangular village green.

Dedicated to St James, the church is stone built and has a western tower graced by a fine octagonal spire. It is specially interesting on account of its rich memorials both inside and out. These monuments are to members of the famous Wilson family. One of these, with sculptures of Charles Henry Wilson of 1907 and his wife, has two angels bowed over a saint, and two women holding vases – a ship on the top of one of them. Charles Henry Wilson, the first Lord Nunburnholme, built up the biggest privately-owned fleet of merchant ships in the world, and was one of Hull's most successful and prominent citizens. Sadly, Warter church has now become a redundant church.

To the west of the village green stand four delightful 19th century thatched cottages. In terrace form, they are red-brick whitewashed, and the thatched roof is richly patterned with gabled windows peeping out.

On the raised, mound-like green stands a memorial to the men of the village who gave their lives in the First and Second World Wars. The monument is in the form of a cross carved with a feast of interlacing work, and a canopied figure of St George.

There was once a mill at Warter. During the 12th century the gift of a mill was presented to Warter Priory by the lord of the manor. The tenants were compelled to have their corn ground in this water mill, and had to pay toll, or 'multure', for the privilege. It has been suggested that in the Domesday survey, the manor of Warter was returned as waste (vasta est), and that at such a time the village may have been entirely deserted.

Watton

The village of Watton lies approximately halfway between Beverley and Driffield on the A164. It is only a small village and has no shops or public houses. The population is around 250, which includes outlying farms and the residents of Tophill Low Pumping Station as well as people living in the main body of the village.

A large part of the parish was originally marsh land and Watton was called 'Wetadun' (Wet Town) by the Saxons. By drainage, the marsh has been converted to good arable land. Wheat and barley are grown, and also oilseed rape, potatoes and peas. Although Watton village is surrounded by quite a number of farms, many people now commute to work to Driffield, Beverley or Hull.

According to Bede, a Saxon nunnery was founded in Watton in the 7th century. This was probably destroyed by the Danes in the mid 9th century. A Gilbertine priory was then founded by Eustace Fitzjohn about 1148. It was unusual in that it was a double house to serve nuns and canons, who were kept strictly apart. The priory was garrisoned by the Royalists in the Civil Wars and attacked by the Cromwellians. The ghost of a lady, murdered during this time, is said to haunt the place. The only surviving building – the prior's lodging – is now a private house and is called Watton Abbey.

St Mary's church dates back to the late 16th century and is built of brick. Very little church building took place during Elizabeth I's reign, so St Mary's is worth a visit. Services are held regularly twice a month, with extra services on special occasions. The village also had a Methodist chapel built in 1887, but this has been converted to a private house in recent years.

During the Second World War, Watton was quite an important place for the RAF. An airfield was created between Watton and Cranswick, and Watton became home to many hundreds of airmen and women. The remains of the officers' campsite with gymnasium and cinema can still be seen and is now part of a local pig farm! A hospital for the RAF was built near the abbey and a huge petrol store was situated at Watton railway crossing. A Salvation Army hut built during the war later became the village hall. This has sadly now gone.

The village post office closed several years ago and the nearest shops are at Cranswick two miles away. However, the village is served by several very good mobile shops including a butcher's, baker's, milkman and library. There is a regular hourly bus service to Driffield, Bridlington and Scarborough; and in the other direction to Beverley and Hull. The nearest railway station is at Cranswick on the Hull to Scarborough line.

Children from the village attend Beswick and Watton school. It was built in 1858 as a National school to take 112 children. At present there are 31 pupils aged five to eleven. The school lies halfway between Watton and Beswick on the A164 and serves children from these two villages and also Kilnwick. At eleven the children transfer to Driffield secondary school.

Despite there being no village hall, there are quite a few school and church events held each year, and there is an active parish council.

Wawne

Wawne is a village on the east bank of the river Hull, roughly midway between Hull and Beverley. Fifty or more years ago, coal was transported by this river on barges to Wawne. A ferry, closed unfortunately about 1946, used to cross with cars and pedestrians, and in later years, just pedestrians. People could travel to Beverley via Woodmansey, and Hull via Dunswell. Wawne was originally an agricultural village until the building programme in the 1960s. From being a village of 200 inhabitants, Wawne has grown to about 1,000.

St Peter's church was built in the 13th/14th century, and later given to the monks of Meaux Abbey, three miles away, of which no ruins remain. The church bells have only recently been restored. The Methodist church, formerly Primitive Methodist, was opened in 1860, the original building now being the Sunday schoolroom. A new chapel was added in 1939.

The present primary school was built in 1910, consisting of two classrooms, and was extended to its present size in the 1960s when the new houses were being built.

At this time, a beautiful old mansion, Wawne Hall, which had been the home of the Windham family and was later used as an army camp during the Second World War, was demolished for housing.

A big event organised by the WI is the Annual Show, open to the village in July and held at the school. In December the Carol Evening has become a tradition, much enjoyed by villagers and friends.

The WI still has one founder member, Mrs Muriel E. Rogerson, who is now in her eighties and still very active. At 80, she was awarded the BEM for her services to the village. She was the inspiration behind the installation of electricity in the church, the cricket pavilion and cricket field, playing field and tennis courts, the choir vestry (built by the 'Mouseman' of Kilburn) in the church, and the provision of the school bus service. She still teaches flower arranging, arranges church flowers for special occasions, and still makes the WI Birthday Cake, in her fireside oven, overnight, judging the heat by feeling the oven door knob! She is also an expert at cake icing. Her latest achievement was the restoration of the church bells, a project which took ten years of fund raising events, raising over £9,000. The service of dedication took place on 9th April 1989.

During this period, £30,000 was also raised by the villagers for a new village hall, which was opened by the hard-working chairman, Mr Michael J. Yates, MA, also present headmaster of the village school. The village boasts its own shop, post office, public house, petrol station and doctors' surgery.

The people of Wawne do their main shopping in Hull or Beverley, but despite its proximity to these, and Bransholme, the largest council estate in England, Wawne still retains its village character.

Welton cum Melton & Wauldby

Welton is reputed to be one of the prettiest villages in East Yorkshire, the population being approximately 1,700 including Melton. Wauldby, a tiny hamlet, has only seven.

Leaving the A63 you enter Cowgate, the main thoroughfare and see immediately the contrasting style of old and new, the old being a beautiful Georgian house known as The Grange. One of the features of this lovely house is a beautifully decorated ceiling, one of the finest of its period. On the opposite side of the road are a number of purpose-built flats for the elderly complete with their own recreation room, where the Darby and Joan meetings take place every week, and other activities such as whist drives and coffee mornings.

Continuing into the village, you pass the local public house, the

Green Dragon, which is famous for the fact that the infamous highwayman Dick Turpin was nearly captured here. He escaped through a small window and fled into the night on the back of his horse Black Beauty.

Opposite the Green Dragon is the village green, in the middle of which is the Fountain, which has long since ceased to discharge water but is a very interesting piece of listed architecture. There is an inscription round this perpendicular fountain which reads 'In memory of Anne Popple AD 1874 "I will give a vow God that if you have a thirst of the fountain of the water of life, drink freely".' Across one corner of the green is a wooden seat donated to the village by the WI. The green itself was once surrounded by heavy black chains but these were removed for the war effort in the Second World War.

The pearl in the crown of the village must be the beautiful St Helen's church standing in the middle of the village, with the lovely mill dam and shallow beck flowing by its side, its ducks swimming lazily around just waiting to be fed by the numerous visitors to Welton.

The church dates back to around 1066 having a tower added in the 15th century. Inside the main door to the left is an effigy of a Knight Templar dating from the 12th century. Outside in the graveyard is an amusing epitaph on a headstone which reads 'Here lieth ye old Jeremy, Who hath 8 times married been. Now in his old age, he lies in his cage. Under the grass so green.' This Jeremiah Simpson departed this life in the 84th year of his age in the year of our Lord 1719.

Leaving the church there is a choice of three delightful walks. Take the middle one up Dale Road passing Cattle Well on the way, one of the many wells which earned Welton its title in the Domesday Book as the Town of Wells. Cattle Well itself is a brick-built creation where water pours continually from an iron pipe, its source being an underground spring.

At the end of Dale Road is a derelict water mill which was used to grind corn, harvested from fertile pastures surrounding the village.

As you enter the Dale there are two lovely springs which house quite a lot of waterfowl and fish. Opposite a quaint old cottage, formerly the gamekeeper's, is the point where the chalk meets the clay and is the start of the Yorkshire Wolds. The water bubbling up through the chalk is popularly known as Jesus Water.

The Dale is a natural breeding ground for pheasants and other game birds. The occasional deer can sometimes be spotted. At the end of the Dale is a heavily wooded area in which stands the mausoleum, the burial ground of the Raikes family who were Quakers. Built in 1818, it houses stone lead-lined coffins which are placed on shelves inside and rumour has it that any unauthorised person who enters may meet their doom!

The hamlet of Wauldby is but a stone's throw from the mausoleum. It has its own tiny church, which was built in 1840 and can hold 60 people. Returning to Welton down a steep hill there is a panoramic view of the river Humber and across to Lincolnshire.

Welton's largest employers are Humber Growers Ltd. The market gardens were originally started by the Bean family and it is now the largest area under glass in England producing approximately 36,000,000 cucumbers a year! They also produce most other salad vegetables. Walk along the banks of the Humber to Melton, and there are some large ponds now used as fishing ponds but which were once the producers of clay used in the manufacture of cement. The cement works closed in 1981 leaving two other industries in Melton, a smelting works, soon to be closed, and a chalk quarry.

The post office-cum-general store is Welton's only shop. It is hard to believe that when there was a population of 700 there were eight shops in the village. Until 50 years ago most of the village people were employed by the estate, as farm workers or domestics, but now the residents commute to Hull and surrounding towns. Like most villages Welton has changed over the years but has still managed to maintain its unique character and beauty and is well worth a visit.

Welwick

Welwick, situated in the east end of Holderness, about two miles south-east of Patrington, is believed to be so named because of its abundance of springs. Judging by old Ordnance Survey maps this could certainly be true, as there is a liberal scattering of P for Pump!

Poulson, in his 1840 *History of Holderness*, declares that Welwick is a pleasant village and has nothing particular in it to arrest attention but the church. Most of the inhabitants would disagree strongly with this. Perhaps there are no stately homes or exquisite examples of fine architecture, but over the years there have been plenty of happenings and characters to make up for this dubious loss. One of the most famous examples of this is the connection of Welwick with the Gunpowder Plot. John and Christopher Wright of Ploughland were two of the plotters and were born at Ploughland Farm. They were half-brothers of William Wright, whose burial place in St Mary's church, alongside his wife Ann, is commemorated with brass effigies which have done well to survive from the early 17th century. John and Christopher had a sister, Ursula, whose daughter Mary Ward, 1585–1645, founded the Institute of the Blessed Virgin Mary, an educational order of nuns. As a girl she lived in Welwick for five years with her grandmother, and worshipped at St Mary's church.

The size of the village does not seem to have altered much over the last 200 years, as the 1851 census lists almost the same number of dwellings, 94, as the present day. This is one of the few local villages not to have had its character or appearance changed or spoilt by large building expansion. Yet, by no stretch of the imagination could this small, friendly place be called a sleepy village. One 19th century joiner announced in his advertising poster – 'there's allus sommat gannin' on'. So much so that children, according to the school log book of 1890, had little time to attend their lessons. Pig-tenting, coursing, following the hounds, soliciting for New Year gifts, going to farm sales, potato picking, making bands, Sunday school outings, village fairs, all took their toll on academic concentration.

The Welwick village fairs of yesteryear have been revived recently in the form of a Heritage Weekend, which comprises a beautifully decorated church, various craft and local history displays, working vintage farm machinery, and many more interesting attractions. The whole village gets together for this festive harvest-time event, with almost everyone 'doing their bit' to contribute to its success.

The village hall, originally the Naafi building from the Second World War army camp at Spurn Point, was bought and re-erected in 1947, and its both well kept and well used. It provides the venue for village meetings and many other local functions.

The Primitive Methodist chapel, built by subscription in 1911, holds its festival in the schoolroom at the rear of the building. There is no religious division as both church and chapel are supported equally, coming together for joint services at regular intervals, especially at Christmas when the chapel is host to a charming Carols, Candles and Coffee evening on the Monday preceding Christmas Day.

Welwick is often referred to by the many drivers who pass through it en route to the BP and British Gas developments at Easington, as 'that little place with traffic lights'. Put temporarily in place in 1982, to the consternation of the inhabitants, they have now become a fact of life, although there is still plenty of debate in the local Coach and Horses as to the value of this technological intrusion. The one public house, since the closure of the Wheatsheaf and Plough in the early 1960s, is well-known in the district for its excellent meals, and hosting the Harvest Festival Auction which has raised thousands of pounds over the years for deserving charities.

The school log book is a reminder of the days when the village school played a leading part in the community. The first recorded educational establishment was sited in Humber Lane in an old Quaker meeting house but was replaced in 1905 by a new building in the centre of the village. At this time the average number of children on the roll was 70, although not all of them lived in the village, but walked from out-lying farms and hamlets up to three miles away. This number gradually lessened until 1977 when a roll of 20 was too small to warrant a school and forced its closure.

Many of the street and house names remind us of Welwick in the past: Mill Hill (a mill was recorded here as early as 1611 and worked until the 1920s), Brick Pond, Blacksmith's Cottage, Moat Farm, Beerhouse Alley, Beacon Hill, Green Lane, Kelk Manor and Wheatsheaf House. However, it should not be thought that the inhabitants dwell on days gone by, but rather that they treasure their inheritance and welcome the future with enthusiasm and co-operation, characteristics peculiar to the friendly folk of Welwick.

Winestead

The attractive village of Winestead lies on the A1033 Hull/Withernsea road, just to the north-west of Patrington. Much of the village is hidden away down a side road, and the church, though visible from the main road, is surrounded by trees and easily missed.

At the time of the Domesday Book, Winestead was under the ownership of the Archbishop of York, but the village passed into the hands of the de Verli family. It then passed by marriage to the Hildyard family. The medieval manor house stood to the west of the church, where the moat still survives. It is said that Sir Christopher Hildyard had this house demolished after his son was drowned in the moat. He built a new three-storey castellated house, Winestead Hall, at the north end of the village street in 1579. About 1720 the house was replaced by a new one of red brick, which became known as Red Hall. The estate eventually passed into the hands of Hull Corporation in 1932, and the Hall was demolished in 1936 and a hospital was built in the grounds. The fine stable block, designed by John Carr in 1762, has survived in the grounds. The hospital has recently been closed.

Another large Georgian house, White Hall, was built by the Maister family of Hull in 1814 to the west of the church, on land which originally formed the park of the medieval manor house.

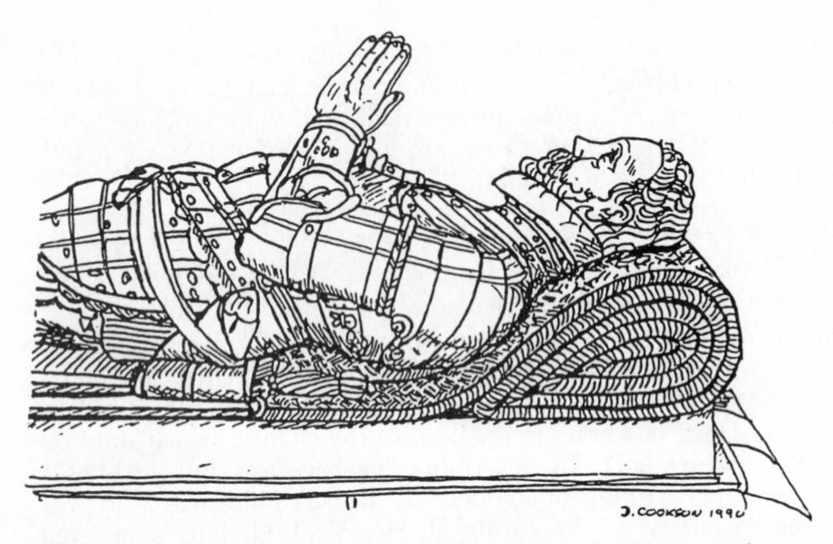

The Hildyard Monument, St Germain's Church, Winestead

The Hildyard family returned to Winestead in 1962 when Captain A. J. C. Hildyard bought the White Hall. The family has recently sold the property and moved to South Humberside.

There was a charity school in Winestead, founded by Anne Hildyard in 1813. The cottage in which this school was held still displays the Hildyard coat of arms in stone, a plaque which is probably from the medieval manor house. A new school was built by H. J. Reckitt in 1903, and was named the Nancie Reckitt school after his daughter. The school closed in 1946, and the few remaining pupils were transferred to Patrington school. The building was used as a village hall, and is now a private house.

St German's church is at first sight a plain building of boulders, bricks and dressed stone, with a red pantiled roof. Stonework discovered during various restorations has dated the original church to the 12th century Norman period. The isolated position of the church leads people to wonder why it was built so far from the houses, but in fact it is the village which has moved, probably after the building of the Hall at the north end of the street. The dedication to St German is unusual. Germanus was a friend of St Patrick who brought the priests and people back to the true faith in the 5th century. Other churches dedicated to him include Selby Abbey, St German's in Cornwall, and the ruined St German's Cathedral in the Isle of Man.

The church is usually kept locked but the key can be obtained in the village, and the trouble entailed is well rewarded, for the interior is of great beauty and interest. The south wall of the chancel contains a very small window which is 14th century work, and is thought to depict St German and rector William Retherby, who built the chancel and who died in 1417. There are many memorials in the church, most of which are to the Hildyard family. There is a brass in the floor of the chancel which shows a knight and his lady. The inscription has been lost, but the man is thought to be Robin of Reddesdale (Robert Hildyard) who was made an outlaw for his loyalty to Henry VI. He later supported Richard III and met Henry VII in his progress to York in 1485. He died in 1490. The largest monument in the church is a full size figure of Sir Christopher Hildyard (1530–1602). He was High Sheriff of Yorkshire and became MP for Hedon in 1563 and 1571–72. Around his tomb are many shields, and at his feet a cockerel, the family crest.

The font was used for the baptism of Andrew Marvell, the Puritan poet and wit, in 1621. The font at some time was taken out of the church and was used as a horse trough in Keyingham. It was recovered and replaced on its original base, which was discovered when the floor of the church was lowered. Two items in the church are thought to have been rescued from the priory at Birstall in the parish of Skeffling, at the Dissolution of the Monasteries. The first is the chancel screen, a very beautiful piece of carved woodwork of 14th century date which was obviously not designed for its present location. Much of the fan vaulting had perished, but was restored as a memorial to Thomas Hildyard. The second survivor from the priory can be found below the arcade which divides the nave from the aisle. It is an effigy of a recumbent priest in full vestments for Holy Communion.

The Old Rectory is the birthplace of Andrew Marvell. In recent years it was the home of the late Sir Rupert Alec Smith, President of the Georgian Society of East Yorkshire. He rescued Georgian doorways and fireplaces from demolished buildings and installed them in this beautiful house.

The story of this village is not yet fully told, for during the past six years an archaeological dig has been in progress at Weldon's Plantation which is unearthing evidence of a settlement here in the Neolithic period.

Withernwick

It is known that a settlement existed here in Roman times called 'With-Forne-Uuic'. The settlement expanded in Anglo-Saxon times to a village, the name having changed many times, all deriving from 'White Thorn'. Withernwick is still truly a village, with a continuingly strong farming community. Modern building has not been allowed to spoil the charm, and apart from the main Beverley and Hull to Aldbrough roads, the village lies away from the main routes.

The manor of Withernwick was held during an early period by the family of Fauconberg, and is said to have passed from this family, by the marriage of an heiress, about the reign of Richard II. It subsequently passed through various hands to the Bethell family of the neighbouring village of Rise.

The present church of St Alban was built in 1855. Records show that a previous church existed in 1115 on the same site, and some stones from the Saxon age exist in the walls of the nave. The Methodist chapel was built in 1843.

Withernwick is still fortunate to have its own school, built in 1846 and enlarged in 1858. Close to the school stood one of the last remaining post mills; the mill was demolished in the early 1900s.

Wold Newton

Wold Newton, or Newton Rochford as it was named in the Domesday Book, is the most northerly village in Humberside with a population of about 200. It is built on what is believed to be an old Anglian settlement and there are two round burial mounds – Ball Hill and Willy Howe, which is one of the largest in the area. It is situated in the Gypsey Race valley, this being a unique stream that is fed by springs and empties into the sea at Bridlington. It can stay dry for many years, then suddenly it becomes fast flowing almost overnight. Its rise is reputed to foretell a national disaster.

The village is mainly agricultural and is enhanced by many mature ash, beech, sycamore and chestnut trees. The pond on the village green is very attractive and was restored to celebrate the Queen's Silver Jubilee in 1977. Everyone was invited to help, from puddling in tons of clay for the base to planting trees and bulbs on the green. Now it is the home of many ducks and a swan.

On the 13th December 1795, a meteorite fell to the south-west of the village, which must have caused much alarm. The remains can now be seen in the Natural History Museum in London.

All Saints' church is tucked away in the centre of the village. The round font and carved doorway are Norman, and the first vicar was appointed on the 20th February 1312. One mile away, in the hamlet of Fordon, is St James' church, which is reputed to be the smallest in Yorkshire.

In 1897 there were two shops, a post office, three wheelwright/joiners, a shoemaker, a rope maker, two dressmakers and a tailor, plus a vicarage, reading room, a chapel and a school. Now alas there is only one shop-cum-post office and a good modern school which serves four villages. The chapel is now the community centre where most village activities take place, including indoor bowls, over sixties club, a day centre, whist drives, and a small but thriving Women's Institute which was formed in 1946.

There is a cricket team, a football team, and a Flower and Produce Show is held every August. A village bonfire is always held on the 5th November, and carols are sung around the tree on Christmas Eve. There is no bus service but the Gypsey Rider, a mini-bus based at Burton Fleming, regularly travels to Bridlington, Driffield and Scarborough.

Woodmansey

Woodmansey, Thearne and Beverley Parks, now usually collectively called Woodmansey, is a large parish to the south-east of Beverley, bordered on the east by the river Hull.

King Street in Woodmansey village was once the main street, comprising about 20 cottages, a farm, two smallholdings, a chapel and the village public house (the Dixons Arms) on the corner of the main Hull-Beverley road. The present pub was built on the site of the old inn in the mid 1930s.

Also in King Street is a residence called Monument House. In the garden is a former bell tower from St Mary's church in Beverley. The tower was erected in the garden as a summer house.

Thearne was also a collection of cottages, farms and a Methodist chapel, which ceased being used for worship in the 1930s. Thearne Hall in Ferry Lane, now a large residence, fell into a state of neglect in the 1920–30s, but the last two owners have restored it to its former glory. Further along Ferry Lane, as the name implies, used to be found the Wawne ferry. The last person to act as ferryman was called Danny Brewer, who was also the landlord of the public house on the Wawne side of the river. The ferry was closed down during the Second World War and has not been used since.

The area has a very fertile soil, so when the Dutch growers came over it provided an ideal place for them to build their intensive glasshouses. A large acreage of horticulture soon developed and has been increased by local growers over the years and become one of the major industries of the parish.

Beverley Parks was and still is a farming area and along with horticulture, creates a rural setting. Sadly the old fashioned mixed farms are giving way to more specialised units – with two or three large dairy herds and the odd intensive livestock unit replacing the family farm.

High House in the parish was the home of the Bainton family, who were responsible for the building of St Peter's church. Most of the local people helped in some way and in 1898 the church was consecrated by the Archbishop of York. Prior to the church being built services were held in the Church of England school on the opposite site of the Beverley-Hull road. Both the church and the school were built in what at that time was a thinly populated area, but was at the centre of the three communities.

Spurn Point lighthouse

Index